A CENTURY OF CONFLICT

WAR, 1914–2014

A CENTURY OF CONFLICT

WAR, 1914–2014

JEREMY BLACK

New York   Oxford
OXFORD UNIVERSITY PRESS

Oxford University Press is a department of the University of Oxford.
It furthers the University's objective of excellence in research,
scholarship, and education by publishing worldwide.

Oxford   New York
Auckland   Cape Town   Dar es Salaam   Hong Kong   Karachi
Kuala Lumpur   Madrid   Melbourne   Mexico City   Nairobi
New Delhi   Shanghai   Taipei   Toronto

With offices in
Argentina   Austria   Brazil   Chile   Czech Republic   France   Greece
Guatemala   Hungary   Italy   Japan   Poland   Portugal   Singapore
South Korea   Switzerland   Thailand   Turkey   Ukraine   Vietnam

For titles covered by Section 112 of the US Higher Education
Opportunity Act, please visit www.oup.com/us/he for the
latest information about pricing and alternate formats.

Published in the United States of America by
Oxford University Press
198 Madison Avenue, New York, NY 10016
http://www.oup.com

Library of Congress Cataloging-in-Publication Data
Black, Jeremy, 1955-
   A century of conflict : war, 1914-2014 / by Jeremy Black.
      pages cm
   Includes bibliographical references.
   ISBN 978-0-19-937232-4 (pbk. : acid-free paper)
  1. War—History—20th century. 2. Military history, Modern—20th century.
3. World politics—20th century. 4. World War, 1914–1918. 5. World War,
1939–1945. 6. Cold War. 7. War—History—21st century. 8. Military history,
Modern—21st century. 9. World politics—21st century. I. Title.
   D431.B53 2014
   355.02—dc23

                                                                    2014020444

Printing number: 9 8 7 6 5 4 3 2 1

Printed in the United States of America
on acid-free paper

For
Nick Kaye

CONTENTS

PREFACE

We prefer to forget the fact that much of human history is a history in which war has played a major role and has also conditioned the human experience. This is true not only of periods of killing, but also of the years of "peace." The latter are years in which the military have prepared and trained for war. The rest of society has paid the costs, ranging from caring for the wounded and bereaved from previous conflicts to dealing with the often crippling financial costs. Anxieties about the next war have also frequently been to the fore.

The centenary of the start of World War I in 1914 provides an opportunity to assess the role and impact of conflict in the history of the past century and also to consider how warfare has changed. This book offers a clear, global study of these topics, one open to general readers and students alike. Clarity, however, does not mean simplicity. Readers must note that, because the global nature of the study is matched by a determination to cover the multiple dimensions and spheres of war, there is no suggestion here that there is one true type or form of warfare and therefore one pattern of development. Instead, the emphasis is on the range of conflict: on regular warfare between large, professional forces that are similarly equipped, but also on conflict that has totally different characteristics. The technical distinction here is that between symmetrical and asymmetrical warfare, but it is easier to think of this contrast as that between sides that are alike in goals, methods, and weaponry (symmetrical warfare) and those that lack such a similarity.

Overlapping this contrast, but not always identical to it, is that of warfare between states and warfare within them. Indeed, by discussing the latter, this book seeks to give due weight to the use of force both to assert the role of the state and to challenge it, whether by resisting government or by contesting control over it. This domestic, internal aspect of force is of great significance, but tends to be underplayed in many works on the history of war.

Moreover, in being conceptually and methodologically up to date, there is a linked determination to be truly global. Due weight is given to Asia, where the bulk of the world's population lived throughout this period and will go on living, as well as to Africa and Latin America. As a result, this book will locate the more conventional cast of conflicts, namely the two world wars and the Cold War, in a wider context. There will not be the standard focus on Europe and on European accounts of the two world wars, the interwar period, and the Cold War.

Related to this goal, there is a determination to treat recent decades not as some aftermath of the world wars, the general pattern indeed within Europe, but, instead, as a period in which war has been important and has also greatly changed. In doing so, there is an "end-loading," so that the 2000s and 2010s receive due attention and are not treated as a sort of sequel to earlier developments. Furthermore, a discussion of the 2000s and 2010s greatly helps both in the explanation of the present situation and in the consideration of the future.

Every reader will appreciate that these are ambitious goals. They are made more so because, instead of treating war and wars as a consequence or product of other developments, notably political, economic, or technological, the argument here is that there were, and are, such links; but also that war has autonomous, indeed independent, characteristics as an activity. As a related, but additional, point, although an author can pretend that, in the face of the range of events and changes that should be covered, there is an obvious pattern of priorities, a clear narrative, and a readily understood explanation of developments, he or she should rather tell the truth and explain that there is no such pattern, narrative, and explanation. Readers, therefore, are invited to consider, as part of the educational nature of this book, how they would vary its priorities. There is, after all, no one military history.

Instead, there is room for debate about what to include and how to cover it. Moreover, as I will discuss in the first chapter, the room for debate is enlarged greatly by the extent to which, in the past, as in the present, discussion about strategy and the procurement of new weapon systems draws heavily on an analysis of current and future tasks in which competing presentations of the recent past play a major role. In short, there never was a clear pattern of narrative and explanation.

While thinking about and writing this book, I have benefited greatly from teaching at Exeter and from the opportunities to speak at a conference, "On the Eve of War," organized by the Research Centre for Communication and Culture of the Catholic University of Portugal in 2013 and to lecture at the (American) Naval War College in Newport, to the World Affairs Council, for the Foreign Policy Research Institute, to the University of Oxford Summer School, at Roger Williams University, and at Rhode Island College. I also profited from visiting Austria, Belgium, France, Germany, Hungary, Portugal, Slovakia, and the United States while working on this book.

I would like to pay tribute to colleagues in the world of military history, notably in the United States, where many fine scholars take the subject forward. When a book appears, the credit is given to the author, but in fact it is shared among those who work in a field, influencing each other directly and indirectly, sometimes in agreement and sometimes in disagreement. I benefited greatly from the comments of Dennis Showalter, Colorado College; Cathal J. Nolan, Boston University; Graydon A. Tunstall, University of South Florida; Steve R. Waddell, United States Military Academy; Devin Pendas, Boston College; Marc Gallicchio, Villanova University; Brian Crim, Lynchburg College; Nicola Foote, Florida Gulf Coast University; Alexander Mikaberidze, Louisiana State University-Shreveport; John Cox, University of North Carolina-Charlotte; and two anonymous readers on the synopsis for this book and those of Christopher Bell and Stephen Morillo on an earlier draft. They are not responsible for any errors that remain. I have also profited enormously from reading the work of other scholars and from discussing the subject with them. Partly as a result, visits to the United States are always a joy. One such visit brought me to breakfast in a New York diner with Charles Cavaliere and I would like to thank him for being a most helpful and thoughtful editor. This book is dedicated to Nick Kaye for keeping the "show on the road," a formidable achievement in the world of British Higher Education.

LIST OF MAPS

ABOUT THE AUTHOR

Jeremy Black, Professor of History at the University of Exeter and senior fellow at the Center for the Study of America and the West at the Foreign Policy Research Institute, has been described as "the most prolific historical scholar of our age." Among his many books are *The War of 1812 in the Age of Napoleon* (2010); *London: A History* (2009); *What If?: Counterfactualism and the Problem of History* (2008); *Eighteenth Century Britain, 1688–1783* (2008); *George III: America's Last King* (2007); *Rethinking Military History* (2004); *World War Two: A Military History* (2003); *War: An Illustrated World History* (2003); *European International Relations 1648–1815* (2002); and *British Diplomats and Diplomacy 1688–1800* (2001).

MAPS

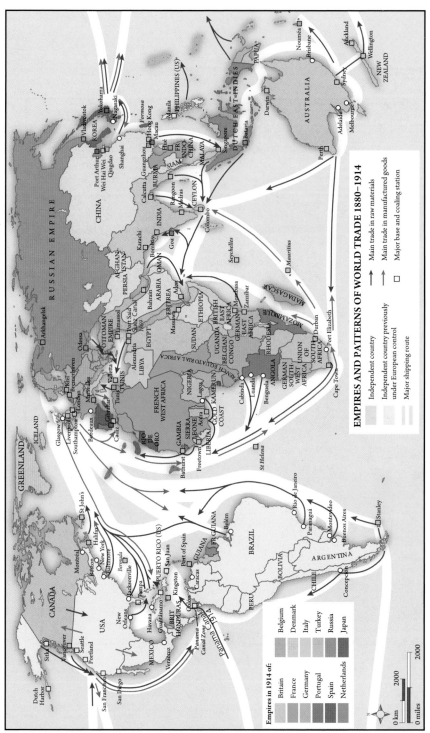

Map 1. Empires and Patterns of World Trade, 1880–1914

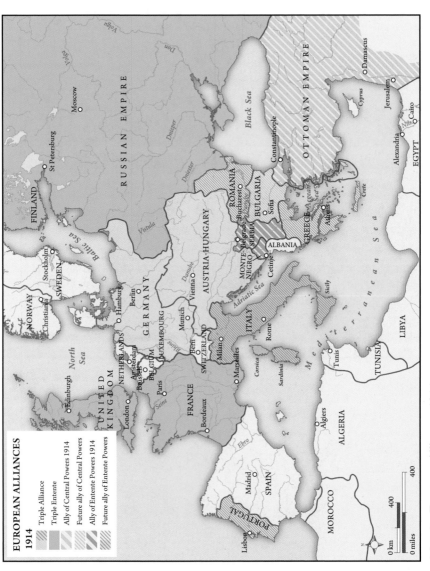

Map 2. European Alliances, 1914

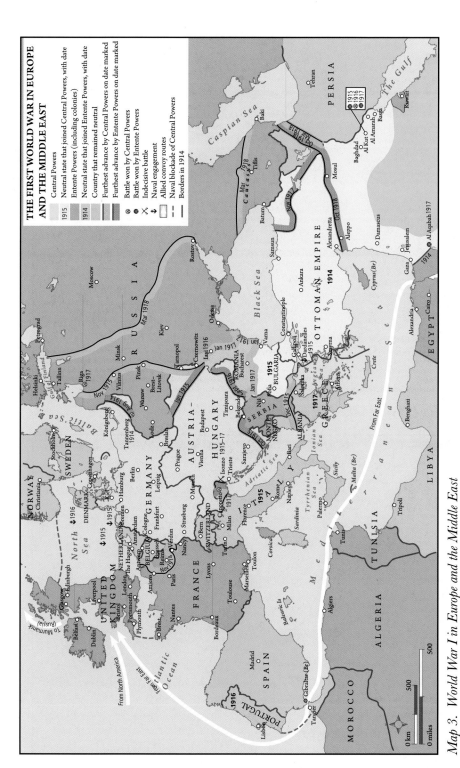

Map 3. *World War I in Europe and the Middle East*

TREATIES BETWEEN ENTENTE POWERS AND DEFEATED COUNTRIES:

Treaty of Versailles 28 June 1919 – Entente Powers (excluding USA) and Germany
Treaty of Saint-Germain 10 September 1919 – Entente Powers and Austria
Treaty of Neuilly 24 November 1919 – Entente Powers and Bulgaria
Treaty of Trianon 4 June 1920 – Entente Powers and Hungary
Treaty of Sèvres 10 August 1920 – Entente Powers (excluding USA and USSR) and Turkey (Sultanate of), superseded by:
Treaty of Lausanne 24 July 1923 with Turkish Republic
Treaty of Berlin 2 July 1921– USA and Germany

Map 4. Treaty Settlements in Europe, 1919–1923

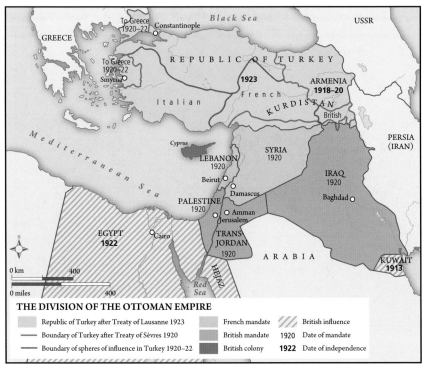

THE DIVISION OF THE OTTOMAN EMPIRE

Republic of Turkey after Treaty of Lausanne 1923
— Boundary of Turkey after Treaty of Sèvres 1920
— Boundary of spheres of influence in Turkey 1920–22
French mandate
British mandate
British colony
British influence
1920 Date of mandate
1922 Date of independence

Map 5. The Division of the Ottoman Empire

Map 6. Revolution and Civil War in Russia

REVOLUTION AND CIVIL WAR IN RUSSIA

— Boundary of the Russian Empire 1914

— German occupation line March 1918

✿ Center of great Bolshevik activity

➜ White Russian and interventionist attacks

Interventionists:

C	Canadian	B	British
F	French	US	American
G	Greek		

— Boundary of area controlled by Bolsheviks August 1918

▨ Area controlled by Bolsheviks October 1919

— Polish advance into Russia May 1920

— Russian advance into Poland August 1920

–·– USSR–Polish boundary established October 1920 by Treaty of Riga

— Other international boundaries 1922

▨ Areas lost to Russia 1914–21

▨ Soviet Union 1922

EXPANSION OF NAZI GERMANY 1933–39

Germany 1933
Saar-region, incorporated 1935
Rhineland demilitarized zone, occupied 1936
Territory annexed by Germany:
on 13 March 1938
on 1 October 1938
in March 1939
by 31 December 1939

SWEDEN

LATVIA
Riga

DENMARK

Baltic Sea

Copenhagen

Memel Territory
23 March 1939

LITHUANIA
Kaunas

Königsberg
EAST PRUSSIA

Hamburg

Danzig
19 Sept 1939

Amsterdam
NETHERLANDS

Hanover

Berlin

Weser

Elbe

Poznan

Vistula

RUSSIAN OCCUPATION

Brussels

Cologne

Rhine

Leipzig

Oder

Warsaw

17 Sept 1939

BELGIUM

Frankfurt

LUX

Saarbrücken

SAAR

G E R M A N Y

P O L A N D

Lvov

GENERAL GOVERNMENT
OF POLAND
12 Oct 1939

Kraków

SUDETENLAND

Prague

PROTECTORATE OF
BOHEMIA–MORAVIA
16 March 1939

Paris

Seine

FRANCE

Stuttgart

Nuremberg

Freiburg

Munich

Danube

Salzburg

Vienna

to Hungary 1939

PROTECTORATE
OF SLOVAKIA
23 March 1939

to Hungary
23 March
1939

Bern

Innsbruck

AUSTRIA

Budapest

HUNGARY

Geneva
SWITZERLAND

Lyons

Saône

Trent

0 km   200

0 miles   200

ITALY

Venice

Po

Trieste

YUGOSLAVIA

ROMANIA

Map 7. Expansion of Nazi Germany, 1933–1939

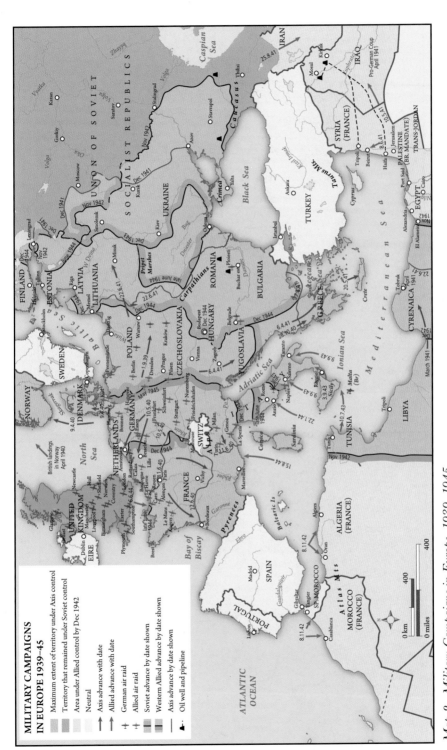

Map 8. *Military Campaigns in Europe, 1939–1945*

MILITARY CAMPAIGNS
IN EUROPE 1939–45

Maximum extent of territory under Axis control

Territory that remained under Axis control

Area under Allied control by Dec 1942

Neutral

Axis advance with date

Allied advance with date

German air raid

Allied air raid

Soviet advance by date shown

Western Allied advance by date shown

Axis advance by date shown

Oil well and pipeline

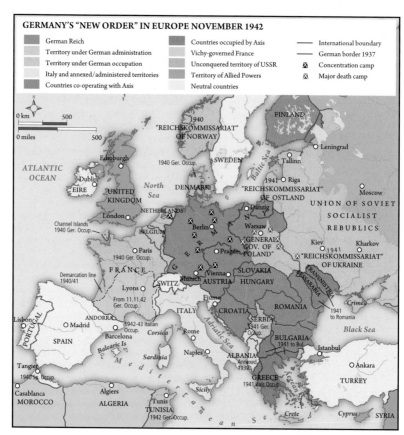

Map 9. Germany's "New Order" in Europe, November 1942

Map 10. The Japanese in China, 1931–1945

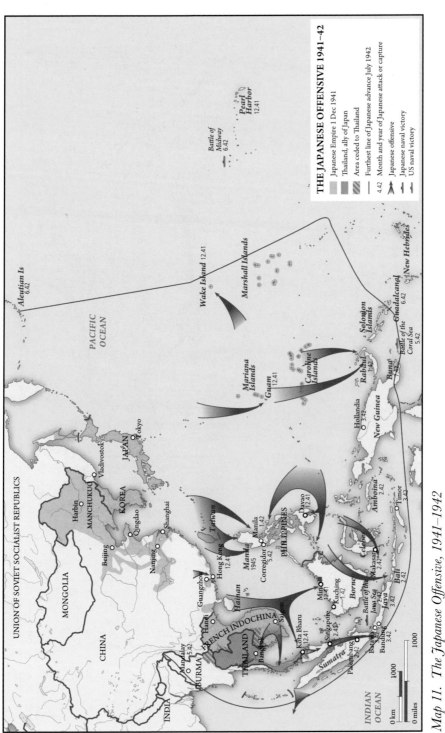

THE JAPANESE OFFENSIVE 1941–42

Japanese Empire 1 Dec 1941

Thailand, ally of Japan

Area ceded to Thailand

Furthest line of Japanese advance July 1942

4.42   Month and year of Japanese attack or capture

Japanese offensive

Japanese naval victory

US naval victory

UNION OF SOVIET SOCIALIST REPUBLICS

MONGOLIA

CHINA

Harbin

MANCHUKUO

Beijing

KOREA

Vladivostok

JAPAN

Tokyo

Qingdao

Nanjing

Shanghai

INDIA

BURMA

Mandalay
5.42

Hanoi

FRENCH INDOCHINA

Guangzhou

Hong Kong
12.41

Hainan

Taiwan

Manila
1.42

PHILIPPINES

Corregidor
5.42

Ma ma
12.41

Davao
12.41

THAILAND

Bangkok

Saigon

Kota Bharu
12.41

Singapore
2.42

Kuching
1.42

Miri
12.41

Borneo

Celebes

Makasar
2.42

Battle of the
Java Sea
2.42

Java

Bali
3.42

Palembang
2.42

Sumatra

Batavia
3.42

Bandung
3.42

Timor
2.42

Amboina
2.42

PACIFIC
OCEAN

Aleutian Is
6.42

Wake Island 12.41

Marshall Islands

Mariana
Islands

Guam
12.41

Caroline
Islands

Rabaul
1.42

Hollandia
3.42

New Guinea

Buna

Solomon
Islands

Guadalcanal
6.42

New Hebrides

Battle of the
Coral Sea
5.42

Battle of
Midway
6.42

Pearl
Harbor
12.41

INDIAN
OCEAN

0 km   1000

0 miles   1000

Map 11. The Japanese Offensive, 1941–1942

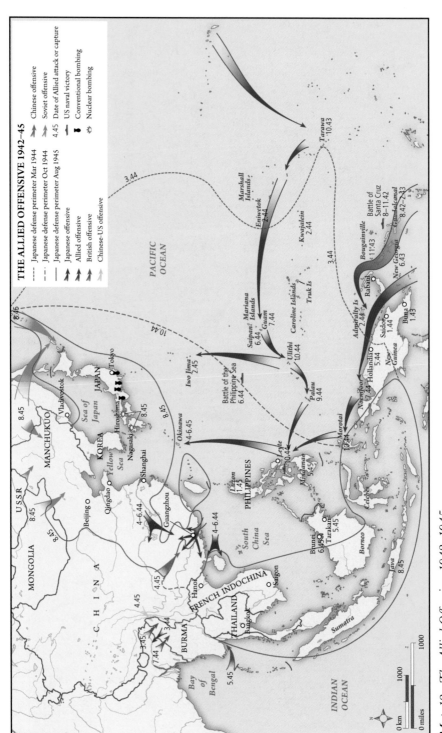

THE ALLIED OFFENSIVE 1942–45

- - - - - Japanese defense perimeter Mar 1944
── ── ── Japanese defense perimeter Oct 1944
─ · ─ · ─ Japanese defense perimeter Aug 1945

Japanese offensive
Allied offensive
British offensive
Chinese-US offensive

Chinese offensive
Soviet offensive
4.45 Date of Allied attack or capture
US naval victory
Conventional bombing
Nuclear bombing

Map 12. The Allied Offensive, 1942–1945

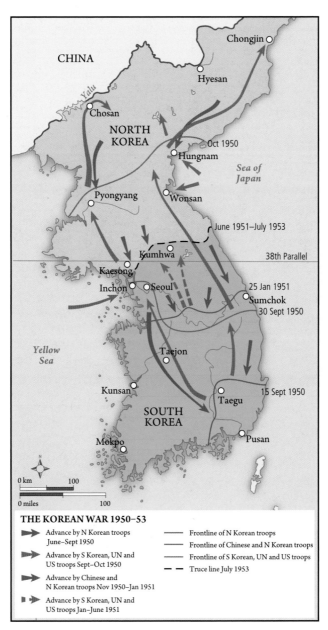

CHINA

Chongjin

Hyesan

Yalu

Chosan

NORTH
KOREA

Oct 1950

Hungnam

*Sea of
Japan*

Pyongyang

Wonsan

June 1951–July 1953

Kumhwa

38th Parallel

Kaesong

Inchon

Seoul

25 Jan 1951

Sumchok

30 Sept 1950

*Yellow
Sea*

Taejon

Kunsan

15 Sept 1950

Taegu

SOUTH
KOREA

Mokpo

Pusan

N

0 km   100

0 miles   100

THE KOREAN WAR 1950–53

Advance by N Korean troops
June–Sept 1950

Frontline of N Korean troops

Advance by S Korean, UN and
US troops Sept–Oct 1950

Frontline of Chinese and N Korean troops

Advance by Chinese and
N Korean troops Nov 1950–Jan 1951

Frontline of S Korean, UN and US troops

Advance by S Korean, UN and
US troops Jan–June 1951

Truce line July 1953

Map 13. The Korean War, 1950–1953

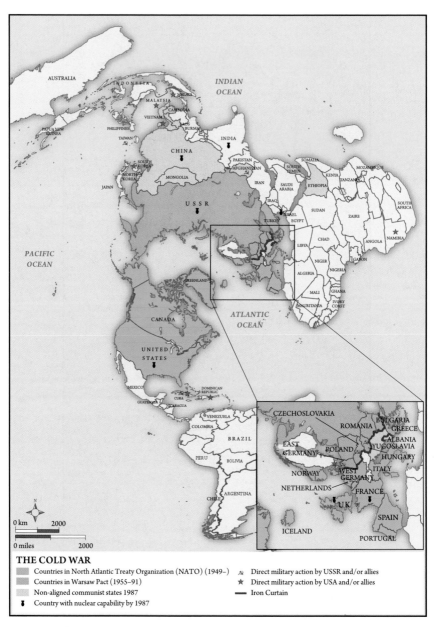

THE COLD WAR

- Countries in North Atlantic Treaty Organization (NATO) (1949–)
- Countries in Warsaw Pact (1955–91)
- Non-aligned communist states 1987
- Country with nuclear capability by 1987

- Direct military action by USSR and/or allies
- ★ Direct military action by USA and/or allies
- — Iron Curtain

Map 14. Cold War Conflicts

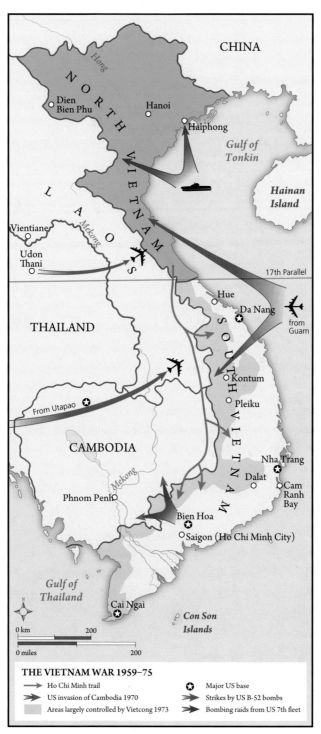

Map 15. The Vietnam War, 1959–1975

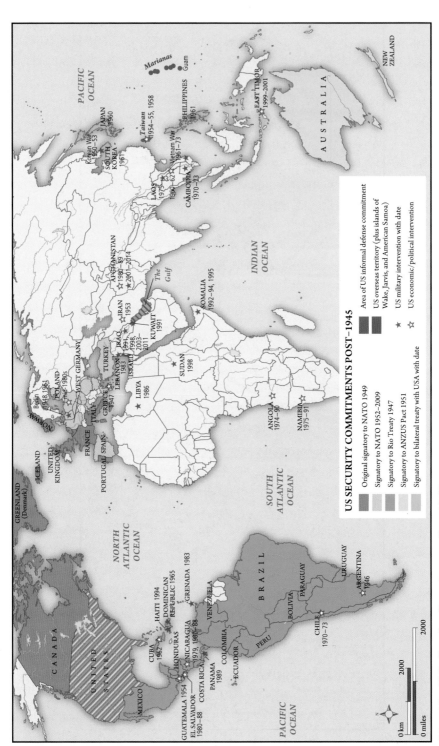

Map 16. *U.S. Security Commitments, Post-1945*

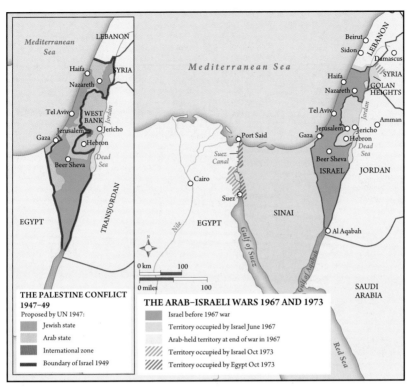

Map 17. The Palestine Conflict, 1947-1949/The Arab–Israeli Wars, 1967 and 1973

Map 18. Wars in the Gulf Region, 1980–1988, 1990–1991, and 2003

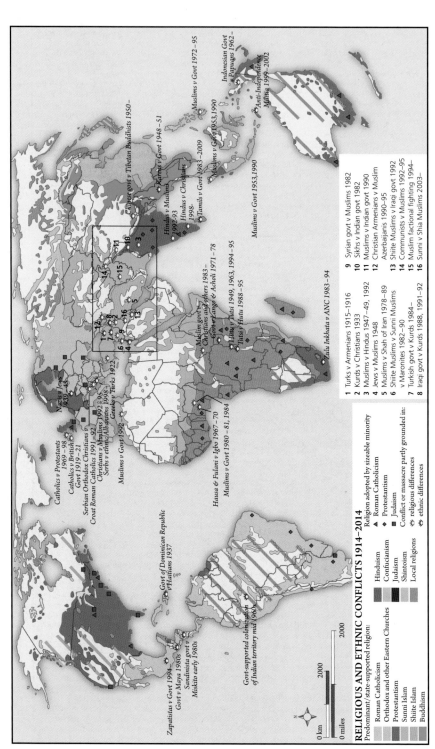

RELIGIOUS AND ETHNIC CONFLICTS 1914–2014

Predominant/ state-supported religion:

Roman Catholicism
Orthodox and other Eastern Churches
Protestantism
Sunni Islam
Shiite Islam
Buddhism

Religion adopted by sizeable minority:

▲ Hinduism
▲ Confucianism
◆ Judaism
■ Protestantism
■ Shintoism
Local religions

Conflict or massacre partly grounded in:
✶ religious differences
✤ ethnic differences

1 Turks v Armenians 1915–1916
2 Kurds v Christians 1933
3 Muslims v Hindus 1947–49, 1992
4 Jews v Muslims 1948
5 Muslims v Shah of Iran 1978–89
6 Shiite Muslims v Sunni Muslims
  v Maronites 1982–90
7 Turkish govt v Kurds 1984–
8 Iraqi govt v Kurds 1988, 1991–92

9 Syrian govt v Muslims 1982
10 Sikhs v Indian govt 1982
11 Muslims v Indian govt 1990
12 Christian Armenians v Muslim
   Azerbaijanis 1990–95
13 Shiite Muslims v Iraqi govt 1992
14 Communists v Muslims 1992–95
15 Muslim factional fighting 1994–
16 Sunni v Shia Muslims 2003–

Map 19. Religious and Ethnic Conflicts, 1917–2008

ONE

THE IMPORTANCE
OF MILITARY HISTORY

九連城大激戰露兵撃退之圖

Japanese and Russian soldiers in combat, Battle of Yalu River, 1904.

War was no add-on to the history of the past century. Instead, as throughout the history of the human species as social beings, war was a formative experience for the peoples of the world. That does not mean that all states were involved in war or that they were involved equally. Indeed, in the limited but very important case of state-to-state conflict, there was scant conflict, for example, in Latin America after 1935, notably the short-lived "Football War" of 1969 between Honduras and El Salvador and the conflict in 1982 between Argentina and Britain over competing claims to the Falkland Islands/Malvinas. In North America, the United States never fought Canada or Mexico during the twentieth century.

In Europe, neither Sweden nor Switzerland was a combatant at any stage during the century, and Spain stayed out of both world wars. Furthermore, the relatively limited number of states that have been combatants in state-to-state war since 1990 has led to discussion of the decline of warfare; so it was also with the absence of conflict between any of the great powers after the struggle between American and Chinese forces as a major (although far from only) part of the Korean War ended in 1953.

THE CONSEQUENCES OF WAR

Yet war had an impact for all, whether or not they were directly involved. To take the examples above, there were bitter civil wars in China, Spain, and several Latin American states. The impact of war, moreover, was seen across the full range of human activity and concern, from economics to environmentalism, from society to politics. This impact was especially present on neighboring states, which were affected in particular by the extent to which civilian populations in combatant states became targets and victims, leading to massive flows of refugees. Thus, the Pakistani army's suppression of opposition in East Pakistan in 1970–1971, a suppression that led to genocidal attacks on the Hindu minority and eventually to Indian invasion, was responsible for the slaughter of more than 300,000 people, and approximately 10 million became refugees.

Similarly, the Syrian civil war that began in 2011 had by October 2013 led to deadly attacks on civilians that not only resulted in much of the population becoming refugees, but also caused 2 million of a population of about 21 million Syrians to flee to neighboring states, especially Jordan and Turkey. This refugee flight posed humanitarian challenges as well as public order issues in these states. In part, the resulting pressures moved on as refugees journeyed farther afield for safety and shelter. This was an extreme instance of the degree to which war had major consequences for social structure and mobility.

The economic consequences of war could also be global. Conflict led to the damage and destruction of economic assets, such as oil wells and refineries (for example, during the Iran–Iraq War of 1980–1988 and the 1991 Gulf War), as well as to serious interruptions to trade. Such events caused global commodity prices to alter as shortages were encountered or anticipated. Moreover, such disruption could become a tool of policy, most notably with oil. Having replaced the United States as the arbiter of oil prices, the Organization of Petroleum Exporting Countries used its collective muscle to harm the Western economy after the Israeli victory over Egypt and Syria in 1973. In addition, oil shipments through the Gulf had to be protected by Western naval action from interference during the Iran–Iraq War of 1980–1988. That war originated, in part, from Saddam Hussein's wish to gain control of neighboring oil fields, as later, in 1990, did the Iraqi conquest of Kuwait. In turn, Western intervention to protect Saudi Arabia from possible pressure and to reconquer Kuwait in 1991 was influenced by concern over a region that was the world's leading source of oil supplies.

In addition to impacting the availability and price of commodities, conflict led to serious pressure on the financial system and the money supply. In need of funds to finance war, states borrowed and printed currency, affecting both the value of money and the confidence in the money supply. Indeed, savage inflation was one of the principal consequences of war during this period. Such inflation proved to be highly disruptive for societies and ensured that those at home far distant from the sphere of hostilities, for example, Americans during the Vietnam War, were still greatly affected by war. Economic dislocation and wartime fundraising took a number of forms, as with the use of "blood diamonds" in Africa and of drugs in Afghanistan and Colombia.

Wartime inflation and debt both left major burdens for the postwar situation. Indeed, whereas societies were greatly affected by the erosion of value and confidence represented by inflation, public finances could be crushed by the impact of wartime debt. The consequences included pressure for higher taxation and for cuts in expenditures on other aspects of public spending. Britain emerged from World War I (1914–1918) with a level of debt that greatly affected policies thereafter, including its ability to discharge military commitments. With the "Geddes Axe" of 1922 in Britain, there was a savage postwar cutting of government expenditure on both social policy, including homes for demobilized troops, and the military. There were to be similar issues after World War II (1939–1945).

Problems with American public finances and debt were greatly exacerbated by the consequences of the interventions in Afghanistan and Iraq from 2001. Because these interventions were not accompanied by tax increases, much of the American public was shielded (in the electoral short term) from the consequences of fighting by government borrowing. At the same time, war contributed to a serious deterioration in American public finances. This deterioration had enormous strategic implications because the gap between income and expenditure had to be filled by borrowing, and the latter required regular foreign currency inflows. As a result, the ability of the American government to operate was closely linked to the stability and views of those East Asian states that were the source of those inflows, notably China and Taiwan.

War therefore affects much of the rest of human activity, and its impact certainly does not cease when the guns fall silent. The cultural consequences could be immense. Most insistently, World War I helped cause a widespread crisis of confidence in human progress, notably in Europe, where its casualties and devastation were concentrated. There were already prewar signs of despair on the part of some commentators, but these became more common after the war and were related to a potent demand for change or at least the challenge to old orthodoxies. This challenge was seen with political radicalism and also in the rejection of conventional forms in the arts.

The impact of specific struggles was but part of the more general manner in which economics, ideology, society, and culture were all entwined with the causes, courses, and consequences of conflict. Moreover, these relationships were far from static. Thus, the changing context of war is an important aspect of the history of the past century. This context speaks to what are held to be fundamental values. For example, despite the world's population rising to unprecedented numbers, indeed, to 7.2 billion people in 2013 and with a continuing upward trend, there is a sensitivity to casualties in many societies, notably, but not only, the West.

Focusing on the fate of individuals, this sensitivity reflects a social shift away from collective obligations to individual rights and experiences. In military terms, this shift led to a reluctance to accept casualties; to greater concern with the condition of the military, including the fate of the wounded, of prisoners, and of the corpses of the slain; and to the abandonment of conscription across much of the world beginning in the 1960s and in Britain from 1957. Around the world, changing gender rights played a role in the rejection of conscription. An obligation restricted to only one sex appeared of dubious legality or social justice, and because there was scant pressure in most societies to extend this obligation to women, it seemed less reasonable only for men.

There were other reasons for the abandonment of conscription, notably the growing complexity of warfare, especially of the weaponry used and the resulting emphasis on military professionalism. This abandonment also reflected a change in the trend of state ideologies. The significance of empire and the necessity of imperial expansion for international strength and for domestic social health were strong themes among the major powers in the first half of the twentieth century. However, these themes became less potent by the second half of the Cold War, which began in the 1970s. Nevertheless, even when imperialism of the traditional type had been put aside, leaders still believed that it was essential to struggle or at least to prepare for struggles that would greatly affect all of society. As a result, war was an aspect of a more general pattern of national mobilization, one that contributed greatly to an adversarial international system. Such mobilization became less acute with the end of the Cold War in 1989–1991, but continues to be strong in societies threatened by neighbors, especially Israel and South Korea (where military service in 2013 was for 21 months) and also in totalitarian states, such as North Korea. A similar situation exists in Eritrea, a dictatorship run by Isaias Afewerki. The leader of the Eritrean People's Liberation Front, a guerrilla movement, prior to independence from Ethiopia in 1993, Afewerki has been president since as well as commander in chief of the armed forces. All Eritrean men up to the age of 50 are compelled to do national service in the army, and those up to age 65 have annual periods of service in the form of a reserve force. Eritrea is in a state of near-permanent mobilization with Ethiopia, against which it fought a bitter war in 1998–2000 that allegedly led to the death of approximately 100,000 Eritreans.

Moves to limit war led to alternative values, not least to a view that war was wrong unless waged for specific reasons and in a particular way. This effort to construct a legal pattern for the causes and course of war was a key aspect of the consequences of conflict. In particular, the two world wars, each of which was waged by alliances, led to attempts at international cooperation, although aspects of international governance generally proved elusive. Established in the aftermath of World War I, the League of Nations was fatally weakened by nonparticipation, notably by the United States, where the Senate was concerned about the consequences entailed for national independence of being a member of an international organization. In contrast, nonparticipation was not the problem for the United Nations (UN), which was established in 1945 in the aftermath of World War II. Instead, the operation of the UN was greatly affected by the rivalries of the Cold War and thereafter, but the organization did represent an attempt to constrain bellicosity.

The resulting need to justify conflict, both domestically and internationally, affected the way in which it was presented. International cooperation was to be linked to moral absolutes, with opponents treated as so evil that societies had to be mobilized to destroy their threat. This theme looked both back to World War I and forward, beyond the Cold War, to ideas about the desirability of interventionist warfare. These ideas entailed an attempt to link war and morality, notably in the conflicts with Iraq in 1991 and 2003 and in the confrontation with Syria in 2013. War therefore posed fundamental questions about the character of the international system, as well as about the nature of civil society within states. Because it bridged the international and the national, war was and is a key element in and of transnationalism.

CONTESTING THE WORLD

The significance of the subject helps explain the importance of military history, but there are two other elements to consider. First, conflict was central to the world question, the dramatic shifts in control over the world's population and land surface that were so apparent in this period. In 1914, much of the world's population, notably in Europe, Africa, and Asia, was ruled by a small number of empires, mostly European, but by 1975, these empires had collapsed. Imperial behavior continued, notably by the Soviet Union, China, and the United States, but also by newly independent states, especially India. Nevertheless, the successive end of the German, Turkish, Italian, Japanese, Dutch, Belgian, French, British, Portuguese, and Spanish empires represented a major change on the world scale.

This change owed much to war. Direct consequences were important in the shape of defeat by rival empires, notably that of Germany in 1918: most of its colonies were acquired for the British, French, and Japanese empires, whereas the Arab lands of the Turkish empire were largely acquired by Britain and France. The Japanese empire lost Pacific islands to the United States as a result of defeat in World War II.

Yet, there was also failure by empires at the hands of native resistance, or at least failure resulting from the inability to suppress this resistance, as with the French in Vietnam in 1954 and in Algeria in 1962.

The role of this resistance ensured that many states presented, and still present, their history in terms of liberation struggles. Moreover, these struggles provide legitimacy and authority today for particular political groupings. Thus, the legacy of war plays a crucial role in explaining domestic political circumstances, languages, and ideas across much of the world, yet another instance of the lasting impact of war.

THE USE OF MILITARY HISTORY

Second, military history is important because it is read into current debates about policy, both military policy in terms of how best to organize the military and foreign policy in terms of what appears practical in military terms. The standard cliché is that generals try to fight the last war, in short, that the instinctive conservatism of the military draws on an understanding of the previous conflict. The clear corollary to this view is that such an approach is flawed and inadequate and that military leadership as a whole is therefore almost a contradiction in terms.

Such a view, however, not only is inaccurate but also, in part, reflects the competition to control military history in the sense of using it to advance particular political and military agendas. The claim that there was incompetence has certainly served the case of those opposed to the military, or at least to particular wars. This antiwar sentiment proved an aspect of the public culture of the past century, although it varied greatly in its incidence, being particularly significant for Britain and France in the 1930s and for the United States during the latter stages of the Vietnam War. Ironically, the military leadership itself could be opposed to wars. For example, it is widely believed that much of the American and British military leadership was reluctant to attack Iraq in 2003.

Along with the criticism of the military, as well as the use of history accordingly, came the arguments of military reformers keen to argue the case for new methods. Their use of recent military history did not have to be critical, but there was often the argument that mistakes had been made and could only be avoided if the remedies suggested by the reformers were adopted. A very important case occurred in the 1920s and 1930s, as the supposed "lessons" of World War I were discussed in accordance with particular views on strategy, operational means, tactical practice, and force structure. For example, it was claimed by those who saw the future in tanks and aircraft that their use by Britain, France, and the United States in 1918 had broken the tactical and operational intractabilities of trench warfare and restored mobility to the battlefield, allowing the Allies to defeat the Germans in the last campaign of World War I. That interpretation encouraged the emphasis on tanks seen in particular in German war making in 1939–1942.

World War I also produced an increasingly powerful "air" lobby, which, driven in part by interservice rivalry, claimed that traditional battlefield victories were no longer necessary to achieve victory because strategic airpower offered a more efficient, cost-effective means to strike directly at the heart of an opponent's war-making capabilities and morale. This belief manifested itself in the heavy commitment of British and American resources to the strategic bombing campaigns in World War II, which fell far short of the expectations of its most ardent supporters. However, nuclear weapons gave airpower enthusiasts a new lease on life after World War II, and their promises of easier victories and lower casualties could be seen again during the Vietnam and Iraq wars and continue to be very popular in the West, most recently with the development of unmanned drones.

Despite their emphasis on the potential of tank attacks, the Germans lost World War II. This occurred for a number of reasons, as we discuss in Chapter 4. They included Allied strengths, but German deficiencies were also significant. The latter deficiencies link to the idea that the enthusiasts for tank warfare derived the wrong lessons from World War I. Their preference for a weapons system that in theory could produce a quick victory led to an inability to plan for a long war. Moreover, insofar as the analysis of the victory in 1918 was concerned, there was a failure to note the limitations of tanks and, instead, the far greater significance in this last campaign of the war of the effective Allied use of artillery, a use that was more effective than in earlier campaigns. Correspondingly, in World War II, artillery, including the mobile artillery provided by ground-support aircraft (for example, "tank busters") and by self-propelled guns, played an important tactical role in the Allied victory, both on the western and on the eastern fronts in Europe, as well as in the war with Japan.

The use of military history to derive an understanding of how to win was also seen in post-1945 military planning. This was scarcely surprising because this history was also important in military education and, indeed, remains so. Thus, the curriculum at the U.S. Military Academy at West Point includes much military history, both American and non-American. More recent military history played a key role in planning because it indicated the capability and methods of opponents. During the Cold War, the American-led forces of the North Atlantic Treaty Organization (NATO, founded in 1949) assessed the reasons why the *Wehrmacht*, the German army, had failed in its conflict with the Soviet Union in 1941–1945, whereas NATO subsequently focused on the nature of the successful Soviet offensives of 1944–1945 and especially on Soviet operational art. This success and capability appeared highly relevant because it was believed that if World War III broke out, it would include a large-scale Soviet tank–led offensive across the North German Plain. Such an offensive indeed featured in Soviet plans, and an attack was contemplated by the Soviet Union as late as 1983.

Military history was also held up as a warning, and new wars were fed by and into the warnings and admonitions that could be offered. The appeasement of "the dictators," the rulers of Germany, Italy, and Japan, in 1931–1941, notably by Britain and France but also by the then-isolationist United States, was subsequently used as a prompt to arming and acting. This was the case with familiar episodes such as the British debate over intervening against Egypt in the Suez Crisis in 1956 and discussion over invading Iraq in 2003 and intervening in Syria in 2013. The failure to stand up against Hitler in the 1930s was also cited in less

Syrian refugees, 2013.

familiar episodes, as in 1971 when Henry Kissinger, the head of the American National Security Council who had been a refugee from Hitler, used the parallel with appeasement to encourage (unsuccessfully) opposition to Indian intervention in East Pakistan.

Conversely, British failure against Egypt in 1956 and American failure in the Vietnam War, failure that culminated in withdrawal in 1973, were both deployed in calls to caution and prudence in subsequent crises, as over Iraq in 2003 and Syria in 2013. The evidence of the past on these points was deployed in 2003 by those who argued in favor of war with Iraq, as well as by those opposed to such a course.

The use of the past could also be sequential. Thus, for American military and civilian planners and commentators, success against Iraq in 1991 encouraged subsequent boldness, notably sending American troops in 1992 into the failed state of Somalia. In turn, failure there led to cautious nonintervention, notably in Rwanda in 1994. However, the rapid and massive slaughter of civilians in genocidal massacres there produced a call to action, which saw America lead successful NATO interventions in crises in Bosnia (1995) and Kosovo (1999), both in the failed state of Yugoslavia.

These achievements encouraged the sense that problems in Afghanistan and Iraq could be overcome, only for the serious difficulties then encountered in the 2000s to lead to an attempt not to get closely involved in the crisis in Syria in 2012–2014. Learning lessons thus feeds into the decision-making process and is an important aspect of the degree to which the past is still present. History, therefore, is part of the way in which issues are addressed for current audiences in order to affect the future.

Many historians like to suggest that they are somehow separate from this process, but that is not the case. Let me give a simple example. If I present the key issue of the 2010s as the growth of Chinese political, economic, and military power and ambitions, then I will necessarily direct attention away from the problems posed by instability in the Arab world or the challenge posed by Iran. Moreover, because the agenda of planning is therefore different, so the change in potential task for the military of the leading power, the United States, will have clear consequences for the type of military that is necessary. Potential confrontation with China requires "high-spectrum" weaponry and a strong modern navy, whereas intervention in the Arab world puts the emphasis on an army trained in COIN, the American term for counterinsurrectionary warfare.

THE BACKGROUND TO WORLD WAR I

Similar questions about emphasis arise for the past, and readers of this book must be aware of them. We will begin with the outbreak of World War I in 1914. This global war rightly commands attention. However, from the perspective of East Asia, a key sphere for rivalry throughout this book, the most significant development of the 1910s occurred closer to home. Beginning with a mutiny by part of the army, the overthrow of the Manchu imperial dynasty in 1911–1912 and the creation of the first Chinese republic brought an embrace of modernity and modernization to the world's most populous state. China's revival and prospects were to excite Japanese concern and activity, or ambition and expansionism, depending on where you wish to place the emphasis, a topic, indeed, that plays a role today in the vexed relations between the two states. The resulting Japanese interventions in Chinese politics looked toward the eventual outbreak of full-scale war between the two powers in 1937.

Western dominance of the international system and the world economy in the early twentieth century, however, were such that events in China then appeared of lesser consequence as tensions rose between the major European powers in the early 1910s. These tensions looked back to earlier conflicts, notably between France and Germany in 1870–1871, a war won by the latter, and the powers prepared so as to be able to win any future war. This preparedness, as well as a more general bellicosity, contributed greatly to the outbreak of World War I in 1914. That was the conflict that began the age of modern warfare, and it is a war that still resonates today, not least in the fears expressed in 2013 that Syria would serve, as the Balkans had done in 1914, to ignite a wider struggle, bringing in other regional powers and the great powers. Similar fears were expressed in 2014 about differences over control of the East and South China Seas.

Because World War I still resonates so much in the collective modern psyche, it is also an appropriate place to begin a history of modern warfare. It was a key conflict in the development of this warfare and in the shaping of the twentieth-century world. In particular, the war led to the Communist takeover in Russia in 1917 (transforming it into the Soviet Union) and thus to the beginning of the

Burying the dead after the Battle of Adrianople, First Balkan War, 1912–1913.

"Cold War" between Communism and capitalism, although that conflict is not usually dated until after World War II ended in 1945.

In addition, it is the role of this war in public attitudes that is significant. There had been terrible struggles earlier and struggles that had absorbed the human and material resources of society, notably the French Revolutionary and Napoleonic Wars in Europe between 1792 and 1815. However, because of its unprecedented scale and destructiveness, World War I was regarded as totally different and, accordingly, was known as the Great War by contemporaries. The very sense of difference and of a new beginning in warfare created a distancing of earlier episodes.

This scale reflected in part the industrialization of the West between 1815 and 1914. That development helps explain the differences between the Napoleonic Wars and the global struggles of the twentieth century. The related rise in growing, wealthier, and more urban and educated societies of public politics helped explain a related change: the cultural factors that turned World War I, World War II, and the Cold War into struggles not only for political control of the world, but also for the cultural and ideological shape of that control.

In practice, there were parallels between the fighting in World War I and earlier conflict, notably with the Russo-Japanese War of 1904–1905. This was particularly so in the character of the fighting on land. That also was a conflict in which attacking infantry was mown down by machine guns and rapid-firing artillery and in which infantry were based in trench systems protected by barbed wire. Initially, it was hoped in 1914 that conflict of the type seen in the Russo-Japanese War of 1904–1905 and in the two Balkan Wars of 1912–1913, all three wars deadly but short, would be repeated. Heavy casualties were predicted, but it was widely believed that the war would be "over by Christmas" of 1914. In the Russo-Japanese War and the Balkan Wars, the sides that had attacked had won, albeit with heavy casualties, and it was anticipated that this would be the pattern again. That this was not to be led to a war on a scale that genuinely changed the nature of conflict and also drove home assumptions about a transformation that represented the terrible birth of a new type of warfare.

READING LIST

Jeremy Black, *War and Technology*, Bloomington, Indiana University Press, 2013.

Azar Gat, *The Development of Military Thought: The Nineteenth Century*, Oxford, Oxford University Press, 1992.

Richard Hall, *The Balkan Wars 1912–1913*, London, Routledge, 2000.

TWO

INDUSTRIAL WAR AS THE HUMAN EXPERIENCE: WORLD WAR I, 1914–1918

A Ugandan color guard, commanded by a British officer.

The age of modern warfare began with World War I as a result of five characteristics of the war. First, this was a global struggle on an unprecedented scale. Second, the nature of combat changed. Third, it proved necessary to transform economic systems and societies to contest the war, in some cases accelerating processes of transformation already occurring, but in others very much proceeding in different directions. Fourth, the war gave rise to a host of other struggles including, ultimately, World War II in 1939. Last, the heavy casualties caused by World War I thereafter affected planners and commentators, who, as a result, sought different ways of fighting, if not the avoidance of war.

There had been wars before that had been far-flung. The French and Indian War between Britain and France (1754–1763) became part of the broader Seven Years' War (1756–1763) and saw conflict from North America and the West Indies to Europe and West Africa and from India to the Philippines. In his *History of the English-Speaking Peoples*, Winston Churchill referred to this conflict as "The First World War." When Britain and her allies fought France and her allies in the French Revolutionary and Napoleonic Wars (1792–1815), there was also fighting from the West Indies to Europe, from South Africa to India, and in modern Indonesia. Moreover, in India, local powers were directly involved in the Seven Years' and the French Revolutionary and Napoleonic Wars. In contrast, during World War I, there was no fighting on land in the West Indies or in North America, although German submarines operated offshore. Moreover, the global range and intensity of the fighting in World War I did not match that in World War II; there was far less combat in the Pacific, in East and Southeast Asia, and in the Horn of Africa (Ethiopia and Somalia), although World War I did involve the conquest of German colonies in East, West, and Southwest Africa; in East Africa this fighting continued until the end of the war.

Nevertheless, the global nature of World War I is striking because of the role of non-European powers, because of the colonial strength of the major European powers, and because of the character of European warfare since the defeat of Napoleon in 1815. A war that saw Japanese warships in the Indian Ocean and the Mediterranean, as well as a large American army in France, was unprecedented. For Japan, which went to war with Germany in 1914, World War I saw a major increase in its ambitions and role, as well as significant expansion in the economy. The United States had flexed its muscles repeatedly from the 1890s and in 1898 had shown its range when it had conquered Cuba, Puerto Rico, and the Philippines from Spain. However, Spain was a weak and declining power, whereas Germany was the second strongest industrial power in the world after the United States and the second greatest naval power after Britain. Germany posed a military challenge greater than any faced by the Americans since the very different War of Independence from Britain in 1775–1783. Moreover, the American response in the dispatch of much of the fleet and most of a rapidly raised army to Europe (as well as aircraft) was unprecedented.

Turkey, formerly part of the Ottoman Empire, is a difficult state to classify. Its former capital, Constantinople (now called Istanbul), was geographically in Europe, and there is a tendency in the early twenty-first century to see Turkey as a European state. That choice, however, speaks more to current political aspirations than to the reality of a country that is mostly now in what used to be called Asia Minor. In 1914, the Ottoman Empire was far more far-flung, but only in Asia, ruling the modern states of Iraq, Syria, Lebanon, Israel, and Palestine as well as the Hejaz, the western part of the Arabian Peninsula, including the sacred Muslim cities of Mecca and Medina. Thanks to his guardianship of these cities, the sultan (ruler) claimed leadership of the Muslim peoples as Caliph, which led in 1914 to the declaration of a holy war (*jihad*) as the Turks sought to stir up opposition among the Muslim subjects of their opponents. Thus, the entry of the Ottoman Empire into the war as part of the German alliance system not only resulted in conflict in the empire, but also threatened the cohesion of British, French, and Russian territories that included such Muslim subjects from British-ruled India to British, French, and Italian-ruled North Africa and the Russian-ruled Caucasus.

The geographical range of the Ottoman Empire created targets and threats for its rivals, and this situation helped bring into play the colonial strength of the Western powers ranged against Germany. The British Empire was the largest colonial system in the world, in terms of both population and territory, and France was the second largest. The British Empire was also a formidable military resource. Whereas the Indian Army mustered 155,423 regular soldiers in August 1914, it had grown to 1,440,337 by December 1918. Australian, New Zealand, and Indian forces from the British Empire played a major role in the attacks on the Ottoman Empire, notably with the unsuccessful Gallipoli offensive of 1915, an attempt by naval and amphibious forces to break through to Constantinople. Imperial forces also played a key role in conquering the German colonies in Africa and the Pacific, operations that helped ensure that the war was indeed far-flung. Thus, troops from South Africa, then part of the British Empire, conquered German Southwest Africa, now Namibia, in 1915.

Imperial forces also played a key role on the western front, with the Canadians being particularly significant. The British forces that played a central part in the defeat of Germany in 1918 included Canadian, Australian, and New Zealand formations. There was also crucial economic support for Britain from the empire, as there also was to be in World War II.

Last, the global character of World War I is significant because the wars between European powers since 1815 had been fought only in Europe, with the exception of the Crimean War involving Russia in 1854–1856, a conflict that had also involved small-scale Anglo-Russian hostilities in the Far East. Moreover, again with that exception, these wars had been short. Germany had defeated France rapidly in 1870–1871, winning the two key battles in the opening month, and the assumption in 1914 was that there would be another quick war, with the results settled on land and without the intervention of non-European powers. This, however, was not to be.

In part, the failure of the opening campaign to provide a quick victory reflected flaws in war planning and execution, as well as changes in the nature of conflict. Other factors were also significant, notably the extent to which Britain and

France could draw on powerful empires, which meant that the ability to rapidly deliver an impressive military result in Europe could be countered using imperial military and economic resources. As in World War II, it proved mistaken to plan for a quick conflict, the idea that helped produce political support for war.

The transition from the unsuccessful opening campaign in 1914 to the fighting at the close of the war in 1918 also indicated the start of the age of modern warfare. In 1914, cavalry was deployed in large numbers, infantry was used without due awareness of the destructive capacity of modern weaponry, notably rapid firing artillery, and the French troops still wore bright red trousers. There were few aircraft and no tanks in 1914. By 1918, as we shall see, the nature, demands, and expectations of fighting were very different.

War arose from the competition between the major European powers, most of which were aligned in competing leagues, particularly those of France–Russia and Germany–Austria, and were arming and preparing their forces for war. Moreover, a series of diplomatic crises had greatly raised tension from the 1900s, notably over the Balkans (Southeast Europe), because the Turkish Empire there was (mostly) partitioned between neighboring powers in 1912–1913.

The war itself began because of an assassination in Sarajevo in Bosnia on June 28, 1914. Bosnia was a province in the Austro-Hungarian Empire (or Austria). The visiting Archduke Franz Ferdinand, the nephew and heir of the elderly emperor, Franz Joseph, was assassinated by terrorists linked to a Serbian nationalist organization that was part of the governmental structure. This assassination led Austria to decide on a show of force against Serbia, the ambitions of which challenged Austria's position in the Balkans. War was seen by military decision makers in Austria as the best way to stabilize the empire in the face of serious nationalist challenges from within and without, notably by the Serbs.

Alliance systems contributed directly to war, rather than helping deter its onset. German support for its ally, Austria, provided crucial encouragement to the latter. The Serb response to an Austrian ultimatum was deemed inadequate, and on July 28, the Austrians declared war, ending the possibility of mediation by the other powers that had been a prospect the previous day. Moreover, military action was to start with the Austrian bombardment of Belgrade, Serbia's capital. In reply to the Austrian declaration, Serbia's ally, Russia, declared general mobilization on July 30, a move that made a major war more likely. With its decision makers confident that war was necessary and could lead to a quick victory, Germany demanded the cancelation of this mobilization, a step that would have identified Russia as an inadequate ally, and thus destroyed the Franco-Russian alliance. When this demand was refused, war on Russia was declared on August 1. Russia's ally, France (elements of whose government had encouraged Russia to act), then became the key element for the Germans. They issued an ultimatum that France must declare neutrality and provide guarantees for it, and French refusal led the Germans to declare war on August 3. Thus, the Germans, who had rejected British and Russian suggestions of mediation, declared war on both Russia and France before either had begun military action against them.

THE INITIAL CAMPAIGN ON
THE WESTERN FRONT

Germany now faced war on both fronts—with France and Russia—as it had not done when it defeated Austria in 1866 and France in 1870–1871. To win, the Germans thought it necessary to focus their efforts on defeating their opponents in sequence. Although Germany shared borders with both France and Russia, France was the only one that apparently could be knocked out rapidly: Paris was far closer to attacking German forces than Moscow. To avoid the fortifications and hilly terrain in eastern France, however, the Germans attacked France via flatter Belgium. Belgian neutrality was guaranteed by the major powers, including Britain. However, on August 4, Belgium was invaded, and the German chancellor declared, "Necessity knows no law."

Britain already felt challenged by Germany's aggressive expansionism and naval buildup and concerned about the balance of power. The invasion of Belgium united most British political opinion behind the war. National honor was an important factor in the political culture and international realities of British politics. The British government had also entered into naval arrangements with France. On August 4, when an ultimatum demanding the German evacuation of Belgium received no answer, Britain entered the war.

The German failure to appreciate the consequences of British entry reflected the wider limitations of German strategic thought. Because the Germans sought, planned in great detail for, and anticipated a swift and decisive victory to avoid the military, political, economic, and social complexities of a large-scale and lengthy war between peoples, the political dimension was not significant for their planners who, in any case, underestimated their opponents' power and resolve.

The focus in 1914 was on winning the initial campaign and, in doing so, by attacking. Heavy casualties were anticipated, but all the major powers, bar Britain and the United States, already had conscription, and armies were large. Moreover, although enthusiasm for war was far from universal and many were shocked by the turn of events, there was a strong sense of patriotism. There was considerable public support for war. Reservists mobilized and volunteers flocked to serve. Moreover, support for war in Britain increased once news spread about German atrocities, notably against civilians in Belgium. Newspapers and posters spread reports and images of these atrocities. Such reports were to be a significant strand in war reporting of the following century.

Popular consent for the war was strongly grounded among all the combatants. The conviction that the war would be short contributed to its popularity, but so did the strength of nationalism in this period. In contrast, the peace movement collapsed in August 1914 and the Socialist parties preferred the nationalist course to the alternative of an international Socialism opposed to war.

The plans of all the armies failed in 1914, bar those of the Serbs, who defended themselves successfully against Austrian attack. The Germans launched the key offensive, advancing through Belgium into northern France. The Belgian fortresses around Liège were blown apart by massive German howitzers: the 420-mm guns fired 2,052 16-pound high-explosive shells able to penetrate 10 feet of concrete. The Germans benefited because initially the French focused not on Belgium, but on advancing farther south against the German-ruled section of Lorraine, annexed by Germany in 1871 after the previous war between France and Germany. Launched in the face of German artillery, the French offensive was unsuccessful and very costly.

Eventually, French and British forces were fed in to resist the German attack via Belgium. The Germans, meanwhile, were slowed down by the need to transport food and ammunition for the formidable number of their advancing forces. Aside from serious faults in German planning and execution, there were also problems with equipment and discipline. These qualify the usual historiographical picture of total German competence, a point also valid for World War II.

German problems gave the French a better opportunity to regroup. Indeed, German war making, with its emphasis on surprise, speed, and overwhelming and dynamic force at the chosen point of contact, was not effective against a French defense that had depth and that retained the capacity to use reserves by redeploying troops by rail during the course of operations: units were moved from the Lorraine front to resist the Germans who had advanced via Belgium. The same issues were to face the Germans when they invaded the Soviet Union in 1941, again achieving initial success but failing to knock out their opponent.

These problems were serious in 1914, as was the mishandled German advance when it neared Paris itself. A gap between the two armies on the advancing German right developed and the French took the opportunity to counterattack, advancing into the gap on September 8 in the Battle of the Marne. The Germans were not defeated, but suffered a failure of nerve and fell back in what became a key failure of impetus.

The Germans had lost their opportunity to win. This strategic defeat also reflected a more general falling apart of prewar plans, a product both of their deficiencies and of mistakes in implementations. The limitations that invading powers faced in maneuver warfare were serious, especially in sustaining mass and maintaining the tempo of attack, and these limitations helped to cause the failure of the German offensive. In contrast, whatever the German deficiencies, the maintenance of the French defense in 1914 was a fundamental Allied strategic achievement. It ensured that Germany would have to fight land wars on two fronts, unlike in 1870 and 1940, when France was defeated. In 1918, the Germans only had to fight on one front and the Allies were put under great pressure by German attack.

After the Battle of the Marne, both sides unsuccessfully sought to outflank the other to the northwest to avoid the high casualties of frontal attacks and to gain the advantage of the open flank and of maneuvering into the opponent's rear. The German attempt to break through to the English Channel, however, was thwarted by the British in the First Battle of Ypres, in which more than 140,000 men were killed in two weeks. The heavy casualties reflected the peril of the modern battlefield, a peril that owed much to enhancements in weaponry since Germany and

France had last fought, in 1870–1871. In particular, the potency of artillery was increased by better sights, new propellants and fuses, steel-coated projectiles, high-explosive fillings, and new recoil/recuperator dual systems whereby one part allowed the barrel to recoil without moving the carriage and the other part allowed the barrel to return to its original position on the carriage. This hydro-pneumatic and hydromechanical system was essential to quick-firing guns.

The enhanced accuracy of artillery helped make the open battleground dangerous to an unprecedented degree, affecting tactics and uniforms. As a result of this danger, soldiers dug in. Field fortifications had long been a feature on battlefields and entrenchment (digging trenches) was scarcely new, but the threat from artillery very much ensured that entrenchments now played the major role in field fortifications. Trenches were designed to protect troops.

By November 1914, there was a stalemate on what had become a fixed western front, with the front line stretching from the Swiss frontier to the North Sea. The maneuver stage of the war in the West, with its emphasis on a strategy of envelopment and on a battle of annihilation to secure total victory, was now over. Trenches became the environment of military life and the center of conflict. Dug into the soil and difficult to keep dry or make warm, trenches represented the extreme discomfort of military service. Soldiers focused on their boots and the means to keep their feet warm, and they also had to deal with rats and lice. Because trench lines were fixed for long periods, the memory of those who had

German artillery shells abandoned after the Battle of the Marne.

already been killed in them played a major role in the sense of site involved. This was a world that was very different from civilian society, at once both disorienting and very frightening.

THE NATURE OF TRENCH WARFARE

Generals were to try repeatedly to recreate the flexibility of the opening stage of the war, indeed to seek to reopen a war of movement by breaking through their opponents' front line, but this goal was to prove elusive year after year. Indeed, it is unclear how far maneuver warfare, as planned prior to the war, was in fact a real possibility for the large and well-equipped armies of major European powers fighting each other in a confined space in this period or whether it was an illusion, so that a quick victory from outmaneuvering the opponent was unlikely. Whether or not trench warfare could have been avoided by better planning, generalship, and tactics, it was established by the end of 1914, creating tactical and operational problems that were to be savage in their consequences in terms of casualties.

The basic strategic fact was that Germany, in the opening campaign, had seized most of Belgium and part of France, which obliged Britain and France to mount offensives against the German trench lines to regain the lost territory. Moreover, gaining the initiative by attacking was seen as necessary for victory.

Successive offensives, however, revealed the defensive strength of trench systems. The concentration of large forces in a relatively small area ensured that any defender was able to call on plenty of reserve troops to stem an advance that was necessarily slow when made by infantry against ground badly cut up by shell fire. The strength of trench positions also owed much to the weaponry available for their protection and that they could protect, especially quick-firing artillery and machine guns, with their impressive and unprecedented range and rapidity of fire. In addition, barbed wire hindered attackers.

Furthermore, even if such trench positions were breached, it was difficult for an attacker to make substantial gains. Local superiority in numbers could not be translated into decisive success. Although it was possible to break through at least some of the opponents' trench lines, as attackers repeatedly demonstrated, albeit at heavy costs, it was hard to exploit such successes, in part because the attacking army had exhausted itself in the first stage.

Moreover, once troops had advanced, it was difficult even to recognize, let alone reinforce and exploit, success. Until wireless technology improved in late 1917, communications remained limited, and this issue stultified the control and direction of forward operations. This problem was part of a more widespread limitation in command structures, specifically poor communication and often cohesion between front-line troops and more senior command levels. Furthermore, the devastating impact of modern shell fire ripped up the terrain to such an extent that it was difficult to bring up supporting artillery and supplies behind any advance, which meant that the impetus of the critical attack could not be sustained.

In addition to local reserves, the defenders could also use railways to bring in reinforcements rapidly in the event of a threatened breakthrough. Thus, defenders could move troops more rapidly by rail to the battlefields than the attackers could advance on foot through the battlefield.

Artillery was the real killer, followed by machine guns. Estimates suggest that high explosive fired by artillery and mortars caused up to 60 percent of all casualties. The relative stability of the trench systems made it worthwhile deploying heavy artillery to bombard them because the guns could be brought up and supplied before the situation changed, as it did in maneuver warfare. It was necessary to provide artillery support to batter an enemy's defensive systems and to subdue opposing artillery.

In 1915, British and French attacks on the western front suffered from a lack of understanding of trench warfare. There was a shortage of heavy artillery and shells arising from the expectation of a short war and the related delays in establishing the necessary industrial and military procurement policies for a sustained war. The earlier reliance on field guns, rather than on heavy guns, proved inappropriate for trench warfare. Attacks, for example, those by the British at Loos, failed, with heavy casualties.

In 1916, in contrast, the combatants benefited to a degree from the gearing up of their economies for war, notably in increasing shell production, and they launched more sustained offensives. The Germans attacked at Verdun, followed by the British (and, to a lesser extent, the French) at the Somme. For both, the

British machine gunners in a trench.

alternative to the pursuit of the strategic breakthrough appeared to be a policy of attrition, which focused primarily on killing large numbers of opponents. The numbers killed were formidable. The Verdun offensive, launched on February 21 and designed to bleed the French army dry in defense of a vulnerable position, had led to the death of 714,000 French and German troops by the end of the year, but the French did not break. Indeed, they recaptured most of the territory near Verdun lost earlier in the year.

In part to take the pressure off the French at Verdun, the British took the major role in the Somme offensive. On July 1, 1916, when the British attacked on the Somme with 120,000 troops, they suffered that day alone 57,470 dead or wounded, many from machine gun fire. In 142 days, the British, who lacked sufficient heavy artillery support, advanced to a maximum depth of about six miles. More generally, in 1916, as in 1915, the deployment by the British of a large, recently raised volunteer army gravely compromised the professionalism that the smaller prewar British army had displayed. However, the Somme offensive also saw a marked improvement in British fighting methods and effectiveness during the course of the campaign; and German casualties, although less than British casualties, were still heavy. As with the major naval battle at Jutland that year, British deficiencies and casualties did not prevent both German losses and a sense on the part of German commanders that they would not prevail in the face of Allied determination and strength.

The year 1917 was another year of failure, with the British and French unable to break into the full depth of the German defenses, to consolidate, and to press home any advantage that arose so that break in could be converted to breakthrough. The French Champagne offensive proved particularly unsuccessful and the heavy casualties led some of the French units to mutiny. This failure put the onus to act on the British.

However, in the Third Battle of Ypres, generally called Passchendaele after a ridge that became a key target, mud became a major problem for the attacking British and Dominion troops. The waterlogged terrain and heavy mud both proved ghastly living and fighting conditions and accentuated the frequent problem on the western front in which tactics swallowed operations. Unduly heavy rainfall ensured that the artillery lacked firm ground from which to fire and on which to move. A total of 70,000 British troops died in that offensive without any breakthrough. All local gains that were made were retaken by the Germans in the Lys offensive of April 1918. This was one of the German spring offensives on the western front that year in which the Germans inflicted serious losses.

THE EASTERN FRONTS

Although the fighting on the western front dominates attention and has molded the subsequent image and understanding of the war, there was more flexible campaigning on a series of fronts in Eastern Europe. Moreover, this campaigning delivered military results that were to be of great political consequence. The offensives launched there in 1914 failed, like those in Western Europe. Russian armies invaded East Prussia, only to be heavily defeated by the Germans at Tannenberg and the Masurian Lakes. The lack of coordination between the invading armies permitted the smaller German forces to defeat the Russian armies separately. The Germans had the advantages of interior lines of communication, but also benefited from their ability to adapt more rapidly to opportunities. The Russians had more success that year in invading the Austrian possessions in southern Poland, whereas the Austrians failed to defeat the Serbs.

In 1915, the Russians were driven out of Poland by the Germans, which encouraged Bulgaria to join the German alliance system. The subsequent overrunning of Serbia by Austrian, German, and Bulgarian forces in October 1915 demonstrated the ability of contemporary armies to achieve decisive victories in the right circumstances. In this campaign, large forces were ably deployed and coordinated over difficult terrain.

In 1916, the Russians under General Brusilov attacked the Austrians in southern Poland, benefiting from the lower density of troops there compared to that on the shorter western front. Lower force-to-space ratios on the eastern front ensured that the defense was weaker, both at the front and in terms of reserves, but it was still possible, if troops could be massed, to mount offensives successfully. In a surprise attack, Brusilov made major gains, but the offensive was pushed on beyond where it should have stopped to consolidate the gains. The Germans and Austrians were able to seal the front and to mount a successful counteroffensive.

Russian prisoners guarded by Austrian forces, Przemysl Fortress (present-day Poland).

Brusilov's initial success encouraged Romania, which had territorial ambitions at the expense of Austria and Bulgaria, to enter the war on the side of the Allies in 1916. However, against Romania, as previously against Serbia, the forces of Austria, Germany, and Bulgaria displayed an impressive ability to deliver a verdict. Most of Romania was rapidly overrun, indicating the potential decisiveness of operations. As with the Americans later in their initial operations on the western front, the Romanians suffered from a lack of experience of conflict of the type of World War I. Their army also lacked the relevant weaponry, and its command style reflected the ethos of aristocratic society, rather than experienced professionalism. Nevertheless, the Romanians fought on in Moldavia, and the need to fight there weakened the Central Powers elsewhere, notably in 1917.

REVOLUTION IN RUSSIA

Russia's failure to protect its territory from invasion contributed directly to the savage socioeconomic crisis there. The organizational weakness of the Russian state was particularly clear in transport and food allocation. Food shortages became more serious in the context of a paranoia that drew on a lack of national unity and on related political and social tensions. Alongside popular discontent, there was significant disillusionment among the elite. Having taken direct charge, Tsar Nicholas II had proved an ineffective war leader. The army failed to act against demonstrators in Petrograd (Leningrad, St Petersburg) in March 1917, and Nicholas was pushed into abdicating.

A republican provisional government took power, but the war went on, although without success. Indeed, the eventual fall of the new government owed much to this failure. In September 1917, a German offensive captured Riga, a major city. The Germans successfully used storm troopers, infiltration tactics, and a heavy neutralization artillery bombardment. Two months later, a Bolshevik (Communist) coup in Petrograd led to the overthrow of the government with little resistance. The Bolshevik leader Lenin, who had been transported to Russia with German connivance, was opposed to the war. He negotiated a peace with Germany in March 1918, the Treaty of Brest Litovsk, a peace that gave Germany rule over much of western Russia. This success suggested that Germany might win the war. It would now only have to fight on one front and it would have access to Russian resources, especially to grain from Ukraine, thus potentially circumventing the Allied naval blockade.

ITALY

The Germans were to try a similar knockout blow against Italy in 1917. Ambitious for territorial gains from Austria, Italy had joined Britain and France in May 1915, mounting a series of costly offensives that failed to break through the Austrian lines. The Italian forces were poorly trained, equipped, supplied, and led, and they fell victim in 1915–1916 on the Isonzo front, the center of operations, to Austrian defensive firepower. Successive Italian offensives led to the gain of little territory and no breakthrough. Troops that were reluctant to advance risked being shot.

In late 1917, the Austrians and Germans employed the tactics the Germans had used at Riga earlier that year when attacking the Italians at Caporetto. The emphasis was on surprise and speed, not attrition. Benefiting from the cover of fog, the Austrians and Germans moved rapidly, with machine guns and light artillery on lorries, avoiding Italian strongpoints as they advanced, and destroyed the coherence and communications of the Italian defense. Poor command contributed greatly to the Italian collapse, but this collapse also indicated the potential effectiveness of the offensive using the new tactical doctrine.

Although no supporting amphibious operation was launched by the Austrians from their possessions in modern Slovenia and Croatia across the Adriatic Sea, Italy was nearly knocked out of the war. Its forces were pushed back 80 miles and lost possibly as many as 700,000 men, as well as nearly 5,000 pieces of artillery. This military disaster was linked to a slower-moving political and social crisis in Italy, one that led to concern that it would collapse, rather as Russia had that year and as France was to do in 1940. A new government was formed, pacifism was repressed, and a new front line was shored up with major British and French contingents despite the opposition of western front generals to this transfer.

WAR WITH THE TURKS

Entering the war against the Allies in October 1914, Turkey greatly extended the geographic range of the Central Powers (the German alliance system). They gained a new front with Russia, in the Caucasus, as well as the possibility of land conflict with the British because the British and Turkish (Ottoman) empires had a common border on the Egypt–Palestine frontier, whereas Turkish rule of Iraq threatened the British position in the (Persian) Gulf. Thus, the strategic problems facing the Allies increased greatly. In particular, Russia no longer had a safe supply route from the Black Sea to the Mediterranean.

The Allies sought to address this in 1915 by attacking Constantinople (Istanbul), the center of Turkish power. To its proponents, notably Winston Churchill, the dynamic First Lord of the Admiralty, this scheme appeared to be a way to use British naval power and avoid too great a focus on the conflict on the western front. Indeed, there was a debate in Britain between the "Westerners," who argued that Germany had to be defeated in the main sphere of operations on the western front, and the "Easterners," who looked for an alternative that would make use of traditional strengths in naval power and amphibious attack, gain the initiative, and avoid the carnage on the western front. Churchill was eager in 1915 to avoid the bloody, indecisive campaign on the western front, but he was, nevertheless, committed to a "Germany First" strategy, rather than focusing on knocking out Germany's weaker allies. This priority is generally lost sight of because of Churchill's extensive efforts to justify the Dardanelles campaign after the war, which has created the mistaken impression that he was a dedicated Easterner throughout the conflict. Churchill's preference was for an amphibious assault against Germany in the North Sea or Baltic, and the attack on the Dardanelles was intended by him initially as a means to employ "surplus" naval forces in a secondary theater in hopes of winning a cheap and easy victory with little risk.

The plan first entailed forcing a passage through the Dardanelles. An Anglo-French naval attempt to force the passage began on February 19 and was stopped on March 18 by mines and shore batteries, with the loss of several battleships to mines. This failure was followed, on April 25, by the Gallipoli expedition, which was designed to gain control of the western shores of the Dardanelles by landing troops on the Gallipoli peninsula. This was the most important amphibious operation of the war and its failure offers an instructive contrast with the greater success of the amphibious expeditions mounted by both sides during World War II.

Flawed in both conception and execution, not least because of a lack of enough powered landing craft (a key contrast with World War II) as well as lack of a relevant planning and command structure, the Gallipoli expedition was badly hindered by an effective Turkish defense that took advantage of the strength of defensive firepower and of holding the higher ground. Both sides dug themselves in. The Gallipoli operation then became an instance of how, repeatedly during the war, strategic conception was not matched by tactical and operational success, which was partially a matter of the absence of marked capability gaps in effectiveness between the combatants. This absence was not the product of military failure, but rather that there was no failure creating such a gap.

Once troops had been landed and his political career was at stake, Churchill started to shift his attention to the eastern theater. The Gallipoli campaign, however, was finally abandoned that winter after very heavy Allied casualties, and Churchill's reputation was badly tarnished.

The Turks also proved a difficult foe elsewhere, notably when the British, to provide forward protection for the Gulf and India, tried to conquer Mesopotamia, modern Iraq. A lunge from Basra toward Baghdad was stopped in November 1915, and the British force, besieged at nearby Kut, had to surrender the following April. This was a humiliating blow, although not on the scale of the British surrender to the Japanese at Singapore in 1942.

As in most wars, both sides faced serious disappointments that reflected not only issues in implementation, but also strategic planning. Thus, alongside failure at Gallipoli, German hopes from the Turks also proved seriously overoptimistic. The Turks were expected to provide the leadership for pan-Islamic revolts, but most of the Muslims in the world did not respond to the declaration of *jihad* (holy war) by the Caliph, the Turkish sultan. There was no supporting rising in Egypt, and the Turkish attack on the Suez Canal was repelled in February 1915 by Indian units, supported by British and French warships. Moreover, the Turkish offensive in the Caucasus in the winter of 1914–1915 was defeated by the Russians.

Turkish soldiers commanded by German officers near the Dardanelles.

Nevertheless, the Turks were still useful to the Germans in that they engaged large Allied forces, rather like Germany's ally in 1940–1943, Italy. Whereas in World War I most of Germany's colonies had fallen rapidly and ceased to absorb large numbers of Allied troops, this was not true of the war with Turkey.

As with Italy in 1943, three years into their war, the Turks were also to suffer from advances by their opponents. In 1917, the British advanced into Palestine and in Iraq. Having checked British attacks on the Gaza front near the Mediterranean in an instance of trench warfare, the Turks were outfought and defeated when the British operated further east, creating an open front in Palestine in late 1917. Jerusalem was captured on December 9. In Iraq, a methodical, logistical campaign by larger British forces, articulated by improved communications, led to the fall of Baghdad in March 1917, the first time it had ever fallen to Western forces. These were welcome victories, but they did not hit the center of Turkish power, as Italy was repeatedly hit in 1943–1944. Moreover, the victories over the Turks in 1917 were outweighed by Germany's success in knocking out Russia that year.

THE NAVAL WAR

The world's leading naval power, Britain, was able to impose an increasingly effective blockade on Germany from the outset of the war, as well as to retain control of its home waters, maintain the flow of men and munitions to the British army in France, and protect trade links that permitted the mobilization of British resources. The blockade, which had many holes but became more comprehensive when the United States came into the war in 1917, was supported by a system of preemptive purchasing that was important to the international control of raw materials; it also greatly influenced neutral economies. In particular, cutting off trade with Germany lessened American economic and financial interest in its success and directed it instead to the Allies. The blockade of Germany affected the availability of food there, which had serious consequences for civilian health.

Britain's supply system was that of a country that could not feed itself: nearly two thirds of Britain's food was imported. Britain also had an imperial economy that relied on global trade and a military system that required troop movements within the vast empire, notably of troops from Australia, Canada, India, and New Zealand. All of this was challenged by German surface raiders, but they were largely hunted down in the opening months of the war. Moreover, Allied sea power supported successful operations against German colonies.

The Atlantic trading system on which the British economy rested was the prime target for the German navy by 1915, with economic warfare the key theme. Trade was important in mobilizing the capital and securing the *matériel* on which Allied war making depended. Neither Britain nor France had an industrial system to match that of Germany, and the Allies were dependent on the United States for machine tools, mass production plants, and much else, including the parts of shells. American industrial output was equivalent to that of the whole of Europe by 1914, and the British ability to keep Atlantic sea lanes open against the assault from German submarines ensured that America made a vital contribution to the Allied war effort before its formal entry into the war in 1917.

Used in particular by the Germans, submarines were a new type of an old challenge, the commerce raider, but their potential had been greatly underestimated by most prewar commentators, and this remained the case during the war. In Germany, there was a lack of commitment from within the navy, which preferred surface warships, and, crucially, a longstanding concentration of industrial resources on the army, a pattern that was to be repeated in World War II. As a result, although submarines swiftly affected the conduct of operations, the Germans did not have the numbers to match their aspirations. Moreover, although they moved while submerged, submarines were dependent on battery motors that had to be recharged on the surface, where they were highly vulnerable to attack. In addition, submarines were slow, which lessened their chance of hitting a warship moving under full steam.

Submarines, however, benefited from the limited effectiveness of antisubmarine weaponry and from the lack of experience in antisubmarine tactics. The submarines could therefore be given a role in strategic planning by attacking merchantmen. The Germans demonstrated that far from being a source of protection for Britain, the sea, as in the past, could in fact be a barrier to safe resupply. In February 1915, the Germans increased the tempo and threat of their attack by beginning unrestricted submarine warfare, which entailed attacking all shipping,

Allied and neutral, and without warning, within the designated zone. When the British ship *Lusitania*, the largest liner on the transatlantic run, was sunk off Ireland on May 7, 1915, there were 128 Americans among those lost.

In response to the risk of American intervention, the Germans abandoned unrestricted submarine warfare. They were also unprepared for such a war because they lacked sufficient submarines, trained crew, or bases to mount an effective blockade of Britain. The Germans sunk 748,000 tons of British shipping in 1915, but Britain and its empire launched 1.3 million tons.

In 1916, the Germans instead hoped for victory in a fleet action. They were seeking to use their main fleet to wear down British naval strength in capital ships as a prelude to a fleet action. Their plan required falling on part of the British Grand Fleet with their entire High Seas Fleet to reduce Britain's crushing numerical superiority in heavy warships. Helped by their effective intelligence system, the British did not fall for this plan; however, although they had the larger fleet at the battle of Jutland of May 31 to June 1, the British suffered from problems with their cautious command style as well as their ships: their battle cruisers proved vulnerable. Nevertheless, although British battle losses in ships and manpower were heavier, the German fleet was badly damaged and its commanders were intimidated by the display of British naval power; the Germans thereafter focused at sea on submarines.

This emphasis altered the nature of the war at sea because, unlike surface fleet action, submarine warfare did not offer the prospect of a decisive victory in a climactic engagement. Instead, the submarine conflict ensured that war at sea became attritional. Combined with the British blockade of Germany, the submarine assault meant that the war was more clearly one between societies, with an attempt to break the resolve of people by challenging not only economic strength, but also social stability and indeed by cutting food movements and demographic health. This challenge necessarily directed attention to the ability of governments to safeguard the home front. Improving agricultural production became a key aspect of the war effort in Britain, as in Germany.

In 1917, the Germans planned a knockout blow against Britain by means of a resumption of unrestricted submarine warfare. Having failed to drive France from the war at Verdun in 1916 and having experienced the lengthy and damaging British attack in the Somme offensive, the Germans sought to force Britain from the war by resuming attempts to destroy its supply system. There was a parallel with the invasion of France via Belgium in 1914, in that the strong risk that a major power would enter the war as a result (Britain in 1914 and America in 1917) was disregarded by Germany on the grounds that success supposedly could be obtained as a result of the German attack. In 1917, however, unlike in 1914, the Germans had had plentiful warnings of the likely consequences of American anger as a result of their earlier use of unrestricted submarine warfare in 1915. There was also a failure of planning on the part of Germany because anticipated outcomes from the submarine assault did not arise, and the projected timetables of success miscarried.

Yet, this account mistakenly assumes a rationalist balance of risks and opportunities on the part of Germany. Such an approach ignores the extent to which the decision to turn to unrestricted submarine warfare reflected an ideology of total war and a powerful Anglophobia based on nationalist right-wing circles that saw British liberalism and capitalism as a threat to German culture. Again, although even more clearly, similar ideological factors were to play a key role with German policy in World War II.

AMERICA ENTERS THE WAR

The German resumption of unconditional submarine warfare on February 2, 1917, led the United States to declare war on April 6. Congress had approved the decision, although 6 senators and 50 congressmen opposed it. The German military leadership, increasingly politically influential, was unsympathetic to American moralizing. In addition, as in December 1941 when Germany declared war on the United States, there was also the view among German policy makers that America was already helping the British and French war effort as much as it could commercially. Moreover, there was a conviction that Britain could be driven out of the war rapidly by heavy sinkings of merchantmen: a belief that the submarines could achieve much and that this achievement would have an obvious consequence. It was claimed that the British would sue for peace on August 1, 1917. Furthermore, many German supporters of submarine warfare assumed that their force would be able seriously to impede the movement of American troops to Europe. More generally, there was a failure on the German part to appreciate American strength. Again, these factors were to play a major role in 1941.

In 1914, there was active hostility in America to the idea of participation in the European war, participation that was seen as alien to American interests and antipathetic to her ideology. However, the unrestricted submarine warfare that sank American ships (and also violated international law) had led to a major shift in attitudes in which Americans became persuaded of the dangerous consequences of German strength and ambitions; this occurred in a highly moralized form that encouraged large-scale commitment. Thus, America came to construct national interest in terms of the freedom of international trade from unrestricted submarine warfare.

Germany's crass wartime diplomacy exacerbated the situation, notably an apparent willingness to divert American strength from war in Europe by encouraging Mexican opposition to the United States. This opposition was attributed to revenge for the major losses suffered in the Mexican–American War of 1846–1848 as well as hostility to the American military intervention in Mexico in 1914. The Americans were made aware of this plan when the British intercepted a telegram to the German ambassador in Mexico from Arthur Zimmermann, the foreign minister. This episode appeared more troubling because of Mexico's instability at this point, instability that affected America directly when, in March 1916, the

Mexican faction leader Pancho Villa raided Columbus, New Mexico, killing 17 Americans. As a result, the threat of German conspiracies involving Mexico seemed particularly menacing.

Asking Congress on April 2, 1917, for a declaration that a state of war existed with Germany, President Woodrow Wilson presented an account of already-existing conflict in which the foundations of American society were challenged. He declared "that from the very outset of the present war [the German government] has . . . set criminal intrigues everywhere afoot against our national unity of counsel, our peace within and without our industries and our commerce." With reference to the Zimmermann telegram, he added, "That [the German government] means to stir up enemies against us at our very doors, the intercepted Zimmermann note to the German Minister at Mexico at Mexico City is eloquent evidence."

America had given neutrality added legitimacy for other states. In turn, influenced by America's power and example, other states followed America in declaring war, including Cuba, Panama, and, more significantly, Brazil in 1917 and other Latin American countries in 1918. Again, the same process was to follow America's entry into World War II in December 1941.

THE SUBMARINES DEFEATED

In the first four months of the unrestricted submarine attacks in 1917, the British lost an average of 630,000 tons of merchant shipping. However, as later in World War II, Britain survived the onslaught thanks both to outfighting the submarines and to success on the home front in the shape of increased food production. These factors were a key instance of the interaction of fighting methods, strategy, and the social and governmental dimensions of war. The introduction beginning May 10, 1917, of a system of escorted convoys cut shipping losses dramatically and helped lead to an increase in the sinking of submarines. Only 393 of the 95,000 ships that were convoyed across the Atlantic were sunk. Moreover, convoys facilitated the transport of over 2 million American troops to Europe, with the loss of just three transports.

U.S. Shipping Board poster celebrates America's increasing naval power during the war.

Convoying was an aspect of the direction on a global scale by the Allies of most of the world's shipping, trade, and troops flow. The Allied Maritime Transport Council oversaw an impressive system of international cooperation at sea, allocating shipping resources so that they could be employed most effectively.

The American contribution was crucial in the struggle against submarines. Although they lacked experience in antisubmarine warfare, the Americans deployed their large fleet to help protect communication routes across the Atlantic. American destroyers were important in this role and the movement of American battleships to British waters helped further shift the balance against Germany in surface shipping, thus leading to a greater focus on the submarine war.

AIR WARFARE

Manned flight by aircraft began in 1903, and the military potential was rapidly grasped. By 1914, the European powers had more than 1,000 aircraft in their armed forces. At the outset of the war, reconnaissance was the key aerial capability, one in which planes replaced cavalry. There was also bombing from the air during the war, initially from German Zeppelin (hydrogen-filled) navigable airships, the first of which had been successfully flown in 1908.

Subsequently, although there were only limited changes in airships, the capabilities of aircraft improved. Improvements in aircraft speed, maneuverability, and ceiling made it easier to attack other planes. Engine power increased and engine size decreased. Synchronizing (interrupter) gear, invented by Fokker, enabled airplanes to fire forward without damaging their propellers.

In 1915, the Germans used Zeppelins to bomb London in an attempt to provide a strategic outcome, but the fragile Zeppelins were vulnerable to British planes. The Germans subsequently switched to bombing from aircraft in an attempt to crush British morale and thus circumvent the impasse in the trenches. An air assault on London from June 1917, however, served only to ensure a hostile popular response. Moreover, in the rapid action–reaction cycle that characterized advances during the war and that was to be seen again during World War II, the raids resulted in Britain in the speedy development of a defensive system involving high-altitude fighters based on airfields linked by telephone to observers, which led to heavy losses among the German planes and to the abandonment of daylight raids.

The British Royal Air Force was established as a separate force on April 1, 1918. This independence from the army was not only a testimony to the argument that such an organization would make it easier to pursue air control, but also a reaction to the demand for retribution for the German raids on Britain. Airpower, moreover, was designed to affect trench warfare and to surmount the deadlock of the trenches by permitting the destruction of the enemy where they were vulnerable.

Alongside bombing, there was a development in aerial ground attack, with the capability and range of ground-support operations expanding. In 1918, the Germans used ground-attack squadrons to support their offensives on the western front, whereas regular Allied air attacks on their supply links inhibited German advances. Aircraft engaged moving tanks.

By the close of the war, the extent and role of airpower had been transformed. By 1918, the British had 22,000 aircraft. Moreover, the combined Franco-American-British force of 1,481 aircraft employed to support the successful American attack on the St. Mihiel salient on September 12 not only was the largest deployment so far, but also gained air control, which was not usually possible during the war. In practice, indeed, many of the hopes of airpower were based on a misleading sense of operational and technological possibilities, and its prime value remained aerial reconnaissance throughout the war.

Because air defense was difficult compared with what was to follow during World War II, it proved easier to attack with fewer losses than in the later war. German cities were bombed, but the purpose of degrading industrial and logistical capability proved difficult in practice. Moreover, there were civilian casualties, which underlined popular bitterness. At any rate, the British exaggerated what their bombers had achieved, and this exaggeration greatly affected interwar discussion of strategic bombing, leading to a misrepresentation of its potential, which fed into the doctrine and practice of British airpower during World War II.

French cavalry, with dirigible providing air support, 1915.

WAR AND SOCIETY

The black-and-white photographs of the wartime devastation of the French city of Rheims are still shocking. Close to the front line, the city was heavily shelled by the Germans from 1914. Most of the city was flattened and the historic cathedral was partly destroyed. This was not an atrocity by troops under no real control, but a deliberate action, and it showed from the outset that this would be a war between peoples.

So, indeed, it turned out to be, in large part because the war lasted far longer, and on a greater scale, than had been anticipated, entailed unprecedented efforts, and involved a major mobilization of the resources of society as a result. The war put enormous pressure on societies not used to the scale of such a conflict. In response, there was a mobilization and organization of resources that greatly expanded the scope of governments and thus changed the nature of the state and its relationship with society. Thus, in Britain, the government took over control of the railways (1914), the coal mines (1917), and the flour mills (1918). Conscription, introduced in Britain in 1916, helped push the size of the armed forces up to 4.5 million in 1917–1918, one in three of the male labor force.

Attempts to rally public opinion include the formation of the Department of Information, which, in 1918, became a ministry. Responding to the propaganda possibilities of film, the War Office created the Cinematograph Committee. Rising amounts of propaganda in Britain and elsewhere were accompanied by a change in the character of propaganda, with the war, toward the demonization of opponents. This change foreshadowed the heightened international ideological struggle that was to be seen until the end of the Cold War in 1989. Surveillance also became more important, with a major growth in numbers and powers: in Britain, the numbers in Special Branch increased from 80 in 1914 to 700 in 1918, and in MI5, the home security service, from 14 to 844. Other states faced comparable pressures and also increased governmental power.

There was a general pattern of social disruption, if not transformation, as a result of the war. The consequences varied by combatant, but the pressures were similar. The social order was affected by higher inflation, greater taxation, an extension of state control, and the spread of trade unionism and female employment.

This process could be readily seen in Britain, where, before the war, pressure from the suffragette movement for women gaining the vote had been vociferous, albeit unsuccessful. During the war, new roles, many in industry, were performed by women. Their part in the war economy was central, not least because large numbers of women workers were recruited by the Ministry of Munitions from 1915. This work was frequently a cause of ill health, if not death, because of trinitroglycerin poisoning. As a result of rising employment in industry (as opposed to domestic service), the female percentage of trade unionists increased from 7.8 in 1900 to 17 in 1917. In factories, women were controlled by male foremen and they received lower wages than male workers; nevertheless, there were more

A 1917 poster depicting French women in wartime.

women earning wages than before and their wages were higher than prewar wages. For agricultural work, the Women's Land Army was established in 1917. There was also a direct role in the war. Whereas only 72 army sisters had been employed in British military hospitals in 1898, a total of 32,000 women served as military nurses in 1914–1919. In this case, women had a place in the command structure: they were able to give orders to male ward orderlies. Founded in 1917, the Women's Army Auxiliary Corps provided clerks, cooks, drivers, and storewomen.

There was a persistence in gender as in class-based attitudes and practices, notably in recruitment and promotion. In Britain, middle-class women tended to be nurses, and working-class women were store-women. Women who served near the front, such as the nurses and telephonists with the American army in 1917–1918, found that the military hierarchy expected them to fulfill traditional gender roles and made scant allowance for their contribution. The latter was also the case for the First Russian Women's Battalion of Death established in July 1917 in an unsuccessful attempt to bolster morale. The unit, which suffered heavy casualties, was not matched by the Western Allies.

More generally, most assumptions about gender were deliberately not disruptive. Thus, female war workers in Britain were regarded as temporary and were not permitted to retain their jobs after the war. Furthermore, the notion of a home front was an aspect of an affirmation of established gender concepts and roles, with women again regarded as nurturers.

At the same time, society changed during the war. Women entering the workplace proved a key element in social change. This was particularly so in Britain, where this process was linked to the extension of voting rights to women immediately after the war. Social change was therefore linked to democratization in Britain, as it also was in the very different context of Germany once it had been defeated and become a republic. The large-scale recruitment of women for the war effort greatly affected social assumptions. The concept of women as occupying a separate sphere, an idea developed in part because of pressure for women winning the vote, buckled under the pressure of major changes in the world of work for women.

New opportunities for women were related to their increased mobility and independence. This included a decline in control and influence over young women by their elders, male and female. As a consequence, there was a new sexual climate. Chaperonage became less comprehensive and effective, and styles of courtship became freer. Illegitimate births in Britain rose to 6 percent in 1918. Furthermore, there was a greater interest in the informed public discussion of sex, with an emphasis on mutual desire as its basis. Marie Stopes's influential *Married Love* was published in Britain in 1918, the same year in which women got the vote in Britain.

WINNING THE WAR

There is a certain symmetry to World War II that is lacking for World War I. In World War II, Axis success rose to a peak and then receded, providing a basic narrative for the war and thus a clear structure for, and prompt to, analysis. All except one of the major Axis offensives in the latter half of the war were counterattacks, like Kursk in 1943, Leyte Gulf in 1944, and the Bulge in 1944, and unsuccessful ones at that. The exception, Operation Ichigo, brought much of southern China, a substantial area, under Japanese control in 1944–1945 and is invariably underplayed in general histories of the war.

In World War I, there is no similar pattern. Central Power attacks were very important, not only in the initial year of the war, but also in 1915 (Eastern Europe), 1916 (western front and Romania), and 1917 (eastern front and Italy). So it was also for 1918. Indeed, insofar as there is the peak referred to above, it occurred in July 1918, with the end of the repeated German attacks on the western front that year. Insofar as there was a symmetry, it was also in 1918, with German power still apparent in the first half of the year and notably increasing in Eastern Europe, in the aftermath of Russian weakness, but the situation then changed radically as Germany lost in the West.

At the beginning of the year, the strategic situation was propitious for the Germans as a result of the Russian Revolution, but it was unclear how rapidly the Revolution would lead to an end of the war in the east and how quickly the Germans would be able to redirect their military effort elsewhere. A total of 62 divisions were moved from the east to take part in the offensives on the western front in 1918, and they comprised close to a quarter of the divisions that took part, although had the Germans not been keen on more territorial gains in Russia, which led them to continue to advance, more troops could have been moved west.

The Germans were to gain major swaths of territory in these spring offensives on the western front, first launched on March 21, in part as a result of the effectiveness of their tactics, which had been used in 1917 at Riga and Caporetto. However, this enhanced German tactical effectiveness was not matched operationally or strategically, and the resilience of the Allies looked toward their success later in the year.

The weight of Allied resources was also apparent in 1918. On July 18, the successful French-led counteroffensive in the Second Battle of the Marne was supported by a creeping barrage, with one heavy shell per 1.27 yards of front and three field artillery shells per yard, as well as an effective use of tanks and aircraft. In the face of this pressure, large numbers of German troops surrendered or reported as too ill to fight. The Allies had now gained the initiative.

Furthermore, there had been no realizable political goals to accompany the German offensives, not least because the army leadership remained opposed to a compromise peace and insisted, instead, on a territorial settlement providing plentiful gains and focused on strategic factors, namely ending German weakness in the face of a future two-front war. The Allies were not going to accept German territorial gains, and political support for the war was sustained in Britain and France during the crises of the German attacks. Insofar as there was growing exhaustion on the part of much of the civilian population in the three powers, it did not affect the politics of the conflict, other than encouraging the view that advantages had to be pressed home.

The failure of the German submarine offensive contributed greatly to the weak German position. By 1918, the rate of Allied tonnage sunk per German submarine lost had fallen, and the strategic irrelevance of the submarine threat was demonstrated by the arrival of the American army. In April–October 1918, more than 1,600,000 American troops crossed the Atlantic, transforming a German superiority on the western front of 300,000 men in March 1918 to an Allied superiority of 200,000 men four months later. From July, the Americans came to play a significant part in Allied operations, but they alone were not decisive. It cannot be said that their attacks inflicted key defeats on the Germans, and the Germans were skeptical of their tactical skill. American troops tended to repeat the British and French mistakes of 1915 and 1916 before they took heed of the lessons and applied the newer tactical methods to the battlefield. Yet, the Americans fought bravely, advanced successfully, and inflicted, as well as suffered, heavy casualties. Moreover, by taking up large sectors of the front, the Americans not only contributed their own efforts, but also freed up French units to fight elsewhere on the western front; and because the Germans were threatened with attacks along the front, they could not produce any reserves to block Allied breakthroughs. Segregated black units were among those that fought well in the American army, although they were not treated fairly, receiving less training and equipment.

The war proved very important in the transition of the American military into a modern, large-scale force able to compete with similar militaries. This had not been the situation over the previous century as America's opponents, principally Native Americans, Mexico, and Spain, had all been weaker militarily, whereas the Civil War had been seen as a short-term emergency that did not establish a pattern for military activity, capability, and organization. The warfare of 1861–1865 also did not see the weaponry in use in 1918, either the range of types or the lethality.

The challenge for the Americans in 1918 therefore was not simply of scale, but also of confronting a new type of war and against an experienced and powerful opponent while, moreover, doing so at a distance and in association with allies. This challenge set the pattern for much subsequent American thinking about war. Because the war ended before American forces could play the major role envisaged for the 1919 campaign, their potential was not yet clear to all contemporaries, although the Germans were well aware of the issue. Having failed to win a quick victory by unrestricted submarine warfare or by attacking in the west in the spring of 1918, Germany had lost. The example and its implications had not been adequately digested by Hitler and his circle when Germany declared war on America in December 1941.

There is a contrast between accounts of Allied victory that focus on the out-fighting of the German army on the western front in 1918 and those that emphasize, instead, the internal crisis created by the strains of the war, specifically as a result of the blockade and the serious problems this created for the German economy and German living standards. The latter approach offers the emphasis on the home front seen in the dominant "war and society" approach to military history. Moreover, the extent to which the Germans were outfought in practice was not one that was to attract adequate subsequent attention at the popular level. The Germans, in particular, preferred the "stab-in-the-back" legend, attributing defeat to left-wing disaffection at home. This was an argument that was to be employed by the Nazis, but not only by them. In fact, although strains on the home front were serious, the key element in 1918 was that German forces were out-fought in the field, defeated, and dramatically driven back on the western front, in the very theater of operations where their strength was concentrated. The same was true for Germany's allies.

This problem does not exhaust the issues posed by Allied victory because, focusing on the fighting, it is necessary to qualify, indeed challenge, the explanation of victory in terms of new weaponry, specifically the British and French use of the tank, but also with an emphasis on aircraft. In practice, some of the statements subsequently made on behalf of the wartime impact of the tank, as of aircraft, reflected not an informed critical assessment of the operations in the war, but the competing claims about weapons systems made by their protagonists in the 1920s and 1930s. There was also to be a projecting back onto 1918 of the role of the tank in World War II and subsequently.

Nevertheless, the tank opened up a clear difference in resources, innovation, adaptability, and tactical outcomes between the Allies and the Germans, who had few tanks. A total of 430 British tanks broke through the German lines near Amiens on August 8, a battle that Ludendorff, the German chief of staff, described as the "Black Day" of the German army. The British captured 12,000 prisoners and advanced seven miles that day, and the Germans were unable to reverse their loss. Tanks overcame one of the major problems with offensives against trenches: the separation of firepower from advancing troops and the consequent lack of

A German tank undergoing repairs, a not-uncommon occurrence.

flexibility. Tank support made it possible for advancing units to confront defended positions and counterattacks. Tanks offered precise tactical fire to exploit the consequences of the massed operational bombardments that preceded attacks.

However, tanks faced a range of issues and problems, including firepower, speed, durability, reliability, and communications, as well as the development of antitank measures. To operate most effectively, tanks needed to support and to be supported by advancing infantry and artillery. This lesson had to be learned repeatedly during the century in the face of pressure from enthusiasts for tanks alone.

Despite the limitations of Allied tanks and airpower, the Germans, thanks to Allied improvements, had lost their advantage in weapons systems. In turn, the Allies had enhanced the strengths and utilization of their earlier weaponry, par-ticularly their artillery. In place of generalized firepower supporting operations, by 1918 there was systematic coordination, reflecting precise control of both infantry and massive artillery support as well as better communications between them. The British had also developed planned, indirect (three-dimensional) firepower. In contrast to direct fire, the use of indirect fire depended on accurate intelligence, including the extensive use of aerial photography as well as of sound ranging (to ascertain the location of opposing guns), surveying, and meteorology.

Technology, tactics, and training were brought together by the Allies in a cooperation that offered major advantages, both with artillery and with infantry. Whereas the armies of 1914 had lacked suitable tactics to cope with firepower and stalemate, the invention and deployment of reliable weapons for trench warfare attacks in the form of grenades, light machine guns, and light trench mortars permitted the effective infantry tactics used by the attacking Germans and then the Allies in 1918. Moreover, the development by the British of deep battle, in which targets beyond the front, including reinforcements and headquarters, were being effectively bombarded, multiplied the impact of firepower, and mobility was restored to troops and the battlefield; it was no longer the case that the strategic level was swallowed up by the operational and the operational by the tactical.

The Germans, in addition, were put under great pressure in 1918 from the successive collapse of their allies as Bulgaria, Turkey, and Austria were defeated. Fighting quality, military morale, and governmental determination all collapsed in these states. In Germany, weak domestic support after the failure of the spring offensives was also a major problem, as were growing problems for military morale. These problems reflected both a German sense that they were being outfought and the pressures of the home front. Large numbers of German troops surrendered as the Germans were pushed back onto the defensive, and the German officers no longer felt they could rely on their units.

Furthermore, the continuation of the Allied offensive from the summer into October 1918 indicated that this campaign was to be different from the others earlier in the war as the impetus of attack could be maintained. This prefigured the marked improvement in Soviet, American, and British operational capability that was to be seen in 1944. Not only did the Allies overcome the tactical problems of trench warfare in 1918, but also they had developed the mechanisms, notably greatly improved logistics, and deployed the resources, especially large numbers of guns, necessary to sustain their advance and offensive in the face of continued German resistance and across a broad front. The contrast with the German offensives in the spring was readily apparent. Successive German defense lines were broken through, with the Americans taking heavy casualties as they fought their way through strong defenses in the Meuse–Argonne offensive.

As confidence in victory collapsed, the Germans accepted President Woodrow Wilson's terms for peace, including that Germany be transformed into a constitutional state and that the armistice terms be such that Germany be unable to renew hostilities. On November 9, Wilhelm II was forced to abdicate, and two days later the armistice was signed. It came into force at 11 AM and the guns fell silent.

CONCLUSIONS

Casualty figures for the war were extreme: 9.45 million men died and millions more were badly injured. About 2 million Germans, 1.8 million Russians, 1.4 million French, 1.3 million Austrians, 1 million from Britain and the British Empire, and 116,000 Americans died. Moreover, casualty rates were high, including 27 percent of all French men between the ages of 18 and 27. For several states, notably France and Britain, the casualties were greater than in World War II, although that was not the case for Germany, Russia, or America, let alone Japan. Although civilian losses were to be far greater in World War II, there was also in World War I the massive civilian loss caused by the destruction, disruption, and disease brought by conflict.

The devastation of World War I was unprecedented and intense, leading to the immediate physical shock arising from the nature of the battlefield, particularly the way in which the scale of the devastation seemingly dwarfed the human experience, including any opportunities for heroism. The direct exposure of large numbers to the fighting was accentuated by its impact on others via newspaper reporting, photography, and newsreels.

The horrors of suffering and loss were to dominate subsequent attention, but that does not mean that the war was a mindless slaughter. Indeed, the frequent failure to distinguish between these factors ensures that World War I is probably the most misunderstood major conflict in history. The horror of what appeared to be the bloody futility of the struggle has distracted attention from the important and worthwhile issues at stake in the conflict and from the eventual effectiveness of the European military system. The former was very much the case as far as the French and the Belgians affected by invasion in 1914 were concerned, as well as for the British who sought to protect international law and stability by intervening and the Americans who acted against unrestricted German submarine warfare.

A focus on trench warfare can lead to a failure to appreciate that the war was not an impasse created by similarities in weapons systems. Moreover, the failure to end the war rapidly did not mean that there was a tactical stasis. The stalemate of the western front was caused by a combination of factors. The firepower of the prewar armies was not understood in 1914, and the consequences of escalating that firepower, as happened during 1915 and 1916, were not anticipated either. Tactics of maneuver and of attack did not take into account the effect of massed artillery or that of modern rifles. The stalemate, however, was not stasis because tactics and munitions continually evolved as part of an unresolved conflict between defense and attack in terms of tactics and technology.

What set World War I apart from previous conflicts in which trench warfare had occurred was the tactical and technological response to it, a response that led to a new mode of warfare. Both sides learned from initial experiences and developed more flexible attack and defense doctrines. The significance of innovation reflected what was to be a characteristic of war over the following century. In the case of World War I, there was also to be a mobilization of economic and social resources that helped sustain the struggle, thus encouraging innovation.

The size of the armies, the proliferation of new weapons, and the extent of entrenchment forced leaders to start thinking about the coordination in time and space of fire, maneuver, obstacles, reserve positions, and so on, largely sight unseen and accomplishing such coordination by topographic maps, aerial photography, and enhanced communications. These were essential first in the defense, but also provided the elementary skills and infrastructure that allowed offensive ideas to grow. Maps, watches, and telephones helped in the coordination of maneuver with artillery: much synchronization had to take place to carry an army through an enemy's defenses.

Along with innovation came decisiveness. The western front was not only a site of stasis, but also the stage for the decisive actions of the war. The blocking of German offensives, in 1914, 1916, and 1918, was decisive in a defensive sense. This blocking was the essential precondition of later Allied victory, and in 1918 the

Germans were finally dramatically driven back in the theater of operations where their strength was concentrated.

In addition to military decisiveness, there were highly significant political, social, economic, and cultural consequences. The old order was swept away as a result of the war and literally so where old-established empires succumbed, as those of Austria, Germany, and Russia did. In each case, imperial control over subject nationalities collapsed and monarchical rule was replaced by republics. There was also a more general process of dislocation. War brought uncertainty, discontent, change, and the demand for change. It challenged values, literally so with widespread inflation.

At the same time, the war presented opportunities for those discontented with the old order, particularly nationalists and Communists. More generally, it led to a reassessment of political relationships both international and domestic. Thus, the United States became more prominent as a great power and Japan became more significant economically and politically. Britain's relative position was also affected by the extent to which the war encouraged a sense of separate identity within the empire, notably in Ireland where the Catholics, by the end, rejected the link with Britain, but also in Canada, Australia, and other dominions and colonies. What the postwar world would bring was far from clear.

READING LIST

Ian Beckett, *The Great War 1914–1918*, Harlow, Longman, 2001.

Jeremy Black, *The Great War and the Making of the Modern World*, London, Continuum, 2011.

Anthony Saunders, *Reinventing Warfare 1914–18: Novel Munitions and Tactics of Trench Warfare*, London, Continuum, 2012.

Larry Sondhaus, *World War One: The Global Revolution*, Cambridge, U.K., Cambridge University Press, 2011.

Huw Strachan, *The First World War*. Volume 1, New York, Oxford University Press, 2000.

THREE

A MULTITUDE OF CONFLICTS, 1918–1939

Poster extolling the Nationalist cause during the Spanish Civil War, 1936–1939.

The outbreak of World War II in 1939 (in 1937 in China) was to lead to the definition of the preceding years that followed World War I as the "interwar" period. In that perspective, much later writing on military affairs focused on two linked elements that indeed occurred in this period: digesting the lessons of World War I and preparing for another great-power conflict, which eventually came in the form of World War II. Although valuable in hindsight, that is not an approach that makes much sense of the experience of large parts of the world, notably so in 1919–1930. The international situation, indeed, became more menacing in 1931, when Japan, under a militaristic and expansionist regime, invaded China's leading industrial province, Manchuria, and more so in 1933 when Adolf Hitler, the Nazi leader, gained power in Germany. However, there were fewer signs earlier that there would be a war between great powers, let alone one that might span the world.

Instead, warfare in 1919–1930 focused on struggles within states, both civil wars and attempts to resist imperial control; these themes remained important in the 1930s. Civil wars greatly affected a number of states, most persistently China, but also Russia, as well as what became Saudi Arabia, Iraq, and Iran. Attempts to resist imperial control could be seen in the established and expanding empires of European powers, notably those of Britain (where there was armed resistance in British Somaliland, Ireland, Palestine, etc., as well as war with Afghanistan), France (Syria), Spain (Morocco), Italy (Libya and Abyssinia/Ethiopia) and Greece (Turkey), but also in the informal American empire in Latin America: American forces were deployed in Haiti (1915–1934), the Dominican Republic (1916–1924), and Nicaragua (1926–1933).

Thus, there was no single shaping comparable to that of moving from one great-power war on a world scale toward another. Nor were these other conflicts similar. For example, the frequent Chinese warlord conflicts of the 1920s were primarily products of a combination of state failure and the rise of independent military fiefdoms run by the warlords, generals who ran their own armies and controlled extensive territories. In contrast, there was a crucial ideological dimension to the conflict in China in the 1930s between the Nationalist Guomindang government and Communist opponents under Mao Zedong. The bitter state-on-state Chaco War over contested territory between the regular armies of Paraguay and Bolivia in 1932–1935 was very different in its character from the Italian conquest of Abyssinia (Ethiopia) in 1935–1936, a colonial expansion, and also to the ideologically highly charged Spanish Civil War in 1935–1936.

This lack of consistency prefigures the situation today. Just as focusing on only one type of conflict or social context or weapons technology today would be offering a limited account, the same is true for 1919–1938.

At the same time, writers and readers must make choices about what appears important to them. In doing so, they must be aware of the significance of present concerns and of how the present changes, often dramatically, bringing the need for a new, usable, and understandable past. The major shift here relates to China. In the aftermath of World War II and during the Cold War, the military history of Europe appeared to be the key issue, with the rivalry there of the United States and the Soviet Union in the Cold War seen as a product of Europe's history. Over the past quarter century, however, the agenda of interest, geopolitical, strategic, and economic, has focused instead on East Asia, particularly China. As a result, we shall begin with its military history in the 1920s and 1930s before looking at a second area of modern concern, the Islamic world, and only thereafter moving to the West, both Europe and the Americas.

CHINA

In terms of the scale of conflict, the wars involving China were the largest conflicts of the period. This was true both of the civil warfare of the 1920s and early 1930s and of the developing struggle with Japan beginning in 1931. Moreover, the partial defeat of regionalism, in the shape of the power bases of the warlords in the 1920s, was a key development in Chinese history; it left the new political–military forces, the Guomindang (Nationalist Party) and the Communists, to battle for control over a country that both wished to keep united. Only Japan, a foreign invader, wanted a divided China, in its case a number of client states. Dispute over the future of China lasted from the end of the direct struggle between the Guomindang and the Communists, with the victory of the latter in 1949, to the present, in which they remain highly armed opponents from their bases in Beijing and Taipei (the capital of Taiwan).

The 1920s are characterized as the warlord era in China, but it is necessary to note that this is a pejorative term reflecting the very failure of the warlords. Elsewhere in the 1920s, successful military leaders, notably Kemal Atatürk in Turkey and Ibn Saud in Arabia, showed that success can lead to a different historical verdict. Long-standing regionalism in China, including historical tensions between north and south, as well as the growing autonomy of regional military units, had helped ensure the rising influence of the military in local society. The 1911 overthrow of the Manchu (Qing) empire was followed by a growing vacuum of power in which prominent generals competed, generally for personal and patronage reasons. Whereas local commanders were essentially regional figures, the leading generals or warlords, notably Zhang Zuolin in Manchuria and Wu Peifu in central China, used territorial bases to contend for power and influence over all of China. Although some figures are open to doubt, the size of their armies grew, with the total number of all the armies increasing from about half a million men in 1916 to about 2 million in 1928. The length of the individual wars rose with these numbers, as did the burden on China's economy and society. Purchasing modern weapons from Europe in the 1920s, the warlords had plenty of artillery and other arms, including aircraft.

In contrast, the large bandit gangs that competed with the warlords to control the localities lacked the ability of the latter to use resources and loans to obtain weapons from abroad. There was, however, an overlap in the social impact, notably with both warlords and bandits oppressing the population. This overlap, which was to be seen in many parts of the world over the past century, for example,

Somalia from the 1990s to the 2010s, meant that bandit forces could be absorbed into the warlord armies, whereas particularly undisciplined warlord units could become bandits. In this way, the traditional Chinese hostility to the soldier, seen as a cause of violence and often no more than a bandit, was perpetuated.

As with the Russian Civil War of 1918–1921, there were not continuous fronts in conflict in China in the 1920s. Their absence contributed to the stress on rapid advances on key positions. There was also an emphasis on seeking to build up support by winning over other warlords. Ideological commitment was limited, and generals, many of whom were former classmates or from a similar military background, changed sides, a process facilitated by payment. Moreover, the poorly integrated armies lacked cohesion. At the same time, military leaders had to display considerable adaptability in responding not only to new technology, but also to different political circumstances.

The growing power of the southern-based Guomindang (Nationalists) was a significant factor. Under Jiang Jieshi (Chiang Kai-shek), the effective head from 1926, the Guomindang came to act as a form of successful warlordism, but one with more concrete national assumptions and pretensions. As commander of the Guomindang forces, Jiang led the Northern Expedition, a drive against independent warlords, launched in 1926 that benefited from Soviet military advisers, money, and equipment. The Soviet Union saw Chinese nationalism as an ally against Western interests, notably seeking to undermine Britain's powerful commercial role in China. Thus, conflict in China was an aspect of the wide-ranging and highly significant "Cold War" (in the sense of ideological struggle) of the 1920s, one that broadened the consequences of the 1917 Russian Revolution. As with the post-1945 Cold War, there were overlaps with other struggles and issues. For example, in the brief Sino-Soviet War of 1929, the forces of the Manchurian warlord, Zhang Xueliang, were trounced with heavy casualties, but the Soviet government preferred to pursue its interests by cultivating the Guomindang.

Success in warfare within China was partly obtained by winning over local warlords, who then became commanders in the army. This means of victory without battle reflected a combination of force and politics that was very important to the Chinese warfare of the 1920s and had also been much used in the past, being a Chinese cultural pattern that was extolled in traditional works on war. This was also the means of operation seen in civil wars in much of the world over the past century, for example, in Afghanistan, including with the triumph of the Northern Alliance over the Taliban in 2001. Ideological alignments of politics and religion, however, offered a different model in civil wars, one that encouraged continual conflict, as with the persistence and revival of the Taliban.

The Northern Expedition was highly successful. Shanghai and Nanjing fell to Jiang in 1927 and Beijing in 1928. In 1930, opposition by a group of warlords was overcome by Jiang in the War of the Central Plains. However, the devastation and cost of the conflicts of the 1920s were great and imposed a heavy burden on Chinese society. The brutalization of the people by troops was commonplace, with killing,

Soldiers patrol the streets of Shanghai in February 1927.

rape, looting, extortion, torture, and abduction for ransom all frequent. There was also serious damage to the economy, especially to food production.

The Communists proved more intractable foes for the Guomindang than the warlords, both militarily and politically. Communism had a political and ideological strength that distinguished the Communists' Red Army from the warlord forces. China thus witnessed the ideological conflict that was so important to the nature of war during the century and that, in East Asia from the 1920s, was far from being a "cold war" in the sense of a confrontation short of large-scale conflict. In 1926–1927, Jiang had turned against the Communists, launching a "White Terror" that was a key aspect of counterinsurrectionary force even if it is difficult to define as warfare. In response, the Communists, far from collapsing, formed a Red Army and rebelled. Their attempts to seize cities failed, but the Red Army was more successful in resisting attack in rural areas, especially in the traditional hideouts of social bandits, remote and mountainous areas, such as the Jinggang highlands on the border between the provinces of Hunan and Jiangxi.

Mao Zedong, a steadily more prominent Communist who regarded the rural base as an essential part of a revolutionary strategy, a thesis he advanced in his March 1927 report on the peasant movement in Hunan, built up a force in the Jinggang highlands. He used violence for political ends from the outset to terrorize others and to destroy potential rival leaders of the rural population. This violence extended to those Communists who did not meet Mao's requirements. Because

Mao was an ally of the Soviet dictator Joseph Stalin, those who could be labeled backers of Leon Trotsky, a prominent Soviet Communist critic of Stalin, were slaughtered in the thousands.

In turn, beginning in 1930, the Guomindang launched "bandit extermination campaigns" against the rural Communists, large-scale operations that distracted Jiang from other foes, notably Japan. As a result, his response to Japanese conquest of Manchuria in 1931–1932 and then to subsequent expansion in 1933–1935 was more limited than it might otherwise have been.

However, the Red Army could trade space for time, survive despite heavy losses, and harry the attackers. Funded and provided with arms by the Soviet Union, Mao became a factor in the complicated negotiations of power in China. In 1937, Mao published *Guerrilla Warfare*, a pamphlet in which he argued that, in response to opposition, unlimited guerrilla warfare based on the mobilization of the whole of society offered a new prospect that was more effective than what was presented as more primitive guerrilla warfare.

JAPANESE EXPANSIONISM

Nevertheless, at this point, the threat to the Guomindang came not from the Communists but from the regular forces and conventional warfare of Imperial Japan. Hit by the global Great Depression and by the accompanying collapse in trade, exports, industry, and employment, Japan became more bellicose in the 1930s. In part, this bellicosity arose because sections of the military followed autonomous policies, ignoring civilian restraint, and in part because the military supported an authoritarian militarism that challenged the democratic ethos of 1920s Japanese civil society and affected government policies.

In 1931–1932, Japanese forces seized control of the Chinese province of Manchuria and, from 1933, there was further Japanese expansionism in northern China. A conviction that large-scale war between Japan and the United States or the Soviet Union was inevitable had developed in Japanese military circles and led to pressure for the strengthening of the military, the state, and Japanese society, with the latter two seen in an authoritarian and militaristic perspective. China was regarded in Japan as a base for the vital resources necessary for preparing for this conflict. To develop these resources, Manchuria, once conquered in 1931–1932, was heavily used as a colony for Japanese emigrants. As well as producing economic wealth, it was planned that the emigrants would act as defenders of what was a strategic asset against the neighboring Soviet Union, as well as protecting Korea, which had been a Japanese colony since 1910.

Alongside discussion of Japanese policy in "rational" terms, there was also a sense of imperial and national mission that drew on religious and racial assumptions in the shape of a radical Shintō ultranationalism and a belief in a divine providential purpose of Japanese superiority and expansion. This point must be underlined for all cultures: ideological factors were important for all states and guided their perception of rational goals and policies.

Ideally, it was felt in Japan that to prepare for conflict with the Soviets, China should be persuaded to accept her fate as a junior partner of Japan; the ensuing diplomacy was designed to show Jiang that he had no alternative. Jiang's uncooperativeness prompted Tokyo to try to give him a short, sharp lesson. An unplanned incident between Chinese and Japanese troops near Beijing in July 1937 led to Japanese pressure to which Jiang did not yield, and full-scale conflict broke out. The Japanese advanced rapidly, with the major cities of Beijing, Shanghai, and Nanjing all captured in 1937 and Guangzhou (Canton) and Wuhan in 1938.

The Guomindang military was badly affected by successive defeats, losing its well-trained units and equipment in 1937, especially in the battle for Shanghai, but resistance continued, both at the front, particularly as the Japanese advanced in southern China in 1939–1941, and in occupied areas where Japanese control outside the cities was limited and episodic. Guerrilla tactics proved particularly effective in these areas. The Japanese were able to secure some collaboration, notably establishing a provisional government under Wang Jingwei at Nanjing, but not enough.

The Japanese army had proved misleadingly confident that China would fall rapidly. The Japanese military despised their opponents and exaggerated the ability of their will (and military machine) to overcome the problems posed by operating in China. These problems were a matter not only of the ratio between Chinese space and Japanese resources, but also of the determination and fighting quality of the Chinese. An assessment by the British chiefs of staff in December 1939 noted, "The Japanese forces have overrun about a quarter of China and control all the major ports. Japanese authority in China is, however, limited to certain main centers and to lines of communication, and Chinese guerrilla forces continue to take considerable toll of Japanese garrison posts."[1]

Moreover, Japanese campaigns in China showed that brutality did not work, a lesson that their racialism prevented the Japanese from learning. The massacre by Japanese troops of large numbers of civilians after the capture of Nanjing in December 1937, including using people for bayonet practice, as well as mass rapes, was the culmination of barbarous Japanese conduct during their advance up the valley of the River Yangzi from Shanghai. This brutality did not break Chinese morale, as had been hoped, but testified to an emerging immoral and callous attitude within the Japanese military and to its failure to provide any other answer to the quagmire of its own making. Precise figures are not available, but the scale of the civilian casualties in China in 1937–1945 probably surpassed that in the Soviet Union in 1941–1945.

Japanese conquests in China indicated a lesson that Hitler would have done well to consider before attacking the Soviet Union in 1941: that high-visibility gains did not necessarily lead to overall victory and that conflicts could develop an insuperable complexity. Although the Japanese initially appeared to have done far better than Jiang had done in the Northern Expedition of 1926–1928, in

---

[1]London, National Archives, Cabinet Papers, 66/4/2 fol. 16.

Chinese men accused of collaborating with the Japanese wait to be executed.

practice their achievement was weaker because their capacity to elicit consent and share success was more limited. In that sense, the Japanese did not understand China.

Japan's ambitions were also seen at sea. Although under the Washington (1922) and London (1930) naval treaties Japan had joined the other major numbers in accepting limits on its naval strength, in December 1934 it provided the required two years' notice of withdrawal from the commitments and, two years later, began a major program of naval expansion. This program was aimed at Britain and the United States, Japan's rivals in Far Eastern and Pacific waters.

Japanese developments provide a key link to the subjects of the next three chapters. Japan's attempt to close off China to Western help and the development of the Japanese navy led Japan to attack the West in 1941. At the same time, Japan's heavy commitment to China meant that the effort Japan could bring to bear upon the British in India was more limited than it would otherwise have been. Moreover, the United States was able to devote more of its resources to a "Europe-first" policy in World War II than if the Japanese were solely operating against the Western powers. Once Japan was defeated and demilitarized in 1945, it was the United States that was to seek to balance Chinese power and Communist ambitions in Eastern Asia, leading the United States into war in Korea in 1950 and in Vietnam in the 1960s.

CONFLICT ACROSS THE ISLAMIC WORLD

Like China, the Islamic world witnessed both warfare within states, as authority was contested, and conflict with imperial forces. In the aftermath of World War I, much of the Ottoman Empire was allocated to Britain, notably Iraq, Palestine (modern Israel and Palestine), and Transjordan (modern Jordan), or to France, which gained Lebanon and Syria. Moreover, new political orders were established within states, especially Turkey, where a republic replaced the Ottoman dynasty.

At the same time, a combination of already-established anti-Western feeling and the spread of a new impulse of reaction against imperial authority affected large portions of the colonial world. This situation was particularly intense in the Muslim world, but was also found elsewhere, particularly in China and Southeast Asia. Opposition had varied causes and consequences. In the 1920s, it included hostility to British hegemony in Iraq; a rising against French rule in Syria; the continuation of resistance in Libya to the rule Italy had sought to impose since 1911; an upsurge, from 1921, in action against Spanish attempts to dominate the part of Morocco allocated to it; and the Turkish refusal to accept a peace settlement that included Greek rule over the Aegean coast and British troops in Constantinople (Istanbul).

The most serious failure occurred in Turkey, where Greek occupation on the Aegean coast provided Turkish nationalists with a rallying point. Mustafa Kemal (later Atatürk) coordinated opposition to the Western forces and their allies, and in 1921 Greek forces advancing into the Turkish interior were defeated. Water and food shortages had hit the Greeks, exacerbating disease and exhaustion. In turn, in 1922 in what is known in Turkey as the Great Offensive, the Turks advanced, outmaneuvered, enveloped, and defeated the Greeks, notably in the battle of Dumlupinar on August 20. This victory was followed by an effective pursuit operation, and the Turks conquered the Aegean coast. There were massacres of the local Christian population. In the Chanak crisis later in 1922, Britain came close to conflict with Turks advancing on Constantinople, but war was avoided. The 1923 peace settlement dramatically revised that of 1920. The Turks were left in control of modern Turkey, and there was a large-scale forced population exchange of Greeks and Turks.

The struggle in Turkey can be seen in terms of this standard narrative, one that remains important to the politics of modern Turkey. The war was the foundation of Atatürk's position and of what was known as Kemalist politics. Success validated a particular strategy of modernization for Turkey, one that rested ultimately on the fact and prestige of victory.

At the same time, there was an important international dimension to the war in Turkey. As an aspect of its opposition to the powers involved in the Russian Civil War and to Western imperialism, Russia provided arms and encouragement to the Turks. Opposed to Greece, Italy also provided arms. France had been given an occupation zone in Turkey and fought the Turks, but rapidly settled because the French had imperial concerns elsewhere, notably in neighboring Syria.

Greek nationalist forces at the port of Smyrna (Izmir), 1919.

In Iraq, a rebellion in 1920 was crushed, in large part by the British use of troops from its major colony, India. British naval strength ensured that these units could be rapidly transferred. In addition, aircraft were used with considerable success, not least because the rebels had no experience in dealing with them. However, this rebellion had revealed the serious military and political weaknesses of British rule. As a result, Britain transferred power to an Iraqi government.

In contrast, in British Somaliland, where opposition was also suppressed in 1920, in part by the use of airpower alongside camel-borne troops, direct control was maintained. The British use of airpower in operations was an aspect of the development of the techniques of imperial warfare. The established practice of combining firepower and mobility in "flying columns" was to be strengthened and supplemented in the interwar period by the use of aircraft, tanks, armored cars, and radio.

In the section of Morocco claimed by Spain, a Spanish advance into the interior led to a battle at Annual in 1921 in which at least 12,000 Spanish troops were killed by the Moors under Muhammed Abd-el-Krim. This struggle served to underline the extent to which World War I did not simply start a new age of international alignments and conflict. Instead, many pre-1914 struggles resumed. Renewed Spanish attacks after Annual were defeated by the mobile Moors who, armed with modern firearms, including machine guns and howitzers, were not dependent on the cumbersome supply routes of their opponents. Suffering food shortages in the harsh terrain, Abd-el-Krim, however, looked toward the most prosperous French-controlled section of Morocco, which he unwisely invaded in 1925. This invasion led to the coordination of major efforts by France and Spain, and in 1926 the rebellion was crushed. The war saw Spain use tanks, aircraft, and poison gas, but also demonstrated the need for massive force and the closure of all routes into the conflict zone if native opposition was to be overcome. In most post-1945 counterinsurgency conflicts, these advantages were not to be present.

Indeed, the availability of Afghanistan as a refuge for Waziri insurgents ensured that large-scale British operations in the late 1930s against the Faqir of Ipi on what is now the northwest frontier of Pakistan could not win complete success. In contrast, the ability to surround the area of Syrian opposition in 1925–1926 enabled France to crush its opponents. The French also used artillery and bombing to reduce opposition in Damascus. Having won, the French consolidated their position in Syria and Lebanon by building up a military and police based on local allies, notably Druze and Maronite Christians, contributing to the sectarian and ethnic strains that were to play a role in violence in the region from the 1970s and, more particularly, in the 2010s.

In Libya, where the Italian invasion launched in 1911 had, in the face of insurrectionary warfare that the Italians could not overcome, only brought control over the coastal strip, the Italians were finally to win in the early 1930s by waging a harsh attritional war. The bases of the opposing society were brought under control by the forcible movement of much of the population.

WAR AND MILITARY DEVELOPMENTS IN EUROPE

Far from being the war to end all wars, as was hoped, World War I led into a period of conflict in Europe. Thereafter, however, far from there being significant preparations for renewed warfare, the decade 1922–1932 was a peaceful one, relatively free from anxieties about international conflict. The situation changed in the mid-1930s, as Adolf Hitler, the Nazi dictator of Germany, began a large-scale rearmament that helped drive international tension. At the same time, the confrontation between right and left that had become a theme from the Russian Revolution, the Cold War of the period, led to a bitter civil war in Spain (1936–1939). Other powers became involved in Spain in a pattern that was to be seen in the classic Cold War of 1945–1989, notably in Southeast Asia, the Middle East, Africa, and Central America. By the time the Spanish Civil War ended in the spring of 1939, the European powers were arming and planning for another major war.

Russian Civil War

The major conflict after World War I was the Russian Civil War. Initially, the November revolution in 1917 led to a coalition government, but the Bolsheviks (Communists) only ever tended to see such government as a means to their end of necessary, absolute control as the exponents of the dictatorship of the prole-tariat. In the spring of 1918, the Communists launched a drive for power that led to a civil war by June. The Communist takeover was followed by radical policies that helped encourage large-scale resistance. This resistance took four forms: White, Green, nationalist, and left wing. The Whites were right-wing opponents of the Communists, led by military figures, such as the generals Denikin and Wrangel and Admiral Kolchak, loyal to the former Tsarist regime. The Greens were peasant opponents who resisted Communist efforts to seize food and also to take control of rural society. Nationalists sought independence for territories that had been conquered by Imperial Russia, notably Estonia, Latvia, Lithuania, Ukraine, Armenia, Georgia, and Azerbaijan, but also in Central Asia. Left-wing opponents objected to the Communist monopolization of power as well as to specific policies.

This list represented a formidable array of forces. However, they were not united, indeed often fought each other (notably Whites versus Greens), and when unity was asserted, as between the Whites, there was no coordination of operations. As a result, the Reds (Communists) were able to focus on their main opponents one at a time. The Reds were also helped by their central position, controlling Moscow and Petrograd (Leningrad/St. Petersburg), the two major cities and the centers of the rail network. Control over communications proved a major element in the war. The Reds exploited their area of control to raise large numbers of troops and, despite the use of much of the army in food requisitioning, enjoyed numerical superiority in their successive victories over opponents. Moreover, in a traditional Russian response, the Communists could afford to trade space for time in what was very much a war of movement. The Whites were weakened by corruption, by a failure to develop policies capable of winning mass support, and by opposition from Greens and nationalists.

The Russian Civil War was to be won by the Soviets and lost by their oppo-nents; as with most struggles, it is possible to put the emphasis on either element—winning or losing—and necessary to put it on both. The brutal tenacity of the Communists was a key element. Indeed, Soviet policy was in some respects a revival of the harsh military politics of internal conflict in Revolutionary France in the 1790s, and this revival lent particular drive to the process by which, as in many other civil wars, military necessity led to a high rate of internal violence.

This necessity stemmed from the requirement to create and sustain forces without the support of a clear-cut, coherent, and uncontested governmental structure or the possibility of eliciting contest through established political chan-nels. The Communists nationalized businesses, seized grain, and imposed a firm dictatorship, and opposition was brutally suppressed, frequently with consider-able violence, violence that was believed necessary to change society. The Com-munist mind-set was very much one of unconstrained struggle, a notion that was also to be seen with the Fascists in Italy and the Nazis in Germany. Analysis of Communist Party internal language indicates that their self-belief readily per-mitted, from the outset, a rationalization of the use of force, not least in the absence of the mass support anticipated or hoped for because of their proclaimed role as vanguards of the people. This stance looked toward the subsequent "peacetime" policy in the Soviet Union of Stalinism (after Joseph Stalin, dictator from 1924 to 1953) in which those who followed different social practices were seen as enemies, irrespective of their degree of political activism.

Communist tenacity in the Civil War was accompanied by determination and the use of terror. The secret police, the Cheka, helped maintain control and used considerable force to do so, but troops were also used to crush opposition within the Soviet-dominated zone. Force and intimidation, moreover, played a role in the raising of a large conscript army in 1918, which ensured numerical superiority for the Reds over the Whites.

As a result, a host of foreign states, principally Britain, France, Japan, and the United States, found that their intervention lacked an adequate basis of support within Russia. Concern about the willingness of the Communists in 1918 to align with the Germans had helped lead to this intervention, notably by Britain, the member of the anti-German alliance best placed to project force into European Russia. Moreover, after the close of World War I, this concern was maintained by a wish to suppress Communism as a real and apparent force and focus for international instability and radicalism.

Fourteen states sent troops and weaponry to help the Whites. British troops were dispatched to the Baltic, the Black Sea, and the Caspian, as well as to Archangel

The Japanese army occupies Khabarovsk, Siberia, in 1919.

and Murmansk in northern Russia, whereas the Americans and the Japanese deployed forces in Siberia and the French in the Baltic and Black Seas and northern Russia. Other participants included Canadians, Italians, and Serbs in northern Russia, former Czech prisoners of war in Siberia, and Finns, Letts, Poles, and Romanians on Russia's western borders. As far as conflict between Western liberal states and the Soviet Union was concerned, this was far more bitter than anything seen after 1945. Indeed, the Cold War in one sense reached its height in the Russian Civil War and thereafter had a long afterlife or, if the Russian Civil War is seen as separate, the afterlife was the Cold War.

Foreign forces focused on the peripheries of Russia, with the Americans being sent to eastern Siberia, in part to check Japanese expansionism. These foreign forces were not therefore able to determine the major clash between Reds and Whites. The limited persistence that came from their war weariness further ensured that the foreign powers were marginal to the struggle within Russia.

The defeat of the Whites led to the overawing of the Greens. The divided and outnumbered nationalists then fell. In the White debacle in 1921, Ukraine was conquered by the Reds, whereas the new states in the Caucasus and Central Asia, such as Armenia and Georgia, were too weak to resist the Red advance. The situation was different from Russia's west, in part because of British intervention, in part because of nationalist determination, and in part because, alongside this opposition, the Red Army focused elsewhere, notably in Ukraine and against Poland. Finland, Estonia, Latvia, and Lithuania were able to establish their independence.

Although the Reds had some skilled commanders, neither side in the Russian Civil War showed much operational or strategic skill. Instead of maneuvering to obtain the most favorable positions, both sides generally chose to fight where they encountered each other, and success usually came to the side that mounted the offensive, a situation also seen in China in the 1920s. Because of relatively low force-to-space ratios, this was warfare in which the emphasis was on attacks, raids, and the seizure of key governmental positions, rather than on staging large-scale battles from well-prepared positions, as on the western front in World War I. The Red Army tended to rely on prepared offensives, albeit crude ones. Forces were massed in a particular sector for a frontal assault that was more or less guaranteed to break a thin enemy line and force the withdrawal of the enemy. The difficulty of sustaining operations, a crucial aspect of logistics, encouraged the emphasis on movement rather than scale and hence the significance of the railroads.

The defensive remained important at the tactical level, not least because the artillery necessary to suppress defenses was in limited supply and was not really useful for fast-moving operations over large areas, in part because the means to move it were limited, which helped explain the importance of armed trains. Their guns provided a form of mobile artillery. Moreover, the absence of continuous fronts made it easier to outflank defensive positions, as was also amply demonstrated in China in the 1920s.

The victory of the Communists over domestic foes and foreign intervention in the Russian Civil War ensured that their regime would not be short lived, as was Communist rule in Hungary in 1919 in the face of successful Romanian invasion and Czech attack, for example. The Communist victory also furthered the identification of the Soviet regime with struggle and provided it with a strong rationale for opposition to Western states, notably the leading European empires, Britain and France, as well as the United States and, indeed, Japan. Born in the experience of civil war, the Soviet Union accordingly took on part of its character in a sense of assault from linked threats, both internal and external, a character that was expressed in part in paranoia.

In many respects, the history of the following decades saw a working out of themes from these years, whether the Soviet attempt to overthrow the British empire or to conquer Poland (which was attempted in 1920, partly carried out in 1939, and achieved in 1944–1945) and the Baltic Republics (Latvia, Lithuania, Estonia), all occupied in 1940, or to overawe Finland. The Soviet Union regarded Poland as a reactionary power, largely carved out of the former Russian empire and willing and able to resist Soviet attempts to influence developments further west. Moreover, the early years of the Russian Revolution and of the revolutionary regime proved crucial in the developing attitudes and experience of individuals who were to play a key role for decades, most notably Joseph Stalin, the Soviet dictator from 1924 until his death in 1953.

EASTERN EUROPE

Having defeated the Whites in Siberia and pushed them back in Ukraine, the Red Army advanced into Poland in 1920, intending to use it to spread Communism further into Europe. Soviet activity and expansionism rested on the belief that Communism was a global need and a worldwide movement and that the legitimacy of the Russian Revolution lay in Russia transforming the world, which was seen as a necessary and inevitable result of the historical process. Institutionally, this belief was expressed in the Comintern, or Communist International, created in 1919. In the situation of great flux that followed World War I and accompanied the Russian Civil War, major efforts were made to spread the revolution and to encourage revolutionary movements elsewhere. If, with hindsight, the idea of the Communist International might seem implausible, Soviet and then also Chinese power was to help enable a major expansion in Communist control in Eastern Europe and Southeast Asia from 1945 to 1954.

However, there was no revolution in Germany, as had been anticipated, whereas in Poland in 1920, far from there being a pro-Soviet rising, the Polish Government of National Defense won support, notably by backing land reform, the step the Whites conspicuously failed to take. Volunteers rallied in a potent display of nationalism and opposition to Communism that lent energy to the Polish counterattack. In the battle of Warsaw between August 16 and 25, the most important battle of the 1920s, the Red Army was defeated and driven back.

This ended the drive west by the Red Army, which had already led to the capture of the cities of Minsk and Vilnius (now capitals of Belarus and Lithuania, respectively) the previous month.

Given that the Red Army had already defeated other opponents and Poland was to be rapidly conquered by Germany in 1939, it is worth considering why the Red Army failed in 1920. It suffered from a lack of coordination among its mutually distrustful generals, from an advance over such a very wide front that it lacked depth and nearby reserves, and because its forces were poorly trained, equipped, and led and had low morale. The Poles also had strengths, including high morale, the ability to gain the initiative and defeat the attacking forces in detail (separately), the availability of French supplies and military advice, and superiority in intelligence, in part thanks to reading Soviet radio traffic.

Nevertheless, Polish campaigning had serious weaknesses and, as is frequent in military history, the conflict was decided by which side was best able to cope with its deficiencies and exploit those of its opponents. It was significant that the Red Army invading central Poland was overextended following a rapid advance. The mobility of operations was seen in the aftermath of the victory with a major Polish offensive then to within 90 miles of Kiev, the capital of Ukraine, before peace was negotiated in March 1921. The failure of the Soviets to conquer Poland, Finland, and the Baltic Republics of Estonia, Latvia, and Lithuania, all of which had broken free from the Russian empire in 1918, owed something to containment by Britain and France, not least in the shape of the British navy in the Baltic, which provided protection for the Baltic Republics.

Moreover, containment was to be an important theme in the 1920s and 1930s, with the prevention of "infection" from the Soviet Union a major goal. Whereas the United States was to play the leading role in containing the Soviet threat in Europe after World War II, the powers in question in the 1920s were Britain and France. In response, the Soviets used a variety of means to weaken Britain and France, encouraging radicalism in the two states and anticolonialism in their empires. In addition, Soviet arms sales to Turkey, Iran, Afghanistan, and China were designed to challenge British interests in each.

In emphasizing containment, however, there was a tendency to underplay the role of local opinion in the shape of the determination of the population not to be engulfed by the Soviets and their local Communist allies. This point exemplifies the more general point about the extent to which the consent of the conquered and to-be-conquered plays a role in imperial (and other) stability and expansion. If there was only limited support for the Whites in Russia, the Communists found even less support in many areas into which they expanded or sought to expand, in large part because of anti-Russian nationalism alongside anti-Communism.

On a smaller scale, there were also conflicts across much of Eastern Europe in the aftermath of World War I. The disruption it had brought combined with the rise of ideological alignments to ensure that political violence became more pronounced in Europe. These changes created a more challenging context for regular armies, in terms both of the tasks they faced and of the control they were supposed to exercise. A stress on swift movement in fighting was encouraged by the need to establish control rapidly in contested areas to present peacemakers and other powers with *fait accomplis*. Fueled by aggressive nationalism, there was a rejection of the attempt by outside bodies to dictate developments.

Sectarian and ethnic violence looked toward more recent patterns of both. What would later be termed ethnic cleansing was practical because of the ethnic basis of the new states in Eastern Europe. The extent to which the regular armies were mostly new forces without any sense of institutional autonomy increased the overlap with politics. Force, however, also settled issues, for example, with invading Romanians overthrowing a Communist regime in Hungary in 1919 while the Czechs took Slovakia from the Hungarians.

The 1920s

By 1925, the political situation across Europe was stabilized. Far from the peace settlement after World War I sowing the seeds of a major new war, as is frequently claimed, the international system it established worked reasonably well in the 1920s. Germany was reassimilated into the international system, much earlier than many could have expected in 1918, and a series of treaties strengthened the system.

Given this situation, as well as the heavy burdens of debt, devastation, and dislocation left after World War I, it was scarcely surprising that investment in the armed forces did not match new military doctrine. Moreover, although tanks and aircraft were embraced by some as force multipliers, calls to take advantage of new technology, both what was available and what might be available, were frequently ignored.

Counterfactualism (what if?) always has its limitations, but it returns us to the unpredictability of the past and the uncertainties of contemporaries. To subtract the failure, protectionism, misery, and extremism produced by the Depression of the 1930s is to suggest that the 1920s' order could have continued, in part because internationalism, liberalism, democracy, and free-market capitalism would have retained more appeal, with both electorates and governments. In the 1920s, with Soviet expansion checked and Germany under the 1919 Versailles peace settlement limited to a 100,000-man army and its rearmament banned, the European order was dominated militarily by France, and France was committed to maintaining peace.

"Never again" was a phrase much used with reference to World War I. For much of the public, it meant "never again a world war," but, for the military, it meant "never again a world war fought in this manner." This idea arose from an understanding of the serious consequences of attritional warfare, as well as from the concern that any further war on this scale would, as in Russia (1917) and Germany (1918), undermine political stability and indeed the entire structure of society.

As a result, there was intellectual inquiry about the nature of war winning, attempts to develop operational doctrine, concern about ensuring maneuverability and what would later be termed "deep battle," and much interest in the potential of tanks, mechanized transport, and air-to-air, air-to-land, and air-to-sea warfare. Meanwhile, the weaponry developments of the war, such as the greater use of hand grenades, were absorbed into tactical doctrine. No post-1918 Western army went back to the prewar ways. Instead, infantry was now equipped and trained to fight a flexible battle with a range of weapons.

A key element in all this military thinking became that of manpower versus machines. Machines cost much money, not only to develop but also to introduce, supply, and maintain. This was true both for complex machines, such as planes, and for simpler equipment such as improved firearms. On the other hand, there were heavy costs involved in training, paying, housing, clothing, equipping, and feeding large numbers of troops. The victorious campaign of 1918 had required both manpower and machines, but the massive expenditure and effort of the war years had left debilitating debts and could not be sustained in peacetime. There was also a key political dimension: Britain abandoned conscription (compulsory military service for young men) by choice, whereas Germany was made to do so as part of the 1919 peace settlement.

Manpower limitations posed a challenge to tactics, operations, and strategies requiring large numbers of troops. The organizational centrality of mass armies could no longer define planning. Instead, machines were seen as a way to deliver increased capability at lower cost and to shorten war by delivering a rapid verdict, arguments pushed particularly hard by advocates for airpower, but also seen with supporters of army mechanization. The resulting preference for an elite, well-equipped force, however, clashed with institutional preferences within armies for continuity and size and with the careers bound up in traditional military structures, a tension that was also to be seen in the 1990s after the end of the Cold War. Other factors also played a major role in the 1920s and 1930s, including the need for numbers, notably for the maintenance of control in colonies; the equivalent in the 1990s–2010s was for power projection and counterinsurgency in the "Third World."

In the 1920s and 1930s, there was also pressure to match the armies of other powers, and many states, notably totalitarian ones, sought a large army, seeing it as an indicator of national strength. In Japan, the Imperial Way faction in the army successfully pressed for an emphasis on manpower and the military spirit, rather than on machines. Their call was for "flesh before steel" and they believed that Japanese manpower had inherent and unique qualities that made them effective.

Moreover, states with smaller populations than those of potential foes, France as opposed to Germany or Japan as opposed to China, sought ways to compensate for the lack of men. So also did states that rejected conscription, such as Britain and the United States. Britain put an emphasis on equipment, notably so in the case of the air force and the navy, and sought to improve the army's effectiveness. Formal training was increasingly seen as important and was not limited to the "home" armies but extended to their colonial forces. Formally inaugurated in 1932, the Indian Military Academy offered formal training for Indians who wanted to be officers. For France, the decision to build the fortifications of the Maginot Line, on which work began in 1930, was part of the equation in offering protection for Eastern France against German attack. The Maginot Line was both an economy of force measure and a means to create jobs. It also reflected the importance of fortifications in the military planning of the powers.

In practice, ideas about new warfare, notably concerning what future war would be like, advanced further than technological capability and resource availability and often much further, as was to be shown in the early campaigns of World War II. There were inherent problems with the application in weaponry and battle of many of the technological ideas and innovations, let alone fundamental questions about effectiveness. Moreover, interwar investment in armed forces, constrained by contemporary economic realities, was too limited to permit an effective implementation of new doctrine in equipment and in training. More than resources, however, were involved in these limitations. For example, thanks to rivalry between specialisms within the army, the Americans found it difficult to develop appropriate combined arms doctrine, and tank warfare was given little role under the National Defense Act of 1920.

The development of mechanized warfare in the latter stages of World War I, as well as the offensive tactics and operational art employed by Germany in 1917–1918, influenced subsequent thinking. An effective combined arms doctrine was developed in Germany under Hans von Seeckt, commander of the army from

Pillbox turrets along the Maginot Line.

1920 to 1926. In Britain, J. F. C. Fuller pressed the case for tanks and argued in favor of deep penetration by attacking tank forces leading to the disruption of opposing units. An emphasis on armored attack was also seen in the writings of Basil Liddell Hart, who associated military doctrine with his eagerness for self-publicity, a frequent pairing. Armor appeared a means to secure a quick outcome and avoid the strains of a long conflict, offering a counterpart to the ambitions (and fears) focused on bombing.

However, the emphasis on land remained on infantry and artillery. In part, this reflected the conservatism of the military leadership, whether in Britain, France, or Germany, but far more was at stake, including the limitations of the tanks of the period. There were also serious problems in coordinating tanks, infantry, and artillery and in deciding how best to employ tanks. Concern with tanks, nevertheless, did encourage an interest in antitank guns. Thus, in Belgium, a 47-mm antitank gun was brought into service three years after the introduction there of a more mobile artillery with the 120-mm tractor-drawn artillery.

The tasks facing the military were also significant. The need to maintain imperial positions meant a requirement for significant numbers of troops, with the key addition of mobile firepower being provided, notably for Britain, by airpower, rather than slower-moving tanks, which were also greatly restricted by the terrain and the absence of many roads. Thus, the British used bombing to overawe Afghanistan in the 1919 Anglo-Afghan War, bombing the capital Kabul, and also to overcome opposition in British Somaliland in 1920. Within Europe, there was also the need for troops to overawe domestic opposition, as in Britain with the General Strike in 1926.

Although the political context differed from that of the maintenance of imperial control, other states faced similar issues, notably in dealing with opposition, if not rebellion, from marginal areas, but also from ethnic and religious minorities, as well as from powerful figures and areas far from marginal that fell out with the government. To a varying degree this was true in the 1920s and 1930s of China, Ethiopia, Iran, Iraq, Turkey, Brazil, and Mexico. As a consequence, although it might have offered a deterrence from such attack or intervention from abroad, the military was primarily used not for war with other states, but for dealing with domestic resistance, discontent, and criminality.

Many of these themes and conflicts, for example, armed opposition from the Kurds to the governments of Iraq and Turkey, linked this interwar period to the past 70 years. In addition to providing a measure of continuity, these conflicts helped explain the problems faced by Western forces when they intervened.

The 1930s

In the 1930s, the European situation became more menacing after Adolf Hitler gained power in 1933. He rapidly set Germany on a path of rearmament, which he saw as necessary for national regeneration, both internally and externally, and which also responded to the mass unemployment of the Depression by creating jobs.

A large arms budget was announced in 1934 and conscription was reintroduced in 1935. Hitler rejected the Versailles peace settlement, took command of the German military, and threatened the stability of the European international system.

As the European powers responded to this threat to peace as well as others, there was the question of what force structure should be developed for individual militaries. For Britain in particular, but also for other powers such as Russia, there was the issue of which power they might fight and therefore what forces would be required. Japan's invasion of Manchuria in 1931 led to the possibility of a war with Japan, which would put the focus on the navy for Britain (and the United States) and on the air force for the Soviet Union, which waged limited frontier struggles with Japan in 1938 and 1939. The possibility of war with Italy led Britain and France to be concerned about the naval situation in the Mediterranean. Conversely, the prospect of war with Germany led to British interest in airpower, which was the focus of British military expenditure in the mid-1930s.

Although the global Depression acted across the world to encourage international economic competition, the politicosocial consequences varied greatly by state, both in terms of government policy and with reference to the ability to take military initiatives, with the mobilization of resources in a militaristic fashion being most pronounced in the Soviet Union. There, industrial capacity was seen as a basis for making war, both offensive and defensive, and the theme of mobilization was a potent one, linking Soviet ideology to a consistent paranoia that was integral to the character of Communism, but to which Stalin was particularly prone. Military industry was greatly expanded as a result of its having a highly placed patron in the shape of the Red Army to push for investment and resources, as well as the presence of Communist military thinkers who, rather than relying on the idea of the people under arms in the shape of a militia, recognized the need for a comprehensive peacetime organization for war. Unlike in Western states, this focus on a military–industrial complex was a drive that was not restricted by pressure limiting investment such as concern for consumer well-being. Moreover, military industry was encouraged by an ideology of hostility to foreign states and influences that characterized even Communist moderates and by the extent to which Stalin's rise to power had been supported by a military high command concerned by the efforts of the fiscally conservative Communists, such as Nicolay Bukharin, to resist the rise in military spending.

The catalyst for full militarization in the Soviet Union was Japan's invasion of Manchuria in 1931, which brought forward concern about Japan as a strategic threat in the Far East and provoked a full-scale industrial mobilization. This mobilization included expanding bases and forces in the Far East and retooling the heart of Soviet heavy industry for armaments production. The cost was immense, but levels of production far ahead of anything else in the world were achieved, notably 4,000 tanks annually, instead of about 1,000 annually until the end of 1931; there was never any meaningful retreat from that level of production. The location of industrial development also influenced Soviet strategic capability. Boosted in all regions, industry in the Urals and Siberia increased in the same proportion as elsewhere, but the already strong metallurgical industry in the Urals served as the basis for an expansion of industrial production that proved to be beyond the range of air attack, which proved a key strategic asset when fighting Germany during World War II. Japan's expansion in Manchuria led to serious clashes with the Red Army at Changkuofeng (1938) and Nomonhan (1939), which showed the effectiveness of Soviet forces when ably led, notably the latter.

In the meantime, the Stalin regime used force to crush all other centers of power and opinion in both the state and the country, notably party rivals and the military leadership. Moreover, the paranoid style of the Stalin regime led it to find enemies readily. Thus, in the so-called "Polish Operation" of 1937–1938, more than 140,000 Poles living in the Soviet Union were arrested as a potential threat. Many were then shot. Stalin's decision to turn against the High Command and then the officer corps in 1937–1938, killing a large number of commanders and officers, had military consequences because it destroyed the High Command's attempt to build up a well-equipped military capable of waging effective offensive warfare using concepts of operational conflict to combine mass and maneuver. At the same time, the purges served as a reminder that one of the key roles of the military was as a reliable arm of the state. This entailed issues of effectiveness different from those of combat readiness.

War had broken out in Europe in 1936, but it was in Spain, not in the Rhineland, which the Germans remilitarized that year in defiance of the Versailles settlement without any armed response from France. A rising by the right-wing Spanish army, the kernel of the Nationalist movement, against the left-wing Republican government touched off a civil war that lasted until 1939. The radicalism of the Republic had offended much of the population, notably property owners and the Catholic interest, and this situation provided support for the army.

Foreign powers intervened in support of their ideological allies: Germany and Italy on behalf of the Nationalists, who were led by Francisco Franco, and the Soviet Union backing the Republicans. As such, the war offered an opportunity to try out new techniques, notably with the German and Italian use of bombing. There was spectacular terror bombing of civilian targets, such as the cities of Madrid (1936), Guernica (1937), and Barcelona (1938). The German destruction of Guernica was intended to destroy the morale of the Republican Basques and, indeed, weakened their resistance to the Nationalist advance, although American military observers correctly raised serious doubts about the alleged effectiveness of bombing in destroying civilian morale.

However, terror bombing captured the imagination of many, sowing fears that the bombing of civilian targets would be decisive in a future war. This affected British thinking during the Munich Crisis in 1938, as British intelligence, building on Hitler's propaganda about the *Luftwaffe* (German air force), exaggerated German air capability. The resulting concentration on air defense, however, helped Britain resist German air attack in 1940.

Nevertheless, most of the fighting in Spain was not cutting edge in terms of the military theorists and doctrine of the period. Instead, as with the Chaco War between Bolivia and Paraguay in 1932–1935, the emphasis was on infantry attacks across fronts that were not as coherent as those of World War I had been. Both sides found it difficult to develop effective mass forces given the lack of sufficient time, training, resources, and cohesive administrative support. The divided Republican government lacked the ability to raise revenue and to ensure sufficient food for its army and for civilians, whereas the Nationalists proved more effective at ensuring a measure of unity and also in providing adequate logistics. The attritional character of the struggle underlined the importance of resources, notably foreign support, and also the issue of competence.

In the case of Spain, there was also the powerful political element that was to be seen in much of the post-1945 conflict of the Cold War. Both Nationalists and Republicans terrorized opponents in the areas they controlled, and there was widespread slaughter of both civilians and prisoners. As a result, at least 300,000 Spaniards were killed in the war. The ideological dimension of the conflict also looked ahead to the bitter struggle between Germany and the Soviet Union in 1941–1945.

While the war was being waged in Spain, matters were moving toward a crisis in Europe. In 1938, Hitler increased the ambition, pace, and tone of German revisionism and expansionism. Intimidated by Germany, the Austrian government was forced to accept the *Anschluss*, or union of the two states. Austria was occupied on March 12. Czechoslovakia's southern frontier was now exposed to German attack, and Germany gained frontiers with Hungary, Italy, and Yugoslavia.

Hitler then turned on Czechoslovakia. Created from the Austrian Empire at the end of World War I, Czechoslovakia included on its western borderlands areas with a majority German population, the *Sudentenland*, and Hitler encouraged local demands for this area to join Germany. He was also bitterly opposed to Czechoslovakia because it was the sole democracy in Eastern Europe, as well as the key player in the French alliance system.

War neared in 1938, with the Czechs resolved to resist German pressure. The response of Britain and France led to what would subsequently be called the Munich Crisis. Rather than support the Czechs, Britain and France successfully leaned on them to cede the *Sudentenland* to maintain the peace in accordance with the Munich agreement Britain and France had reached with Hitler on September 29. This outcome left Czechoslovakia vulnerable, and the Germans were able to occupy much of it easily in March 1939: the rest became an independent, pro-German Slovakia. Pacifism in British and French society and opinion affected their government's policies in what has since been regarded as the prime instance of the Appeasement of the dictators. The most appeasing of the powers was in fact isolationist America, the world's wealthiest state, which adopted an important role in the crisis by taking no real part.

Anglo-French fears of Germany in 1938 may have been excessive given the weakness of the Nazi regime, not least an absence of enthusiasm for large-scale war among the German generals, as well as the deficiencies of the German military, the weaknesses of the German frontier defenses, and the lack of German strength for any attritional conflict, the latter a point that was to emerge during World War II. The British and French certainly exaggerated German military strength.

However, it is all too easy in hindsight to criticize the leaders of the period and to underrate their genuine and understandable fear of causing a second "Great War." Indeed, in many respects, the Munich agreement was part of the legacy of the Great War. Germany may have been weaker than was thought, but, under Hitler, the country was determined to gain its objectives. There were also serious weaknesses in the British and French militaries. Their armies were not ready to attack and their air forces were weak. Moreover, whereas the Soviet Union was to play the key role in destroying the German army in 1944–1945 as part of an alliance including Britain and the United States, in 1938–1939 this role was not militarily or diplomatically feasible.

The crisis of 1938 was both consequence and cause of greater radicalization in German policy, a radicalization linked to Hitler wielding greater power and with less restraint. His disgrace and removal of senior military figures he distrusted were important to his drive for supreme control, a control he was determined to use. Territorial expansion and anti-Semitic (anti-Jewish) violence were central aspects of this drive for ascendancy. The seizure of Bohemia and Moravia in March 1939 and Hitler's renunciation of the guarantees he had made at Munich showed both that his ambitions were not restricted to bringing all Germans under one state and that he was increasingly willing to pursue opportunities without considering the risks involved.

Britain and France responded by pressing ahead with rearmament while seeking to create an alliance system capable of deterring and intimidating Hitler. This policy led to guarantees to Poland and Romania. Nevertheless, Hitler persisted with his plan for an attack on Poland. To give substance to the British and French guarantees, it seemed necessary to bring in the Soviet Union, but Poland and Romania were distrustful of the neighboring Soviets. In light of the Soviet invasion of Poland in 1920 and Soviet policy toward Poland from 1939, Polish concerns are understandable. However, the Poles were also naive in imagining that Germany could be restrained by the threat of British and French intervention without active Soviet assistance.

Stalin agreed to a nonaggression pact with Hitler, named after their manipulative foreign ministers, Molotov and Ribbentrop. The pact stipulated no war between the two powers for 10 years, and secret clauses determined their respective spheres of influence in Eastern Europe. Hitler was therefore freed from the prospect of a two-front war against major powers. As such, it appeared possible for Germany to avoid the stalemate of the Great War. Nevertheless, Poland stood firm against German pressure, whereas Britain and France felt war necessary to preserve honor and the international system and to stop Hitler. The German attack on Poland on September 1, 1939, led Britain and France to declare war two days later.

READING LIST

Jeremy Black, *Avoiding Armageddon: From the Great War to the Fall of France, 1918–40*, London, Bloomsbury, 2012.

David Edgerton, *Warfare State: Britain, 1920–1970*, Cambridge, U.K., Cambridge University Press, 2006.

Eugenia Kiesling, *Arming against Hitler: France and the Limits of Military Planning*, Lawrence, University Press of Kansas, 1996.

Alan Millett and Williamson Murray (eds.), *Military Effectiveness: The Interwar Period*, Cambridge, U.K., Cambridge University Press, 1988.

David Omissi, *Air Power and Colonial Control: The Royal Air Force 1919–1939*, Manchester, U.K., Manchester University Press, 1990.

FOUR

A GLOBAL WAR: WORLD WAR II, 1939–1945

American ashtray encouraging smokers to "jam their butts" into Hideki Tojo, prime minister of Japan from 1941 to 1944.

Large-scale conflict between China and Japan from 1937, conflict that continued until the end of World War II in 1945, might suggest that a chapter on the war should begin then, but its global character really started in 1939 because it was then that Britain and France went to war, mobilizing their global empires in doing so. Moreover, war between these powers and Germany added a far-flung naval dimension that was missing in the case of that between Japan and China. Although Germany no longer had colonies and therefore the Allied attacks on them seen in World War I did not occur, 1939 saw a German pocket battleship, the *Graf Spee*, and British warships fighting in the estuary of the River Plate in South America, just as 1914 had seen a battle between German and British warships off the Falkland Islands.

That this war, although a global and industrial conflict like World War I, was to be totally different in its course was dramatically demonstrated in 1940. Unlike in 1914, France fell rapidly to invading German forces in June 1940, with British forces also forced to retreat from France and Britain now vulnerable to German invasion. This outcome brought to a final end the interwar period, both militarily and politically. The defeat of the imperial systems of France and Britain in their European heartland ensured that Germany would only be stopped as a super-power if the Soviet Union and America came into the war and also meant that a major American role would be necessary to defeat Japan once it entered the war in December 1941: Britain and China would be able to deny Japan victory, but not to defeat Japan.

The fall of France also marked the end of limited war because the new British government under Winston Churchill was not interested in a compromise peace dictated by a victorious Germany, the option to close the war that was on offer via Hitler's ally, Italy. Churchill's decision meant that the conflict would continue until the actions of the Soviet Union and the United States could play a decisive role. The British fought the war with a national-unity coalition gov-ernment, and once the political crisis in 1940 surrounding the change in gov-ernment was surmounted, there was no serious political pressure for a settlement with Germany.

THE FALL OF POLAND, 1939

The 1940 German campaign might appear to demonstrate the wisdom of those who had seen the future of war in tanks, mobility, and the offensive, what was to be called *blitzkrieg* (lightning war). In practice, military change is far from straightforward. The Germans were not really preparing for *blitzkrieg* prior to 1939 and instead learned what could be achieved from their successful war of maneuver in Poland that September. The Germans were also helped in that con-flict by the Polish deployment, notably defending the full extent of their lengthy borders and lacking defense in depth, as well as by complete German air superi-ority and eventual Soviet intervention on the German side.

Although they declared war on Germany in response to its invasion of Poland, the campaign there did not involve France or Britain directly. Their emphasis on resting on the defensive and using the indirect means of an attritional economic warfare based on the strength of the Western economies and naval blockade to weaken Germany could not save Poland.

The deficiencies of Germany's opponents and the *ad hoc* nature of the develop-ment and practice of *blitzkrieg* put supposed German operational and doctrinal brilliance in its proper, more qualified, context. In 1939, far from being mecha-nized, much of the German army was heavily reliant on railways and draught animals, and a lack of training was also apparent. Moving toward *blitzkrieg*, in practice, was linked to retraining actively after the Poland campaign. In this, the Germans made more profitable use than France and Britain of the "Phoney War," the lull in the fighting on the Western Front in the harsh winter of 1939–1940. Moreover, Hitler now felt emboldened to promote particular generals who backed mechanized attacks.

THE FALL OF FRANCE, 1940

The Germans launched their offensive on the western front on May 10, 1940, pushed across the Meuse River on May 13, splitting the French defensive line, and exploited this success to advance through the Allied center to reach the English Channel on May 21. A separate advance farther north took the surrender of the Dutch on May 14 and of the Belgians on May 27. Regrouping to advance anew against the French, the Germans broke through against now weaker resistance, entered Paris on June 14, and dictated terms to France on June 22.

For fewer than 30,000 of their own troops killed, Germany had transformed the situation in Western Europe and taken toward fruition the quest for a continent-based empire, a quest that reflected the belief in the inherent competitiveness of international relations, the system of racist geopolitics, and the conviction that widely flung power was necessary for effective competition with the other empires: Britain, the Soviet Union, and the United States.

This triumph reflected German military strengths at the tactical and operational levels that helped overcome the larger numbers of well-equipped opponents including a commitment to a war of movement. However, the effectiveness of the *blitzkrieg* was exaggerated by contemporary and later commentators under the spell cast by the sheer shock and drama of the German offensives. As a result, commentators then and subsequently have overrated the impact on the war of military ideas and methods that in practice represented more of an improvisation than the fruition of a coherent doctrine. The potential of weaponry and logistics based on the internal combustion engine was less fully grasped than talk of *blitzkrieg* might suggest and than the American army was to demonstrate comprehensively in France in 1944, not least because much of the German army was unmechanized and walked into battle. Alongside the highly effective tactical and operational use of the armored tip of the army, the contribution and quality of the German infantry and artillery were significant.

As another qualification of the standard *blitzkrieg* approach, the Germans encountered serious problems in fighting their way across the Meuse River against French resistance, and the German success in breaking through the French positions there was far from assured. Conversely, the success of the risky German strategy owed much to the serious deficiencies of French strategy and planning, especially the deployment of France's mechanized reserves on the advancing French left flank in Belgium, so that they were not available in a reserve capacity to counter the German breakthrough on the Meuse in the French center. Linked to this, there was an absence of defense in depth on the part of the French and their failure to devise an adequate plan for effective mobile warfare. The French *Armée de l'Air* lacked the sustainability crucial to maintaining operational effectiveness.

In 1918, the Allies had responded more effectively to German attack than they were to do in 1940. Greater German mobility was an important factor in 1940, not least the triumph of a German operational war of movement over French more positional warfare, but this contrast was made more significant by French strategic and operational inadequacies. The French were outmaneuvered in 1940, in part because their very attempt to take the initiative contributed to a disastrous position. The German army's key advantage was not superior equipment but greater intellectual flexibility. The French development of mechanized and motorized divisions was intended to provide a mobility capable of countering the German advance in Belgium as a prelude to an engagement by the mass army with its infantry and artillery. That this was not to work in 1940 was largely the result of poor French command decisions and the German ability to sustain a breakthrough, a key element of *blitzkrieg*. The French failure was not a product of any unwillingness to engage with the likely nature of conflict, but occurred because the emphasis on carefully controlled operations failed to provide sufficient room for decision making at lower levels and therefore greatly compromised flexibility. German training and practice were far better in this respect, which was a consequence both of methods developed in the German army in the nineteenth century and of the emphasis in the 1930s on employing flexibility to ensure mobility by making the best use of armor.

A key element in 1939–1941 was that of politics because it set the tasking for militaries. In 1939, by allying with Hitler, Stalin proved more than willing to subordinate the cause of international Communism to that of state expansion in concert with Germany. This process was facilitated by a shared hostility to Britain that stemmed from a rejection of democratic capitalism as a domestic agenda for liberty and freedom, but also hostility to it as an international agenda focused on opposition to dictatorial expansionism. Stalin also wanted to buy time while encouraging the Germans, British, and French to exhaust each other.

The resulting German–Soviet system proved short lived, as Hitler attacked the Soviet Union in June 1941; in the meantime, despite hostility and the Soviet invasion of Poland and Finland, Britain and the Soviet Union did not fight each other. Nevertheless, the combination of Germany and the Soviet Union underlined the extent to which military considerations, such as the force structures of the British, French, and German militaries, were secondary to the goals set by political alignments. For example, whereas Britain went to war with Germany in September 1939, Germany's allies, Italy and Japan, did not enter the war until June 1940 and December 1941, respectively. Thus, the British navy focused on German submarines and surface raiders, rather than on fleet action with the Italian and Japanese navies.

In June 1940, the Italian dictator, Benito Mussolini, an ally of Hitler in the Pact of Steel, joined in the war with France and Britain once the French had been clearly defeated by the Germans because he feared that he would otherwise lose the opportunity to gain glory and territories. Longer-term ambitions also played a major role. German victory brought to a head Mussolini's ideological affinity with

Hitler, his contempt for the democracies, and the inherent violence and aggressive expansionism of a regime that had already played a brutal role in suppressing rebellion in Libya and in the conquest of Ethiopia in 1935–1936. Mussolini's vision of Italian greatness required domination of the Mediterranean, which led him to want Britain's defeat and also resulted in war with Greece in October 1940.

BRITAIN ATTACKED, 1940–1941

Having conquered France, Germany now prepared to invade Britain. A key moment of national defeat and vulnerability in the face of the threat of invasion led not to the acceptance of German peace terms, as might have been expected in the aftermath of defeat, but to a determination to fight on, a determination voiced resolutely by Winston Churchill, the new prime minister. Combined with political will, popular support, potent air defense, and the backing of the empire, the British navy's strength was to ensure that German strategy failed in 1940. To try to counter this strength, the Germans sought air superiority over the English Channel.

Gaining that entailed defeating the Royal Air Force (RAF), but the latter had been greatly improved in the late 1930s. In July 1934, Parliament had backed a major increase in the RAF by 1939, and to counter the growing threat from German air attack, the British developed two effective monoplane fighters. In December 1937, the Hawker Hurricane I entered service, beginning a new period of eight-machine-gun monoplane fighters that could fly faster than 300 mph. The Supermarine Spitfire followed into service in June 1938. Improvements in fighters began to undermine the doctrine of the invincibility, and thus paramountcy, of the bomber. Thanks to the Rolls Royce Merlin engines developed beginning in 1932 and part of the major British advance in aeroengines, by 1939 British fighters could intercept the fastest German bombers. By September 1939, the RAF had replaced its biplanes, and new air bases were built in eastern England in response to the German threat.

The British also invested heavily in the new technology of radar, using radio to detect the presence of distant metallic objects. From 1936, the British built a chain of radar early-warning stations able to spot planes 100 miles off the coast; by 1940, these had been linked into an integrated air-defense system. At the centralized control rooms, data from radar stations and the observer corps, which continued to track German aircraft once they had crossed the coast, were analyzed and then fed through into instructions for fighters. No other state had that capability at this stage.

The failure of the Germans to destroy the RAF in the Battle of Britain in August–September 1940 and gain air superiority led to an attempt to break British resolve by means of the *Blitz*, an air assault on British cities, particularly ports and notably London, from September 1940. The strength of the RAF ensured that the German focus was on night bombing, and great damage and heavy civilian casualties were inflicted, not least because of the weakness of British antiaircraft defenses. However,

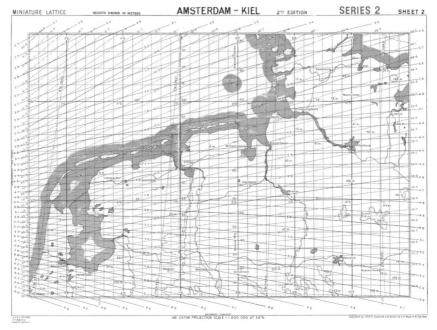

Navigation chart showing radio signals, which RAF pilots used to bomb northern Germany in 1943.

aside from the British response, the Germans had failed to develop a strategic bombing force centered on four-engine bombers. The German focus on quick wars had encouraged an air force designed for ground support. *Blitzkrieg* entailed no obvious requirement for a strategic bombing force. Moreover, the Germans lacked a strong aero industry, notably in terms of producing the engines necessary for heavy bombers. The Germans also faced problems with pilot training and the availability of aviation fuel. More generally, there was a lack of adequate infrastructure that reflected poor leadership. The net result was a weakness in German force structure that exacerbated a failure of strategy. Britain fought on and Germany was deprived of the quick victory it had prepared for. As with Japan in 1938–1939, a strategy of quick victory and reliance on force proved flawed. In Britain, the German air assault helped fashion a renewed patriotism.

At sea, once British resolve indicated a long war, the Germans placed greater reliance on submarines. Prior to the war, the Germans had a weak submarine force. However, the conquest of France provided them with submarine bases from which they were able to attack Atlantic trade routes. The German submarines could not be restricted by minefields across the Straits of Dover and the North Sea as they eventually had been in World War I.

Moreover, Karl Dönitz, chief of the submarine force from 1935, had developed wolf-pack tactics in which a group of submarines, coordinated by radio, attacked convoys on the surface (which allowed them to avoid detection by sonar) at nighttime (which helped to conceal their movements, at least until escort vessels could be equipped with radar sets). The wolf-pack tactic was used with considerable success, overwhelming the escorts.

Yet, again demonstrating the importance of political factors, American entry into the war in December 1941 led to an alliance with the United States that proved crucial to Britain at sea, both providing security for Australasia against Japan and helping ensure the maintenance of control over the Atlantic against Germany. Prior to Japan's attack on the United States and Hitler's declaration of war a day later, the United States had already moved closer to Britain. Concerned about German intentions and about the global balance of power after the fall of France, President Franklin Delano Roosevelt sought naval rearmament as a means to deter Germany as well as Japan. The six battleships of the *Iowa* class laid down under the 1939 and 1940 programs were impressive, with massive armor and high speed (33 knots). Worried about German submarines blockading Britain into submission, Roosevelt was ready for the United States to take over convoy duty in the western Atlantic. In August 1941, Churchill and Roosevelt met on warships in Placentia Bay, Newfoundland, part of the process by which the two powers moved together prior to Pearl Harbor.

This meeting saw both traditional and new themes and means of mobilizing support for conflict. The meeting included a church service in which the idea of a chosen army resisting evil in the cause of God was clearly enunciated. From a pulpit draped with the Union Jack and the Stars and Stripes, Wilfred Parker, the chaplain of the *Prince of Wales*, a British battleship, referred to fighting "against the powers of darkness enslaving the souls of men." Another theme was offered by the attempt to use the meeting to raise and direct morale. Photographers and film cameramen provided a clear account of unity and purpose and helped in two separate tasks of public encouragement: Churchill's need to maintain morale and Roosevelt's attempt to overcome American isolationism, the wish to avoid involvement in the war.

While Britain fought on and indeed made major gains in 1940–1941 at the expense of the African colonies of Germany's ally, Italy, the Germans expanded their power in Eastern Europe, rapidly conquering Yugoslavia and Greece in April 1941. Germany had apparently won the war as then conducted. Soviet backing had proved crucial to Germany's ability to gain control of Eastern Europe because it removed any effective counter, and British military support was ineffective, as the disastrous failure of an attempt to help Greece demonstrated. With the United States moreover neutral, there appeared no way for Britain to be able to reverse the verdict of recent defeats. Indeed, the British were concerned that their position in the Middle East might be compromised by German successes in the Mediterranean region. This led to British interest in fallback positions in Iraq and Iran and therefore in the occupation of both, which was accomplished in 1941 and 1942, respectively.

INVADING THE SOVIET UNION, 1941

These concerns were to be accentuated when the Soviet Union fared poorly in the early stages of the conflict launched by German attack on June 22, 1941. Hitler's contempt for Slavs and for Communism and his belief that Germany had to conquer the Soviet Union and enslave its peoples to fulfil its destiny and obtain *Lebensraum* (living space for settlement and food production) had led to preparations beginning in July 1940 for an invasion initially planned for May 1941. Hitler's decision before Britain had been defeated to embark on a new war with the Soviets demonstrated the importance of political factors. This was the point where Hitler clearly overextended Germany, taking on political objectives greater than could be accomplished by operational success on the battlefield.

Confident that the Soviet system would collapse rapidly, Hitler was happy to accept misleading intelligence assessments of the size and mobilization potential of the Red Army and of the damage inflicted by Stalin's purges. The Germans were convinced from observing the difficulties the Soviets had encountered in the Winter War with Finland (1939–1940) that the Soviet military was weak, although Finland had eventually been defeated. Hitler's adventurism and conceit were a reflection of his warped personality, as well as the product of a political–ideological system in which conflict and hatred appeared necessary and natural. Furthermore, Russian military defeat and political collapse in 1917 encouraged the Germans to feel that victory could again be had. Nevertheless, appreciable casualties were anticipated by the Germans, who deployed as many troops as they could. Delayed by the conquest of Yugoslavia and Greece, the surprise attack

German soldiers in winter uniform, Finland, 1942.

involved nearly 3.6 million German and allied troops supported by 3,350 tanks and 1,950 planes.

The German plan represented an attempt to seize all objectives simultaneously, a source of confusion that reflected both the failure to settle the core target of the operation and the mistaken assumption that the Soviet Union would rapidly fall. The inconsistently conceived and executed offensive (a description also appropriate for the unsuccessful German continuation offensive in 1942) reflected the deficiencies of Hitler as a supreme commander, not least his unwillingness to shut out unwelcome information and advice, but there was also a more general failure of German war making. As in 1914, aggression, overconfidence, and the emphasis on a will to win could not be a substitute for a failure to set sensible military and political goals, specifically the inability to make opposing states and peoples accept German assumptions. Even if the Soviet Union was defeated, there was no viable peace policy on offer for its leadership or people other than complete submission. Alongside a lack of well-grounded goals, there was a failure to define and implement clear strategic objectives.

These strategic and political failures matched those that were already apparent, namely Hitler's failure to persuade Britain to end resistance or to ground the European empire he had created in 1938–1941 in popular support from the conquered. In another strategic context, Japan's willingness to negotiate a nonaggression pact meant that the Soviets did not have to fight a war on two fronts.

Moreover, the German military had serious deficiencies, and Soviet fighting quality was also both significant and underrated by the Germans. In 1941, the Germans were able to inflict heavy casualties on the Soviets, not least by being more effective at the tactical level in linking firepower and mobility, while operationally they outmaneuvered and encircled Soviet defenders and were more successful in imposing their tempo on the flow of conflict. Yet, the Red Army learned to cope with German tactics, notably by negating the impact of German tank attacks with the skillful use of antitank guns. As a result of the hard fighting of the battle for the Yelnya Bulge near Smolensk from July 23 to August 21, German mechanized forces, although victorious, were already badly battered.

The Soviets, moreover, learned to deal with German operational methods, especially coping with German breakthroughs by establishing defenses in depth, which affected the prospect of a drive on Moscow. The Germans also suffered from inadequate logistics, including the difficulties of regauging the Soviet railways and a shortage of trucks. Moreover, most of the German army still traveled on foot and brought up supplies with draught animals.

The impact of the winter on operations proved a particular problem for Operation Typhoon, the drive on Moscow launched on September 30 with newly available tank divisions, a drive where initial success could not be sustained. There was a panic, involving popular disturbances in Moscow in mid-October, as ministries and factories were moved in the face of German advance. However, Stalin decided not to flee, there was no military or political collapse comparable to that of France in 1940, and the ruthless NKVD (Secret Police) was used to prevent anarchy and restore order. By December 1941, the Germans were stalled in hard fighting by defending Soviet forces outside Moscow and Leningrad (St. Petersburg), and the Soviets were about to launch a major counteroffensive near Moscow that recaptured some of the recently lost territory.

JAPAN ENTERS THE WAR, 1941–1942

The Japanese attacked the United States and Britain on December 7, 1941. They did so because Britain seemed weak, and the American attempt to limit Japan's expansionism in Southeast Asia was unacceptable to Japan. So also were the continuing supply of China by Britain and the United States. A quest for resources, notably oil in the Dutch East Indies, was also significant.

After Japanese aircraft from six carriers sank five American battleships at Pearl Harbor on December 7, the Japanese rapidly overran much of the Western Pacific and Southeast Asia. Japanese successes reflected the advantage of surprise, as well as a marked capability in amphibious operations and the effective use of airpower against land and, in particular, sea targets. The Japanese also benefited from poor Allied operational command, particularly in the Philippines, Malaya, and Burma, and from the range of British commitments. Concerned about the war with Germany, the British mistakenly hoped that the defense of Malaya and Singapore would benefit from the strength of the American fleet in the western Pacific and seriously mishandled their own naval units, leading to the sinking of the battleship *Prince of Wales* and the battle cruiser *Repulse* by Japanese land-based bombers off Malaya on December 10, 1941. This was the first time capital ships had been sunk solely by airpower while underway in the open sea.

More generally, the folly of underestimating the Japanese, particularly Japanese airpower, emerged. Rapid Japanese advances against inadequately prepared and poorly commanded defenders led to the humiliation of Western, particularly British, imperial power. Successfully attacked by the Japanese, Singapore, the major British base, surrendered on February 15, 1942, to a smaller Japanese attacking force.

Germany declared war on the United States, although Hitler was under no obligation to do so and despite the fact that Germany was already badly extended in its war with Britain and the Soviet Union, a fresh demonstration of the significance of political factors. Hitler took the view that clashes between American warships and German submarines in the Western Atlantic indicated that the two powers were already in effect at war. Hitler had sought to encourage the Japanese attack on the United States by pressing forward military operations against Moscow.

This declaration of war, however, did not lead to any concerted attempt at grand strategy. Germany and Japan were unable to create a military partnership or to provide mutual economic assistance that in any way matched that of the Allies, seriously strained as relations among the latter were. Germany and Japan indeed fought what were in essence two separate wars.

The Americans decided to focus on the war with Germany, in line with pre-war planning. The American Rainbow 5 War Plan and the Anglo-American-Canadian ABC-1 Plan talks in early 1941 had envisaged a defensive strategy in the Pacific in the event of conflict with Germany and Japan. Roosevelt supported this emphasis because of his concern that Britain might otherwise collapse in the face of German pressure. Such a collapse would have increased American vulnerability to Japan as well as Germany, which indicated the relationship between different spheres of the conflict. This strategy led the American army maneuvers in 1941 to focus on preparing for European-theater conflict and was confirmed after Pearl Harbor in the Anglo-American Arcadia Conference in Washington, D.C., which resulted in the creation of an Anglo-American planning mechanism based on the combined chiefs of staff, as well as the establishment of the Anglo-American Combined Raw Materials Board.

An emphasis on fighting Germany also helped the Soviet Union by diverting German resources to resist American attacks and the potential of such an attack, both of which greatly magnified the strategic challenge to Germany from Britain, not least by giving it offensive capability as far as Atlantic Europe was concerned. Britain became the basis from which the Americans would invade France. The American focus on Germany also accorded with the need to destroy the stronger adversary first.

There was also a major American commitment in the Pacific to stop further Japanese advances. The Japanese were checked in the indecisive Battle of the Coral Sea on May 7–8, 1942; this was a new kind of naval battle, one of carrier airpower from fleets beyond the reach of gunpower. The battle also demonstrated the failure of the Pearl Harbor attack to destroy American naval power: the American carriers had not been in Pearl Harbor when the Japanese struck.

After Coral Sea, the Japanese sought a decisive naval battle aimed at destroying American carriers. Admiral Isoroku Yamamoto, the Japanese naval commander, aimed to lure the American carriers to destruction under the guns of his battleships, a tactic that had long been planned. In what became the battle of Midway on June 4, 1942,

Severely damaged American warships at Pearl Harbor after the Japanese attack.

initial American attacks by torpedo bombers on the Japanese carriers failed, but as a result of these attacks, the Japanese fighters were unable to respond to the subsequent arrival of the American dive-bombers, which destroyed four Japanese carriers, much of their fleet strike force. The American carriers then retired to avoid the approach of the Japanese battleships. The Japanese defeat at Midway owed much to American command quality, to the American ability to seize advantage of unexpected opportunities, and to the more general resilience of American naval capability.

Midway changed the arithmetic of Pacific airpower, not least because the Americans proved far more able to replace trained pilots. More generally, in addition to the availability of superior resources, the effective use of American airpower and the development not only of carrier tactics but also of successful air–naval cooperation was instrumental in the defeat of the Japanese navy. Midway also ensured that the congressional elections took place against a more benign background than if they had been held earlier in the year: the bulk of the political critique of Roosevelt was directed against his New Deal domestic policies.

THE STALINGRAD CAMPAIGN, 1942

The year 1942 also saw a decisive shift in the war against Germany. The large-scale Soviet counteroffensive in the winter of 1941–1942 had eventually run out of steam, in part because, like the German offensives on the western front in 1918, it was on too broad a front. Weakened by poor staff work, logistics, and intelligence, the subsequent Soviet Kharkov offensive in May was a failure.

In turn, the Germans, on June 28, 1942, launched Operation Blue, a major offensive in southern Russia. They no longer had the resources to mount an offensive across their entire front, which was now longer than when the war had begun, but 1 million troops took part. German goals were confused, including an advance to the oil fields on the Caspian Sea, as well as the destruction of Soviet forces in the lower Don–lower Volga region and subsequent exploitation northeastward across the Volga. However, the offensive became totally focused on a struggle to gain Stalingrad, a city on the River Volga that acquired totemic significance for Hitler both because the city was seen as an alleged icon of Communism and because the Germans were held off amid costly, bitter street fighting. This focus squandered German advantages in mobile warfare and the pursuit of the open flank.

The Soviets then launched Operation Uranus, the encirclement of the German Sixth Army in and near Stalingrad on November 19, 1942. The Soviets benefited greatly in this operation from resource factors, notably the development of their arms industry, especially in tank production. Soviet advantages in Operation Uranus were also magnified by the success of their planning and preparations and thanks to the poor quality of German command decisions, including the allocation of what became key flank positions to weak Romanian forces, which rapidly collapsed. An inadequate German response to the Soviet breakthrough was also crucial. On November 23, the Soviet spearheads met west of Stalingrad, creating a large pocket containing the German Sixth Army. Attempts to relieve it failed and the army, with 110,000 troops, surrounded in early 1943.

WAR AT SEA, 1943

In 1943, in the Soviet Union, the Pacific, and the Atlantic, there were clear shifts toward the Allies, not only in success and resources, but also in fighting ability. In the Pacific, the Americans benefited from the strength and nature of their industrial base. The Japanese were outbuilt in all ship types, as well as in merchant shipping. Moreover, the use to which resources were put was crucial. The Americans created self-sufficient carrier task groups supported by at-sea-logistics groups that did not depend on a string of bases. This capability permitted rapid advances across unprecedented distances (with a great deal of island hopping) that destroyed any hope that the Japanese might retain a defensive perimeter in the Pacific. The Japanese proved less effective than the Americans at convoy protection and antisubmarine warfare, whereas in the Southwest and Central Pacific, the Americans in 1943 acquired considerable experience of amphibious operations, experience that was to stand them in good stead in 1944, both in the Pacific and in Europe. The advantage the Americans had on land in the Pacific was increased by the tactics used by the Japanese. The firepower advantage proved particularly useful in dealing with Japanese mass attacks, attacks encouraged by the Japanese belief in the determining role of spirit or morale, a belief that greatly influenced Japanese doctrine. At the same time, it was necessary for Western forces to devise and implement appropriate tactics such as all-round fire zones.

In the Atlantic, the Allies also benefited from resources, notably in the shape of the American shipbuilding industry with its effective prefabrication and flow-production methods. The strategic issue posed for the Germans by Allied shipbuilding interacted with the tactical and operational challenges offered by improved Allied proficiency in antisubmarine warfare, not least in the use of air support, enhanced ship-based weaponry, signals intelligence, and effective tactics. By late 1942, there were enough German submarines to organize comprehensive patrol lines across North Atlantic convoy routes.

However, in the face of contrary RAF pressure to concentrate aircraft on bombing Germany, the British decision to focus attention on deploying very-long-range aircraft against the submarines helped in closing the mid-Atlantic air gap in the spring of 1943. This was important to the success in clashes with U-boats from March to May 1943, clashes that led to the sinking of many German submarines and to the German decision to reduce the pace of their operations in the Atlantic. The RAF was told that the supplies, notably aluminum, required by the British aircraft industry had to be imported across the Atlantic. An account of submarine capability based on the German U-boat campaign in the Atlantic would suggest (eventual) failure, whereas one focused on the (eventually) successful

American submarine assault on the Japanese would be far more favorable about the tactical, operational, and strategic capabilities of submarine warfare.

SOVIET ADVANCE, 1943

The year 1943 also saw the last major German offensive on the eastern front. In accordance with the German conviction that successful offensive operations could counter the strength of an opposing coalition, a seriously misguided view by 1942 and still more by 1943, this was an attempt to break through the flanks of the Soviet Kursk salient and to achieve an encirclement triumph to match the Soviet success at Stalingrad. Hitler also hoped that victory would undermine the Allied coalition by lessening Western confidence in the likelihood of Soviet victory, as well as impressing his own wavering allies. In 1943, the Germans had their largest number of troops under arms—7 million men—and there were more German troops on the eastern front than when the war there had started in June 1941.

However, forewarned by accurate intelligence information, a product of the intelligence war that the Germans were losing, the Soviets had an effective defense in depth, and this defense blunted the German attack in July 1943. The Soviets then launched what proved to be a more effective offensive of their own, one that showed the failure of the Germans on the defensive.

The campaign of 1943 reflected a shift in the relationship of the two armies, notably the enhanced operational capability of the Soviet army. This capability was inspired by Soviet theories of deep operations advanced in the 1930s, but now refined in the cauldron of war. Rather than seek encirclements, the Soviets deployed their forces along broad fronts, launching a number of front assaults designed to smash opposing forces and maintain continued pressure. The Soviets denied the Germans the possibility of recovering from attacks, lessened their ability to move units to badly threatened positions, and searched out the weakest points in their opposing front line. By the end of 1943, the Germans had been driven back beyond the River Dnieper.

Soviet improvements in fighting effectiveness reflected the more general Allied success in directing resources and in appreciating the interdependence of weapons and operations. The Allies did not win success at the rate they hoped for in 1943. On the eastern front, Soviet advances in the south were not matched farther north. In the Mediterranean, Anglo-American forces defeated the German and Italian forces in North Africa in May, conquered Sicily in July–August, and invaded mainland Italy in September. However, although Mussolini was overthrown and Italy also later surrendered, rapid German intervention held the Allied advance south of Rome in 1943. Moreover, the air assault on Germany, in part designed to counter Soviet pressure for a speedy Anglo-American invasion of France, proved more costly and less successful than had been anticipated. Nevertheless, the direction of travel was clear: the Germans were being driven back.

WAR IN THE AIR

On March 13, 1943, Joseph Goebbels, the head of the German propaganda ministry, wrote in his diary that the Anglo-American air assault was Germany's greatest worry at that time. This assault faced many problems and has continued to be controversial. At the time it was costly, in terms of the planes and crew shot down and killed by the Germans, of the diversion of aircraft from other tasks, notably ground support, and of the extent of the military budget and the military–industrial complex and related scientific manpower devoted to this air assault. Subsequently, the deliberate use of airpower against the civilian population has been controversial, as have been the casualties, for example, 37,000 people killed in a firestorm in Hamburg.

The Anglo-American bombers' success in hitting German industrial production, particularly in the latter half of 1944, is also of note, as are the strategic goals of the Allied offensive. Attacks on German rail links and on the production of synthetic oil were especially important to the disruption of the German war economy. The crucial drive for economic output to fuel Hitler's determination to break through to world-power status from a limited base underlined the value of this air assault. In particular, hitting marshaling yards, rail bridges, and barge traffic crippled the movement of coal and oil and thus disrupted the integration of the German war economy. For example, the city of Dresden, the target of particularly deadly attack in February 1945, was also a major center in the military–industrial complex, as well as a communications node, especially railway, which was seen as significant for German operations. Oil refining in 1944–1945 was hit hard by Allied bombing, as was the construction of a new, faster class of German submarine.

Moreover, the air assault gravely weakened the *Luftwaffe*, notably with the death of experienced pilots, and thus greatly helped the process of defeating German forces on the ground, particularly in the Normandy campaign of 1944. This interrelationship of action was also indicated by the impact of air attack on German land operations. For example, close to a third of German artillery production was devoted to antiaircraft guns.

As with other branches of military activity in a given conflict or over a longer period, the air war should not be treated as a single episode. Indeed, there was a learning curve in tactics, weaponry, operational means, and strategy and as part of a learning curve characterized by an action–reaction process that was more generally characteristic of Allied war making. Initial assumptions about the ease of gaining and using air superiority to provide a war-winning means to destroy the German war economy, crush German morale, and lead to the overthrow of Hitler proved wrong, just as German assumptions about the consequences of their air assault on Britain in 1940–1941 had been misguided. These failures are then used to characterize the air war as a whole, and it is certainly the case that for all its versatility, flexibility, and potential impact, serious tactical, operational, and strategic limitations were revealed. At one level, night operations, poor weather, and limited accuracy in bombing were all serious problems, but so was governmental determination and civilian resolve on the part of those bombed.

Yet, from 1943, there was an increasing effectiveness both with the use of airpower at sea, notably against submarines, and with the air assault on Germany and, from 1944, Japan. The provision of effective long-range fighter escorts, notably the American Mustang, was highly significant. At the same time, however, the prediction that Berlin could be bombed enough to cause rebellion there proved wrong. Instead, the bombing

B-17 bombers pound the industrial city of Subotica in northern Yugoslavia, September 1944.

of Germany saw a militarization of society there as civil protection and the dependence on the authoritarian state increased. Moreover, Nazi propagandists presented the air attacks as if the Germans were victims of a barbaric assault, an approach that ignored not only the inherent barbarities of the German war effort and state, but also the role of the Germans in beginning large-scale air attacks on civilian targets from the very first campaign against Poland.

THE GERMANS DRIVEN BACK, 1944

In 1944, the range of conflict broadened as the "Second Front" against Germany was launched when American, British, and Canadian forces landed in Normandy on June 6, "D-Day." There had been pressure from Stalin and Roosevelt for this Second Front to be opened up earlier, notably in 1943. Discussion as to the viability of an earlier invasion, which the British opposed, remains controversial. There is a strong argument for considering that an invasion of France before 1944 could have failed. At the start of that year, there was only limited Allied equipment for, and experience in, amphibious operations, and it was still unclear how far, and how speedily, it would be possible to overcome the submarine threat and thus control the Atlantic shipping lanes. There was also the requirement of assured air superiority. By delaying until 1944, the Allies benefited from the serious problems that hit the Germans in 1943: failure at Kursk, large-scale Soviet advances, and the Combined Bomber Offensive together chewed up part of the German army and air force.

In 1944, Hitler was misled by Allied dummy preparations into assuming that the invasion would be launched farther east (and closer to Germany) in the Pas de Calais, and German forces in Normandy were therefore weaker than they might have been. Moreover, the Allied air campaign against the French rail system that spring had greatly lessened German mobility. The Allied success on June 6 in overcoming the coastal defenses of the Atlantic Wall indicated that, as with other weapon systems, fortifications proved most effective as part of a combined arms force, requiring, as they did, a flexible, supporting counter-attack capacity to be part of the defense. Although ferroconcrete proved resistant to high explosives, all bunkers and casemates needed apertures for guns, access for their crews, and ventilation, which left them vulnerable. On June 6, the Germans lacked sufficient mobile forces forward enough in Normandy to act in cooperation with the coastal defenses, which were damaged or rapidly outflanked. Thus, the German plan as part of a war on the coast to drive the invaders into the sea failed.

In the subsequent Battle of Normandy, the Germans initially repeated their (limited) success in resisting invading Anglo-American forces in Italy the previous year because the fronts were far more constricted than those on the eastern front. Moreover, in both Italy and France, Anglo-American forces proved less adept than the Soviets in switching to the exploitation phase of battles and, subsequently, in maintaining the advance when it encountered resistance. This reflected a lack of understanding of operational art, as well as less experience compared with the Soviets in large-scale maneuver battles with the Germans.

At the same time, there was a marked improvement in Anglo-American fighting quality. In initial clashes during the war, there were serious problems in fighting the Germans: the British conspicuously so in Norway in 1940 and the Americans in the battle of the Kasserine Pass in Tunisia in February 1943. With time, however, improved Allied training and the benefits of experience told, notably at the command level but also in fighting quality. Moreover, the Allies became far more skilled at integrating their forces. Thus, air support played a major role in the eventual Allied success in the Battle of Normandy as German resistance there collapsed in August.

This success was followed by the Germans being rapidly driven from most of France and Belgium. Hitler's wish to hold a defensive line on the River Seine proved abortive. The German commander in Paris surrendered on August 25, and on September 3 Brussels was captured. Similarly, having landed in southern France on August 15, the Allies liberated Marseille on August 28.

However, Allied hopes of an end to the war that year proved premature. German resistance became more coherent and stiffened markedly in September as the German frontier was neared, as well as near Antwerp and in the Netherlands. The terrain and weather helped the defenders, as did a strengthening of morale as the war became a question of defending Germany itself. The threat to court-martial and execute officers and troops who retreated may also have played a role. The skill of the Germans in defensive operations was ably demonstrated, notably against the Americans in the Hürtgen Forest and against the British at Arnhem.

In turn, the Allies, who lacked much experience in military maneuvering, were affected by serious logistical problems as supply lines lengthened. There was also a degree of strategic confusion over the preference for a broad or narrow front advance on Germany. In any event, both failed in late 1944. The maneuver stage was succeeded by static warfare.

Anglo-American forces also drove the Germans back in Italy, although again without a decisive victory. Indeed, in early 1944, the German defense of the Monte Cassino front saw conflict similar to that in the western front in World War I, with an adroit defense denying a large Allied force the capacity to maneuver. Nevertheless, an eventual breakthrough led to the conquest of central Italy that summer.

The Germans were also driven back on the eastern front. In 1944, the Red Army proved adept at developing good cooperation among armor, artillery, and infantry and at making the latter two mobile. The Germans were outnumbered, particularly in artillery and aircraft, although not so much as to make the result obvious. The campaign was less well handled by German commanders than that of early 1943, although the different verdict also reflected an increase in Soviet operational effectiveness and tactical skill; as a consequence, German counterattacks were less successful than hitherto, which affected the flow as well as the

Soviet soldiers pose in a captured Manchurian factory, 1945.

tempo of the Soviet advance. The Soviets used their reserves (more plentiful than those of the British and Americans) to maintain the pace of the advance and to thwart counterattacks.

The Soviets showed in Operation Bagration—the 1944 overrunning of Belarus, the destruction of the German Army Group Center and the subsequent advance into central Poland—as well as in their advance into the Balkans the same year and finally in the Manchuria campaign of 1945 against Japan that they had mastered the capabilities of their weaponry and fighting systems, learned how to outfight their opponents, and acquired not only a Deep War doctrine, but also the ability to maintain the pace of a rapid fighting advance. The provision of American trucks helped to operationalize Soviet concepts for the offensive. In contrast, there was a "demodernization" of the German army on the eastern front, with falling equipment levels (and less fuel for vehicles), as well as a shift to the defensive and an emphasis on ideological commitment and conflict that was associated with atrocities, leading to a different style of conflict than that which had characterized initial German operations.

WAR IN THE PACIFIC, 1944

As with the Red Army on the eastern front, the American advance in the Pacific gathered pace and inflicted more serious defeats in 1944 than in 1943. The American conquest of the islands of Saipan, Tinian, and Guam brought Japan within bombing distance. Both Japan and the United States saw Saipan, the island in the Marianas best suited as a bomber base against Japan, as vital, and its fall on July 7 led to the resignation of the Japanese government on July 18. The invasion of the island of Leyte in the Philippines in October was followed by the Battle of Leyte Gulf of October 23–26, in which, despite dividing strength in the face of Japanese attack, the Americans inflicted a major defeat, including the destruction of four Japanese carriers and three battleships. On November 7, Roosevelt won the presidential election for the fourth time: by 432 to 99 votes in the Electoral College.

THE DEFEAT OF THE AXIS POWERS

By 1944, the Axis powers were being repeatedly outfought. Spheres in which they had once posed a major threat, for example, submarine warfare in the Atlantic and in European waters, became instead areas of conflict in which the Allies, although needing vigilance, were nevertheless successful.

In response, German and Japanese leaders, far from considering surrender or negotiations, placed their faith in miracle weapons and methods and in the hope of a political transformation, an approach that was later to be seen with terrorist groups, most prominently al-Qaeda. Miracle weapons that proved particularly attractive were rockets and jet aircraft for the Germans; they achieved a technological lead with both. Rockets capable of delivering a considerable payload, the V-1 and, even more, the V-2, were used beginning in 1944. Considerable damage was inflicted, notably on London, but the destructive impact of the rockets was not capable of destroying the political will to fight on. Moreover, the guidance systems did not match those of a (later) cruise missile, and therefore it was not possible to aim the rockets with any precision. As a result, the rockets could be destructive, but were not an operationally significant weapon.

The same was true of the German development of jet fighters. These jets might have posed a serious challenge to Allied air superiority over Germany, offering a new set of specifications, much as the German use of the interrupter mechanism when firing through the propeller had led to a major shift in relative capability during World War I, albeit a short-term one. However, the capability gap in the case of jet fighters was not as great and thereby not as tactically significant as their speed suggested, in part because of design faults that would have taken time to overcome. Moreover, there was not time to manufacture enough planes, which lessened the possibility of their operational significance. Hitler also mismanaged their use. Nevertheless, the development of such weaponry encouraged the Allied desire for a quick victory.

Along with supposedly transformative weapons came allegedly transformative methods. The suicide tactics of the Japanese, especially the *kamikaze* pilots, were significant because it was assumed that these methods would both destroy Allied targets, notably ships, and establish the superiority of the Japanese will. Damage was indeed inflicted, but the method did not prove effective at the tactical, operational, or strategic level. In particular, the tactics were attempted at a time of massive Allied superiority in resources, and the Allies also developed appropriate deployments and tactics, not least greatly increasing the antiaircraft firepower of warships. Warships such as the American battleship the *Wisconsin* came to carry many antiaircraft guns and thus a far larger crew.

Such weapons and tactics were designed to accompany a wholesale mobilization of society. In Germany, the *Volkssturm*, a Nazi-run compulsory local defense militia that reflected the mobilization for total war ordered in July 1944 and comprised males between the ages of 16 and 60, was intended to inflict

Nazi poster promoting the *Volkssturm:* "For Freedom and Life".

casualties on the advancing Allies such that their morale could not tolerate, as well as to indoctrinate the civilian population for a total struggle.

The political hopes of the Axis, however, proved fruitless. As late as 1945, both Germany and Japan hoped use the differences between the Soviet Union and the Western Allies (Britain and the United States) to negotiate a separate peace in the case of Germany and to keep the Soviet Union out of the war in the case of Japan. The German attack, in Operation Autumn Mist, on American and British forces in Belgium in December 1944, the Battle of the Bulge, was designed to encourage a war weariness that would then enable the Germans to focus on the Soviet Union. In marked contrast to the Germans attack in April 1940, Anglo-American air superiority ensured that the German attack on December 16, 1944, occurred when heavy cloud restricted the effects of this superiority. The attack placed considerable strain on the American forces, requiring the commitment of most of their strategic reserve on the western front, but was soon held. Hitler still hoped for a collapse in the Alliance as late as the spring of 1945.

In practice, although there were serious rivalries and grave suspicions in the Alliance, there was a short-term determination to defeat the Axis. Moreover, the undertaking announced in January 1943 to fight on until unconditional surrender had been obtained from Germany (and then for the Soviet Union to join the war with Japan) proved the necessary political agreement among the Allies to close down Axis options and, instead, keep the Allies cooperating, at least in the short term.

Germany collapsed first. Remorseless Soviet pressure led to the fall of Berlin in an offensive launched on April 16, 1945, which left the city encircled by April 25. Hitler committed suicide on April 30 and the remaining German forces in the city surrendered on May 2. Other Soviet forces defeated German forces elsewhere in Eastern and Central Europe, capturing Vienna. Meanwhile, helped by the exhaustion of German units in the Battle of the Bulge, American and British forces had fought their way into Germany and across the River Rhine in March 1945. The rest of Germany was rapidly conquered, with the Americans overrunning the South, and Hamburg surrendered to the British on May 3. The Germans continued to kill Jews and prisoners until the end, which came when Hitler's designated successor, Admiral Dönitz, unconditionally surrendered the remaining German forces. Hitler's "Thousand Year Reich (Empire)" had lasted 12 years.

The last six months of the war in Europe saw no decisive single battle—no repetition, for example, of Napoleon's defeat in 1815 at Waterloo or a settlement before the total defeat of the German military—as at the close of World War I, or the use of dramatic paradigm-shifting weaponry—as with the end of the war with Japan in 1945. The last stage of the war, instead, was a matter of hard-fought conventional campaigns, waged with particular determination.

American operations against Japanese forces in early 1945, although successful, were also costly. This was true both of the campaign in the Philippines and of the conquest of the islands of Iwo Jima and Okinawa. As a result, the invasion of Japan appeared a daunting prospect in terms of the casualties that American forces were likely to suffer. There was also the problem posed by the need to make Japan surrender its conquests. Although the British in a very impressive campaign in December 1944–May 1945 drove the Japanese from Burma (Myanmar) after bitter fighting, Japan still controlled Malaya, Java, Sumatra, Taiwan, and much of China. The Soviet entry into the war on August 8 led to a rapid conquest of Manchuria, but, although Japan was clearly beaten and under remorseless American air attack, it proved a difficult target and one that posed a far greater challenge than had Germany at the beginning of 1945. The challenge of conquering Japan helped explain the continued expansion of the American military. The army alone grew from fewer than 200,000 troops in 1939 to more than 8 million in 1945.

The American use of the atom bomb solved serious military and political problems. Bombs dropped on Hiroshima and Nagasaki on August 6 and 9, respectively, led Japan on August 14 to agree to surrender unconditionally, ending the need to carry out what would have been a highly destructive and costly invasion. More than 280,000 people died as a result of the two atomic bombs, either immediately or eventually as a result of radiation poisoning.

WAR AND SOCIETY

The American development of the atomic bomb also reflected the extent to which war saw the mobilization of societies across the full range of their capabilities. The destruction of the Japanese cites proved a particularly dramatic instance of a more general process in which bombing brought war home to civilians to a degree not seen in World War I. As part of the escalation of strategies in wartime, this reflected the deliberate use of bombing to hit civilian morale and to dislocate war economics. Thus, the home front was to be as one with the armies operating on the front line. More than half a million Europeans were killed from the air during the war. In Britain, more than 67,000 civilians were killed in air and missile attacks, nearly half of them in London, much of which was devastated. In 1942, 3 of the 12 houses in the street in which I live in the city of Exeter were destroyed in one raid, as was much of the city center.

Targeting civilians was taken to more brutal levels by the harsh occupation policies of Axis forces. Both Germany and Japan ran at least part of their new empires as slave societies, with the inhabitants brutalized and their resources, notably food, seized. As a result, there was mass starvation in Java, which the Japanese had conquered in 1942, with as many as 2 million deaths as a result.

These policies reflected a racism and racist sense of mission that were central to German and Japanese attitudes and policies. A belief that rival peoples represented races in a battle for mastery led to a marked savagery, especially by the Japanese toward the Chinese and by the Germans toward the Slavs. Thus, in 1939, there were harsh reprisals by the German army against armed resistance from Polish civilians. This savagery culminated in the German wish to kill all Jews, which led in the Holocaust to the mass murder of over 6 million Jews.

The Holocaust was not separate from World War II, but integral to it. The ideal of race
struggle and practice of mass
slaughter were both central to
Hitler's view of the conflict.
Moreover, far from only a minority of Germans knowing, still
less being involved, the numbers
in question were enormous.
Moreover, the army was more
involved in the killing of Jews
than was argued during the Cold
War when, from the mid-1950s,
West Germany was a key member of the West and the German
army was important in the
planned defense against a possible Soviet Union. Thus, the treatment of the Holocaust as a part
of the war and the nature of that

SS officers executing a civilian.

treatment reflect, as so much history does, the tendency to present the past from
the perspective of the present. The significance of the Holocaust to World War II
is now more apparent and emphasized than it was during the Cold War.

The SS, the paramilitary Nazi organization that included major combat units,
represented the bridging of the genocidal policies toward the Jews and the general German war effort. The SS also provided many German military leaders, and
the SS leader, Heinrich Himmler, was given military posts, including command
of the Reserve Army and of Army Group Vistula. Brutality to civilians was a
particular characteristic of Axis governments and forces. Thus, in Hungary, the
pro-German Fascist Arrow Cross staged massacres, and not only of Jews, in
1944–1945.

The Holocaust, although exceptional in its scale and evil, was also part of a
more persistent strand in modern warfare, one in which there was an attempt to
destroy, subjugate, or drive out ethnic groups judged dangerous. This was not the
purpose of the Allies. Keen to overthrow the German and Japanese regimes, the
Allies sought to rebuild their politics, not to destroy their people. The United
States, Britain, and the Soviet Union offered ideologies that were seen as able to
redeem the Germans and Japanese once defeated. The Anglo-Americans propa-
gated democratic capitalism and the Soviets Communism. In moral terms, neither was as iniquitous as the race violence of the German and Japanese regimes,
although the Soviet advance in Eastern Europe saw a sociopolitical warfare
directed against those deemed hostile to Communism. This included the impris-
onment and execution of those who had resisted the Germans.

ТРАКТОР В ПОЛЕ—
ЧТО ТАНК В БОЮ!

Soviet poster from 1942 proclaims the importance of women's work and the agricultural sector in the war effort; it proclaims, "A Tractor in the Field Is Worth a Tank in Battle".

Individual national characteristics affected the nature of the wartime mobilization of society, but in each case there was such a mobilization, which, indeed, was an aspect of the degree to which the scale of the war and the nature of operations, especially bombing and submarine attacks on trade, put unprecedented pressure on societies. As a result, the role of states increased at the same time that they faced major challenges in directing economies and in maintaining social cohesion. Inherent differences were also revealed, as with the contrast on the home front between totalitarian labor mobilization and direction in the Soviet Union and a reliance on individual choice and the guidance of the labor market in the United States.

In both cases, the Allies mobilized far more effectively than the Axis powers because of a willingness to use female labor in the economy. Women workers proved crucial across the economy. In Britain, they were employed in large numbers in agriculture. As in World War I, however, women proved particularly valuable in armaments manufacture. They rapidly adapted to working in the factories despite the frequent lack of resources, such as sufficient appropriate work clothes. Moreover, the manual dexterity, labor discipline, and diligence of female workers proved frequently better than that of their male counterparts. In America, women played a major role in the economy and others served in the military, including ferrying planes. The Soviet Union was ready to see women as a direct resource for the war effort and one that should be controlled by the state. All able-bodied city women from the ages of 16 to 50 who were not students or looking after children under age 8 were put under government direction in 1942. Uniquely, thousands fought on the front line. Soviet propaganda made much of this, as it also did of women partisans. This contributed to the idea of an all-inclusive war effort. The number of women working in Soviet industry greatly increased, and many worked in heavy industry.

In contrast, although the Germans were quite happy to use forced labor of non-German women, Hitler was reluctant to conscript women for the industrial workforce. His conservative social politics led him to see German women as wives and mothers. In Japan, unmarried young women were used to replace skilled male workers who entered the Japanese military, and nonworking women were encouraged to do volunteer and civil-defense work, contributing to the regimentation of Japanese society.

Work environments changed. In New Zealand, where female factory and white-collar work increased, some women were promoted to positions of authority in the workplace rarely reached before. However, in the United States, women at work faced a male-dominated environment and suffered accordingly in working practices and relative pay.

For all the combatants, women bore the brunt of waiting in line, balancing the family budget, coping with the black market, and feeding and cooking with few resources. Aside from numerous losses through bombing, bombardment, and other acts of war, large numbers of women were casualties in other ways. Malnutrition affected many, reducing resistance to disease and leading to skeletal deformities, difficulties in childbirth, and other problems. In occupied countries, women faced more arduous circumstances, and many played a major role in resistance activities, as in France.

In addition, there was a conviction that popular support had to be wooed. Thus, in Britain, where food rationing was regarded as crucial in helping survive the German submarine assault, the public was encouraged to eat the rather gray "National Loaf," as well as other dishes, by means of propaganda. For all the combatants, the mobilization of societies involved the dissemination of opinion and news through institutions such as the Ministry of Information established in Britain in 1939. There was also close attention paid on the part of governments to national mood and morale.

In the United States, popular support for the war was encouraged by government efforts. Norman Rockwell was one of the many artists enlisted to help by producing posters that were used to assist the military and to persuade all Americans to help the war effort, and Frank Capra produced the *Why We Fight* series of public education films. Warner Brothers played a role, with Bugs Bunny and Daffy Duck bolstering support for the war effort.

Wartime propaganda created and strengthened national images. These looked toward postwar rivalry in the Cold War. The perception of World War II proved highly significant in the creation of national understandings of character and identity. The "Good War" and "Greatest Generation" for the United States, the "People's War" and the "Spirit of the Blitz" for Britain, and the "Great Patriotic War" for the Soviet Union all played a key role in the molding and presentation of national character. Government propaganda in Britain emphasized national resilience in the face of bombing and the threat of invasion, notably with the "Britain Can Take It" approach. The theme of unity and the role of the state in confronting the problems of wartime society, notably with food rationing and the evacuation of children from the threat of bombing, encouraged raised public expectations of greater activism on the part of the state.

These expectations affected the contents and debate of postwar politics. Britain had been a society where government powers were limited, but instead, as in World War One, wartime controls over wages, prices, resources, and civil liberties saw major growth in state power. At the same time, these accounts concealed a more complex situation. Thus, in Britain, the wartime presentation of social cohesion, greater equality, and solidarity was subsequently employed to justify and explain postwar policies, notably those of the Labor governments of 1945–1951. Subsequently, there has been a contradictory analysis, one involving major wartime social and ideological divisions.

The impact of World War II on power relationships also looked toward the Cold War. In part, the war confirmed earlier developments, notably the rise of the United States in the Pacific and more generally. Communist success in the Russian Civil War had already ensured that the Soviet Union would be a key Eurasian power. At the same time, both of these powers were greatly strengthened by World War II. The Soviet Union became more powerful in East Asia and Eastern Europe as a result of the defeat of Japan and Germany, respectively, and the prestige of the Red Army increased greatly.

The United States became notably stronger in the Pacific during and as a result of the war. Aside from territorial gains from Japan in the western Pacific and the postwar occupation of Japan itself, there was also a greater tendency for American

Women workers install fixtures and assemblies to a tail fuselage section of a B-17F Bomber at the Long Beach, California plant of the Douglas Aircraft Company, October 1942.

policy makers to see the Pacific as an area of strategic concern and engagement. The United States also acquired a significant military and political role in Western Europe as a result of victory over Germany and of America's subsequent place as an occupying power in Germany and Austria. Moreover, the war had left Britain and France much weakened, whereas America had become an even stronger economic force. Truly the "arsenal of democracy" as Roosevelt had promised his radio audience in December 1943, the United States benefited from its already sophisticated economic infrastructure, which helped in the shift to war production, a process that became better organized as a result of the establishment of the Office of War Mobilization in May 1943. The United States produced 86,000 tanks during the war. Gross corporate profits rose markedly, helping fund investment in production, and workers benefited from a rise in real wages, which ensured good labor relations as well as labor mobility, including the large-scale movement of African Americans from the South into industrial cities. Greater prosperity provided a growing tax base for rising federal expenditure that, in turn, led to economic expansion.

As a result of World War II, it would be America that presided over the West and confronted the Soviet Union in the Cold War. Although it was a victor, Britain had been greatly weakened, as had China. Japan and Germany had ceased to be powers. This settlement was not to last, but it proved decisive for several decades and still greatly affects the world order.

READING LIST

Jeremy Black, *World War Two*, London, Routledge, 2003.

John Buckley, *Air Power in the Age of Total War*, London, UCL Press, 1999.

Williamson Murray and Alan Millett, *A War to Be Won: Fighting the Second World War*, Cambridge, Mass., Belknap Press of Harvard University Press, 2000.

A. W. Purdue, *The Second World War*, Basingstoke, Palgrave Macmillan, 2011.

Gerhard Weinberg, *A World at Arms: A Global History of World War II*, Cambridge, U.K., Cambridge University Press, 1994.

FIVE

DECOLONIZATION AND THE EARLY COLD WAR, 1945–1960

Egyptian women train for war, Cairo, 1956.

The Cold War, the rivalry between American-led democratic capitalism and Soviet-led Communism, dominates attention in the period 1946–1989. The numerous wars of the period, most prominently the Vietnam War, but also conflicts in the Middle East, sub-Saharan Africa, and Central America, tend to be considered in terms of this rivalry. There is, indeed, a considerable basis for this interpretation, but it fails to allow for the distinctive and different nature of these struggles and for the extent to which there was no directing conflict between the superpowers that affected struggles elsewhere, for example, to the extent of the two world wars. Moreover, decolonization, the cause of many of the conflicts in the period, and the Cold War had contrasting origins, causes, courses, and consequences, and it is important not to run them together.

WARS OF DECOLONIZATION

Decolonization reflected the exhaustion of the European colonial powers (notably Britain, France, the Dutch, and Belgium) after World War II ended in 1945 and was therefore, to a degree, a consequence of the military history of that struggle, rather than simply a new set of conflicts defined by equations of strength that were postwar and clear-cut. At the same time, this exhaustion also led on the part of the colonial powers to a determination to hold onto empires that were seen as a protection to prestige and prosperity in a world in which status was threatened by the American-directed free-enterprise economic system. Rule of the Dutch East Indies gave the Netherlands prestige and prospects, and the same was true for both France and Britain in Southeast Asia and Africa and for Portugal and Belgium in Africa.

The wars of decolonization were also a product of the breakdown of earlier practices and ideologies of imperial incorporation, practices and ideologies that had been both called on for help and weakened during World War II. This breakdown did not involve the whole, or even the bulk, of the population, but there was sufficient rejection of imperial rule to give weight to political opposition and make a military solution by the colonial powers to resistance at least difficult. Moreover, the breakdown of imperial incorporation simultaneously reflected the role of Cold War hostilities, as well as already significant patterns of indigenous opposition to imperial rule.

The late 1940s saw a major success for decolonization in the Dutch East Indies, now Indonesia, an important country (the fourth largest in terms of population) that does not tend to feature much in accounts of military history. The Dutch devoted considerable efforts to suppressing opposition, notably on Java, the most populous island, but found it difficult to move from holding on to major positions toward ending resistance. Moreover, the United States adopted a critical position that weakened the financially vulnerable Dutch. The American position was to be significant for all Western colonial powers, for example, for the French in Algeria and for the British at the time of the Suez Crisis in 1956; this position is a reminder of the dependence of warfare on political contexts. Drawing on a view of the anachronism of colonialism and the danger that it would lead the population in colonies to turn to the Soviet Union, American policy was based on encouraging the end of colonial rule and instead moving colonies toward independence as pro-Western, capitalist democracies, states that would be open to American influence and economic activity. The Americans pressed the Dutch to abandon the struggle and, although still in control of much of the East Indies, the Dutch did so in 1949. The Dutch East Indies became Indonesia.

The struggle in Vietnam, a French colony, proved more intractable, not least because the militarily stronger French made a major attempt to retain their position. Initially, after negotiations with the French failed in 1946, the Viet Minh, the nationalist movement, relied on guerrilla operations, but in accordance with Maoist theories of insurrectionary warfare, it then moved to more conventional operations. This move was encouraged by another aspect of the political dimension, the situation in neighboring states. In 1949, the Communists won the civil war in China and, in doing so, overran the part of China along the Vietnamese frontier. This success provided an opportunity to reinforce the Viet Minh and also gave them a nearby safe refuge. The Democratic Republic of Vietnam was recognized by the Chinese in January 1950. As a result, the pace of Viet Minh operations increased. Similarly, this victory in China was to be highly important to the subsequent Korean War.

The move to conventional operations in Vietnam, notably attacking French positions, also exposed the insurgents to the responses of French conventional forces, particularly airpower, and French operational effectiveness revived in 1951 under a new commander. As a result, the success of the Viet Minh offensive slackened until, in November 1953, French parachute forces established a major forward base at Dien Bien Phu in northwestern Vietnam that was designed to stop a possible Viet Minh invasion of French-ruled Laos and to provoke a battle the French could win.

This base became the focus of Viet Minh assaults, not least because its isolated character, dependent on air-dropped supplies and reinforcements, robbed it of many of the advantages of positions close to the center of French power.

French paratroopers land at Dien Bien Phu in January 1953.

In a surprising reversal of the usual pattern of counterinsurrectionary operations, the French were outgunned, notably because the Chinese had provided the
Viet Minh with American artillery seized from the defeated Chinese Nationalists. In May 1954, the outnumbered and heavily bombarded French positions
were overrun.

Most of Vietnam was still under French control, especially, but not only, the
cities, but this defeat led to a major shift in opinion in France, another reminder
of the importance of the political situation. Domestic political support for a continuation of the war slackened, and the government, under financial pressure and
unable to obtain the American military support it sought, decided to abandon
the struggle. A total of 110,000 troops on the French side had been killed since
1945 and about 200,000 Viet Minh. In July 1954, by the Geneva Agreements,
Vietnam was partitioned by a cease-fire line along the 17th Parallel, with the
North coming under Communist control, whereas the South, a new state without
organic roots, was ruled by a corrupt pro-Western dictator, Ngo Dinh Diem. This
was the crucial background to the later Vietnam War because both states claimed
to represent the whole of Vietnam, and in October 1954, President Eisenhower
promised Diem direct military assistance.

The French next found themselves opposed to a nationalist rebellion in Algeria, their leading colony and one with a long history of opposition. Brutal suppression of violent anticolonial riots in May 1945 began a new cycle of violence in
which there was no success in finding a middle way. The pattern of developments
was similar to that in Vietnam from 1954 to 1962, with the important exception
that there was no defeat comparable to Dien Bien Phu. However, counterinsurgency policies, including sealing the borders, focusing on the people, using the
army for police tasks, forcibly resettling approximately a quarter of the peasantry
into guarded camps, and employing considerable brutality, including torture,
did not end opposition by the National Liberation Front. The nationalists proved
brutal and ruthless, both in destroying the prospects for a middle way advanced
by the French government in 1956 and in terrorizing different Muslim political
forces. The apparently intractable nature of the struggle built up political pressure for a solution, and in 1962 France gave Algeria independence.

Again, a change of opinion in France was crucial. The large-scale call up of
reservists to help wage the war made it more politically sensitive. As a result of this
call up, France came to deploy over half a million troops as well as about 200,000
harkis, loyal Muslim militia. The French white settler population in Algeria as well
as much of the military was determined to retain the colony, and in 1958 their
mutiny helped bring down the government and install a new one under Charles de
Gaulle, the hero of World War II. However, in the face of a lack of victory, de Gaulle
eventually proved willing to cut the link with Algeria. In part, this was because he
saw France's destiny as European rather than colonial, but he also believed that
France's military options would improve when France acquired nuclear status and,
therefore, that it would not be necessary to retain a source of North African troops.
An attempt by rebellious generals to overthrow de Gaulle in 1961 failed.

This account suggests that anti-imperial insurrections were bound to succeed, but there were also failures, notably with risings against British rule in Malaya and Kenya in the 1950s. In each case, the insurrections were weakened by their location in sectional (rather than general) opposition to imperial rule, for example, by the Chinese population of Malaya, rather than the Malays. Moreover, the British developed effective counterinsurrectionary policies ranging from the use of airpower and a forward offensive policy to the movement of apparently hostile civilians out of areas of operation. There was little evidence of the policy of minimum force that was subsequently to become important in British military doctrine. Collective punishment and large-scale arrests rested ultimately on the availability of overwhelming force. The mistreatment of civilians was a side effect. The British were also to be successful in resisting an insurrection in Cyprus.

Again, the political context was crucial, notably the absence in Britain in the 1950s of domestic opposition to the maintenance of imperial rule. In contrast, in 1956, when Britain, alongside France and Israel, attacked Egypt in the Suez Crisis, domestic criticism within Britain combined with a response to apparent American opposition to the step led the British to abandon the operation.

POST-IMPERIAL WARS

The wars of decolonization were joined by others in which the position once held by the imperial power was contested by newly independent states. This was the case, in particular, in South Asia and the Middle East. In the former, India and Pakistan competed to dominate what had once been British India and fought three wars as a result, in 1948–1949, 1965, and 1971. These conflicts overlapped with opposition to the two powers, indeed rebellion. Thus, Pakistan sought to intervene on behalf of Muslim opponents of India in Kashmir, whereas Indian intervention in 1971 led to the success of a rebellion in East Pakistan, which became the independent state of Bangladesh.

These wars do not tend to attract attention in general works on military history, which underrates both the significance of South Asia and the interest of these conflicts. The scale was considerable. In the third of the wars, a total of 160,000 Indian troops were sent into East Pakistan in 1971; at the same time, other Indian units fought Pakistani forces in West Pakistan. Regular warfare took place in a variety of forms, notably large-scale tank conflict on the India–West Pakistan frontier, as well as in the air and, to a lesser extent, at sea. Moreover, there was an overlap with insurrectionary warfare and, indeed, conflict between peoples. In East Pakistan, there was a large-scale slaughter of local Bengalis, notably but not only in Hindu, by both the Pakistani army and the allied irregulars.

There was also the question of how best to succeed the colonial powers in the Middle East: France and more so Britain. These wars of succession were seen in Israel/Palestine, Lebanon, and Jordan and also involved neighboring Egypt and Syria. There was also to be confrontation in the Gulf, where the power of the once hegemonic Britain declined markedly from the 1960s: in 1961, the threat of British intervention had helped to deter Iraq from invading Kuwait. This role was subsequently to be taken by the United States.

The wars that attracted most attention were those between Israel and Arab neighbors, although they should also be seen in wider contexts, both regional and global. These contexts were very much affected by the Cold War.

The Arabs proved unwilling to accept the culmination of the Zionist movement in the form of an independent Israel. Rejecting the United Nations (UN) partition resolution of November 29, 1947, the Arabs sought to drive the Jews from Palestine as Britain, the colonial power from World War I on, withdrew. Fighting broke out throughout Palestine in December 1947 and became full-scale when the British mandate ended on May 14, 1948.

From 1948 to 1949, Israel was able to establish its independence and gain more territory than in the abortive partition plan, showing that conflict could deliver a decisive military and political verdict. Fighting well, the Israelis faced poorly coordinated and badly prepared advances by the regular forces of Egypt, Iraq, Jordan, and Syria and the irregular forces of the Palestinians and the Arab Liberation Army. The course of the conflict was important for the creation of a Jewish state and for its shape. In particular, the Israelis proved more successful in conflict with the Palestinians, the Arab Liberation Army, and the Egyptians than with Iraqi, Jordanian, and Syrian forces. This complexity did not prove welcome to commentators who sought to provide a simple equation of Arab and Israeli capability.

The war ended with the partition of Palestine among Israel, Egypt, and Jordan. Tension continued and was exacerbated from the mid-1950s by the Arab nationalism and expansionism of the Egyptian dictator, Gamal Abdel Nasser. This threat helped lead Israel into two wars, in 1956 and 1967. In 1956, as part of the Suez Crisis, Israel conquered the Egyptian-ruled Sinai Peninsula. The Israelis benefited from Nasser's focus on the Anglo-French threat to the Suez Canal zone, but there were also tactical and operational differences that contributed to Israel's success. In particular, the Egyptians fought in a more rigid fashion, relying on prepared positions, but lacking the flexibility to handle the mobility of tank warfare and the possibilities of combined arms operations.

There were also cultural factors of note. The Egyptian forces, largely made up of conscripted peasants, suffered from distant relations between the bulk of the army and the officer corps, a situation that was to be repeated with the Iraqi army in 1991, although there was the additional difference in Iraq that most of the soldiers were Shia Muslims, whereas the officers were Sunnis. As again with Iraq in 1991, the hierarchical nature of Egyptian military society led naturally to the inflexibility of Egyptian military methods. This is a key indication of the value of the "war and society" approach. The latter is usually applied to the wider social context and consequences of conflict, which were readily apparent in the case of Israel. The democratic and participatory nature of Israeli society gave a character to its conscript forces that was different from that seen with Egypt. There was a powerful ideological drive drawing on a conviction that the Arabs intended

Jewish girls learning to march after the establishment of the state of Israel, June 1948.

ethnic cleansing, if not genocide, and that the Jews must avoid the vulnerability seen with the Nazi Holocaust. Moreover, the flexibility of Israeli society helped ensure the effectiveness of both peacetime training and warlike operations. In particular, the reserve system, which provided the bulk of the Israeli army, reflected the reality of a motivated "people under arms" as opposed to the rhetoric to that effect by many totalitarian regimes.

In 1967, rising regional tension, especially Nasser's saber rattling and the related withdrawal of UN peacekeepers, led to a preemptive Israeli attack on Egypt on June 5. As the war spread, it resulted in the Israeli conquest not only of the Gaza Strip and Sinai from Egypt, but also of the West Bank section of Jordan and the Golan Heights from Syria. Gaining air superiority by a surprise attack proved crucial to the subsequent land conflict because opposing ground forces were badly affected by Israeli ground-support attacks. The Israelis also benefited greatly from the sequential nature of their campaigning, being able to focus first on Egypt.

The war led to major Israeli territorial gains in the Gaza Strip, the Sinai Peninsula, the West Bank of the Jordan, and the Golan Heights and to a subsequent situation that was far from peace. Moreover, the Soviet Union rearmed its allies Egypt and Syria, and in 1968, the United States decided to provide Israel with F-4 Phantom jets. This was an important step in the definition of the Arab–Israeli struggle in terms of the Cold War.

This process of growing alignment on Cold War lines was seen not only with the wars of postcolonialism, but also with the surviving wars of decolonization. By the late 1960s, when there were fewer colonies, the wars of decolonization were largely restricted to the fate of the Portuguese colonies in Africa: Angola, Mozambique, and Guinea-Bissau. Advisers and arms from the Soviet Union, China, and Cuba, notably antiaircraft missiles that hindered the Portuguese use of ground-support aircraft and helicopters, greatly complicated the struggle for the Portuguese.

THE COLD WAR

Before considering how these conflicts, the wars of decolonization and the postcolonial wars in Africa and the Middle East, came to a peak in the early 1970s, it is necessary to turn back to discuss the Cold War and more particularly its opening paradox, so that this struggle should not be defined as a whole in terms of the confrontation short of large-scale warfare seen in Europe. There was conflict there, notably the defeat of the Communists in the Greek Civil War, but it did not occur on the scale seen in Asia. Indeed, the Cold War was very much "hot" from an Asian perspective—with the Chinese Civil War leading to the Korean War and then to the Vietnam War, both of the latter directly involving large-scale American commitments.

CHINESE CIVIL WAR

The success of Communism in China transformed the broader geopolitical situation in East Asia and further afield. The small, urban-based Chinese Communist Party had been largely destroyed in the 1927 Harvest Moon Uprising, after which control over the party was increasingly taken by agrarian reformers under Mao Zedong, who pressed for a rural revolution. Despite a series of offensives, the forces of the Nationalist government were unable to destroy the Communists in the 1930s, although they did bring damaging pressure to bear. However, the Nationalist position was increasingly challenged by Japanese aggression, with full-scale war breaking out in 1937. Once Japan overran China's coasts and river valleys, destroying the Nationalists' urban power bases and capturing Shanghai and Nanjing in 1937 and Canton in 1938, the Communists were able to make a greater impact in rural areas, where the Nationalists had little interest and control.

In opposition to the Nationalists, Mao had developed a three-stage revolutionary war model and, during World War II, was able to use a combination of clandestine political–social organization (stage 1) and guerrilla warfare (stage 2) to advance the Communist position; however, he was unable to move successfully into the conventional realm (stage 3) until after the Japanese withdrawal.[1]

---

[1] *Selected Military Writings of Mao Tse-tung* (Beijing, Foreign Languages Press, 1963).

The Nationalist government was gravely weakened by the long war with Japan, being particularly hard hit by large-scale Japanese advances in 1944 and 1945, which overran much of southern China.

Despite American support, the Nationalists were defeated anew after World War II: by the Soviet-backed Communists in the Chinese Civil War. This defeat would have been less likely bar World War II: prior to the Japanese attack on China, the Communists had been in a vulnerable position in their conflict with the Nationalists, but following that attack, the Communists benefited from having become the dominant anti-Japanese force in northern China during the 1930s and early 1940s.

The Chinese Civil War has been the largest conflict, in terms of number of combatants and area fought over, since World War II, and it proves an instructive counterpoint to the latter, indicating the difficulty of drawing clear lessons from the conflicts of the 1940s. It should be stressed, however, that there has been far less scholarship on the Chinese Civil War than on the Korean and Vietnam wars, let alone World War II, and much of the work published has reflected ideological bias. In China, technology and the quantity of *matériel* did not triumph because the Communists were inferior in weaponry and, in particular, lacked air and sea power. However, their strategic conceptions, operational planning and execution, army morale, and political leadership proved superior, and they were able to make the transfer from guerrilla warfare to large-scale conventional operations, from denying their opponents control over territory to seizing and securing it.

Members of the People's Liberation Army undergoing training in ballistics, China, late 1940.

The Nationalist cause was weakened by poor leadership, partisanship, inept strategy, and, because the war went badly, poor morale, whereas serious corruption, terrible inflation, and a lack of land reform greatly affected civilian support. Indeed, the *China White Paper* published by the American State Department in 1950 blamed the Nationalists' failure on their own incompetence and corruption. Their emphasis on command as a result of, and through, *guanxi*, or personal networks and individual favors, did not provide effective military direction. This emphasis on clientage and personal loyalty was to be true of the nonprofessional military across the world, and these factors could also be significant for their more professional counterparts. The overlap between such networks and politics helped to drive the role of the military in many societies.

Since the 2000s, the classic treatment of the war as a Communist victory of "hearts and minds" that indicated the supposedly superior virtues of Communism over the Nationalists, as well as the strength of the People's Liberation Army and its brave peasant fighters, has been qualified by a greater emphasis on the importance of what actually happened in the fighting. Indeed, until 1948, the Nationalists largely held their own. When the American use of atomic bombs led to Japan's sudden surrender in August 1945, the Communists, encouraged by the Soviet Union, liberated much of the north of China from Japanese forces, capturing large quantities of weaponry. Negotiations with the Nationalists were actively sponsored by the United States, which sought a unity government for China, but they broke down and full-scale civil war resumed in October 1945. By December, there was fighting in 11 provinces. In late 1945, the Nationalists decided to deploy much of their army to Manchuria, China's industrial heartland. They were helped by the United States, not least because the Americans flew in Nationalist troops, thus circumventing a Soviet naval presence off Manchuria. However, Manchuria was a zone of conflict that benefited the Communists because of the proximity of the Soviet Union and also because it was distant from the Nationalist bases in south and central China. The Soviets provided arms and advisors to the Communists.

In 1947, Communist guerrilla tactics had an increasing impact in isolating Nationalist garrisons in the north, although further south, the Nationalists overran the Communist-dominated province of Shensi, also capturing Yenan in March. Communist fighting effectiveness increased and in May 1947, for the first time, a Communist field army defeated an elite Nationalist force. Communist offensives led to a series of significant gains, and Nationalist reserves were used up. Like the Japanese in 1937–1945, the Nationalists controlled the cities and the coastal region, but found it difficult to sustain their position elsewhere. Despite pressure in the United States to intervene on the Nationalist side, particularly from the Republican opposition, which raised the charge of weakness toward Communism, the Truman government decided not to do so and took a lesser role than in the Greek Civil War, where Communist pressure was successfully resisted, although that conflict was more containable and more propitious for Western intervention.

In 1948, as the Communists increasingly switched to conventional but mobile operations, the Nationalist forces in Manchuria were isolated and then, with their supplies running out, sequentially destroyed. Moreover, the Communists regained Shensi and conquered much of China north of the Yellow River. Communist victory in Manchuria, the abandonment of which the Americans had recommended, had led to a crucial shift in advantage and was followed by the rapid collapse of the Nationalists the following year. The Nationalists lost large numbers of men, and the Communists made major gains of *matérial* in Manchuria, which also served as a base for raising supplies for operations elsewhere.[2] The Communists now had large, well-equipped armies.

After overrunning Manchuria, the Communists, seeking victories of annihilation, focused on the large Nationalist concentration in the Suchow-Kaifeng region. In the Huai Hai campaign, beginning on November 6, 1948, each side committed about 600,000 men. The Nationalists suffered from poor generalship, including insufficient coordination of units and inadequate use of air support, and were also hit by defections, an important factor in many civil wars. Much of the Nationalist force was encircled thanks to effective Communist envelopment methods, and in December 1948 and January 1949 it collapsed as a result of defections and combat losses. In this and other battles in November 1948 to January 1949, the Nationalists lost 1.5 million men through casualties or defections. These defections increased rapidly in 1949.

Jiang Jieshi, the Nationalist leader, resigned as president (although staying as party leader) on January 21, 1949, and the Communists captured Beijing without opposition the following day. The Communists responded to the new president's offer of negotiation by demanding unconditional surrender, and the war continued. The Communist victories that winter had opened the way to advances further south, not least by enabling them to build up resources. The Communists crossed the Yangzi river on April 20, 1949, the planned defense of this river line destroyed by rivalry between Jiang and his successor. Jiang was increasingly concerned with a safe retreat to Taiwan rather than in helping secure a rump state in South China under his Nationalist rivals. The Communist advance benefited from the mutiny of much of the unpaid Nationalist navy in April.

The rapid overrunning of much of southern China over the following six months testified not only to the potential speed of operations, but also to the impact of success in winning over support. Nanjing fell on April 22 and Shanghai on May 27, and the Communists pressed on to overrun rapidly the other major centers, with distant Chonqqing, which had never fallen to the Japanese, falling in November 1949. The Communists ignored Nationalist requests for a cease-fire. Within China, a sense that the Nationalist failure was inevitable, which in part reflected the cyclical nature of Chinese ideas of history, became self-fulfilling.

---

[2]S. I. Levine, *Anvil of Victory: The Communist Revolution in Manchuria, 1945–1948* (New York, Columbia University Press, 1987).

Jiang had alienated American support and exhausted American options for intervention. A key possibility that had not been developed as an option was the use of nuclear weaponry. Between 1945 and 1949, when the Soviet Union revealed its development of nuclear weaponry, the United States alone had had such weapons, a unique position in the history of the atom bomb. Despite this, there had been no use of the atom bomb, either in China or, indeed, in Europe to deter the Soviet Union during the Berlin crisis of 1948–1949 when the Soviets blockaded the Western occupation zones in West Berlin. This nonuse demonstrated the difficulty of deriving benefit from the possession of overwhelming force, a point that was also to be true of the subsequent years of nuclear deterrence when both the United States and the Soviet Union had the weaponry.

In December 1949, Jiang Jieshi took refuge on the island of Formosa (Taiwan), which was to be the sole significant territory over which he retained control. It was protected by the limited aerial and naval capability of the Communists, such that an invasion was initially implausible, and eventually by American naval power; but, until he intervened in Korea in 1950, Mao Zedong prepared for an invasion of Formosa, creating an air force to that end. Jiang, in turn, used Formosa and the other offshore islands he still controlled as a base for raids on the mainland. Meanwhile, in the spring of 1950, Xinjiang, the poorly defended island of Hainan, and Tibet in 1950–1951 were conquered by the Communists, with Lhasa, the capital of Tibet, being occupied on October 7, 1950. The new strategic order in Asia was underlined in January 1950 when China and the Soviet Union signed a mutual security agreement.

THE KOREAN WAR

Although the Berlin Crisis of 1948–1949 had raised the prospect of war between the Soviet Union and the Western powers in Europe, as the rival alliance systems defined and consolidated their zones, in fact the Western powers were tested not in Europe but in distant Korea. The Communists had won in the Chinese Civil War, but the Americans were determined that they should not be allowed further gains in East Asia. At the close of World War II, in a partition of Korea, a hitherto united territory that had been conquered by Japan and taken into its empire in the 1900s, northern Korea had been occupied by Soviet forces and southern Korea by the Americans. In the context of the difficulties posed by Korean political divisions and growing American–Soviet distrust, both of which sapped attempts to create a united Korea, they each, in 1948, established authoritarian regimes: under Syngman Rhee in South Korea and Kim Il-Sung in North Korea. There was no historical foundation for this division, each regime had supporters across Korea, and both wished to govern the entire peninsula. The regime in North Korea, whose military buildup was helped by the Soviet Union, was convinced that its counterpart in the South was weak and could be overthrown and was likely to be denied American support. The

South Korean army, indeed, lacked military experience and adequate equipment, and the Korean Military Assistance Group provided by the United States was only 500 strong.

The bitter rivalry between the two states, as each sought to destabilize the other, included, from 1948, guerrilla operations in South Korea supported by the Communist North. Having created a South Korean army, the Americans provided air and artillery support for its operations against the insurgents. On June 25, 1950, in contrast, the effective North launched a surprise, full-scale invasion of South Korea, attacking with about 135,000 troops and using T34 tanks and Yak airplanes provided by the Soviets that gave them an advantage over their lightly armed opponents. In February, Stalin had agreed to provide heavy guns to North Korea, in contrast to his position in March and September 1949 when he had rejected Kim Il-Sung's suggestion that an attack be mounted.

In March–April 1950, Stalin moved toward Kim Il-Sung's position, telling him that the Soviet explosion of an atomic device on August 29, 1949, and the treaty of alliance between China and the Soviet Union had made the situation more propitious for action. Stalin made agreement, however, conditional on Chinese support and said that if the Americans intervened, he would not send troops, which increased North Korea's need for Chinese backing. Given Stalin's position, Mao agreed, although he would have preferred an emphasis on gaining Taiwan; indeed, the Korean War helped save Taiwan from a Communist takeover, in large part by assuring American protection.

In June 1950, the South Koreans were pushed back and badly battered, with the capital, Seoul, falling on June 28, but enough units fought sufficiently well in their delaying actions during their retreat south to give time for the arrival of American troops. American forces entered combat in Korea from June 30 because the North Korean invasion led to intervention by an American-led UN coalition, which was determined to maintain policies of collective security and containment and was concerned that a successful invasion of South Korea would be followed by Communist pressure elsewhere, possibly on West Berlin or Taiwan. After the South Koreans, the leading UN contingent was American and the second largest was British. Among the large number of international participants, the Canadians and Turks were prominent. The Americans also provided most of the air and naval power, as well as the commander, General Douglas MacArthur, their commander in chief far east. The UN forces benefited from the backing of a stable South Korean civilian government and from a unified command: MacArthur's position as supreme commander of UN forces in Korea gave control over all military forces, including the South Korean army, and provided a coherence that would be lacking in the Vietnam War. American capability was enhanced by the presence of their occupation forces in nearby Japan and by the logistical infrastructure and support services provided by Japanese facilities and resources.

Thanks to their major role in World War II, the Americans were better able than they would have been in the 1930s to fight in Korea, but since 1945, because of postwar demobilization as the "peace dividend" was taken, there had been a dramatic decline of available manpower and *matériel*. The number of amphibious ships had fallen from 610 in 1945 to 81 in 1950, there was a grave shortage of artillery units, and in 1949 the American army only contained one armored division. American fighting effectiveness had also declined, as shown by the experience of some American units in the first year of the Korean War, notably those rapidly transferred from the garrison in Japan. Moreover, many of the National Guard units sent to Korea were inadequately trained and equipped. In contrast, there was a formidable power projection capability, notably with the airlift of men and supplies to Korea.

After almost being driven into the sea at the end of the peninsula in the first North Korean onslaught, the South Koreans and Americans held the Pusan perimeter there against attack. The Americans then reversed the situation by Operation Chromite, a daring and unrehearsed landing on the Korean west coast at Inchon on September 15, 1950, that applied American force at a decisive point. Carried out far behind the front and with limited information about the conditions, physical and military, that they would encounter, notably the difficult tides, about 83,000 troops were successfully landed, and they pressed on to capture nearby Seoul.

This success destroyed both the coherence of North Korean forces and their supply system, which had already been put under great strain by the advance toward Pusan, and also achieved a major psychological victory that was not to be matched by the Americans in the Vietnam War. The capture of Seoul enabled the American forces in the Pusan area in the south, which, once reinforced, had convincingly held the perimeter, to drive the North Koreans back into their own half of the peninsula and north toward the Chinese frontier, advancing across a broad front against limited resistance. On October 7, 1950, American forces crossed the 38° North Parallel dividing North and South Korea. However, the UN advance was affected by serious logistical problems that owed much to a lack of adequate harbors, but even more to the poor nature of ground routes, especially in the mountainous interior.

The UN advance was not welcome to the Chinese, who suddenly intervened in Korea in October 1950, exploiting American overconfidence. From July, the Chinese appear to have begun preparing for intervention and certainly built up large forces near the border. Success in the Chinese Civil War had encouraged Mao to believe that technological advantages, especially in airpower, which the Americans dominated, could be countered, not least by determination. However, as with the Japanese in World War II, American resilience, resources, and fighting quality were underestimated by the Chinese in this the sole war between any of the world's leading military powers since 1945.

Mao felt that UN support for Korean unification threatened China and might lead to a Nationalist *revanche*, saw American support for Taiwan as provocative, and was also keen to present China as a major force; Stalin, to whom Mao appealed for help, wanted to see China committed against the United States. This was the

price for meeting Chinese requirements for assistance with military modernization. Stalin pressed Mao to send troops into Korea and promised help in the event
of the Americans invading China as a result.

In an instance of poor planning, Chinese intervention had not been anticipated by MacArthur, who had believed that by maintaining the pace of the
offensive and advancing to the Korean–Chinese frontier at the Yalu River, he
would end the war. This advance had been authorized by the Joint Chiefs of Staff,
and there was encouragement from reports of the Central Intelligence Agency
(CIA) that direct intervention by China and the Soviet Union was unlikely.
Despite a Chinese warning on October 3 via the Indian envoy in Beijing of action
if the UN forces advanced into North Korea, it was believed that the Communist
leadership was intent on strengthening its position within China and that China
lacked the resources for intervention abroad.

The opinionated MacArthur ignored the more cautious approach taken by
Truman and his secretary of state, Dean Acheson. Concerned about the Chinese
response, Truman instructed MacArthur to use only South Korean forces close
to the Chinese border, but MacArthur was insistent that American troops be
employed. MacArthur told Truman that it was too late in the year for the Chinese
to act in strength, and after they initially intervened from October 19 in fairly
small numbers, he ignored evidence of Chinese troops in Korea. The operational
success MacArthur had shown in the Inchon operation was not matched by adequate strategic assessment. Although his hubris was partly responsible, there were
also weaknesses in American command and control reflecting the improvised
way in which the conflict was being fought. In addition, the belief that airpower
could isolate the battlefield led to misplaced confidence. These points throw sug-
gestive light on the extent to which the architecture of nuclear deterrence might
later have been operated had there been conflict between the major powers.

Attacking in force from October 25 against the overextended and, because of
an advance on different axes, poorly coordinated UN forces, the Chinese, most
veterans of the recent civil war, drove them out of North Korea in late 1950, capturing Seoul in January 1951. The Chinese, nominally Chinese People's Volunteers,
not regulars, proved better able to take advantage of the terrain and outmaneuvered the UN forces, who were more closely tied to their road links. The fighting
quality and heroism of some retreating units, including British forces, limited the
scale of the defeat, but, nevertheless, it was a serious one. Thanks to control of the
sea, however, it was possible to evacuate by sea some units that had been cut off
by the Communist advance, thus limiting the losses. Control of the sea was
always to be an aspect of postwar American geopolitics and military power. It
was particularly apparent in Asian waters and in the first half of the Cold War,
but even when the Soviet navy had grown in strength, this control remained a
dominant element.

Control of the sea provided power projection but also more specific operational and tactical elements. The firepower of naval ordnance from Task Force 95
and from the carrier aircraft of Task Force 77 was of operational and tactical

value, not least for ground support, and naval control permitted resupply from Japan. Concerned with limiting the war, the Soviet Union did not attack the American naval supply routes, not that they would have been able to do so successfully, and the small North Korean and Chinese navies were in no position to do so: in the Chinese Civil War, the Nationalists, not the Communists, had controlled Chinese naval power until April 1949. Equally, during the Korean War, there was no American or UN blockade of China, and the Chinese forces deployed in coastal regions that appeared threatened with an American invasion, for example, near Tianjin, were not tested in battle.

Unlike at sea, the Korean War involved much conflict in the air because the Americans encountered resistance in the air space over North Korea. The Chinese, who had only created an air force in November 1949 and whose Soviet-trained pilots lacked adequate training and were equipped with out-of-date Soviet planes, were supported, however, by the advanced MIG-15 fighters of the Manchurian-based Soviet "Group 64," and the war saw the first dogfights between jet aircraft, with MIG-15s fighting American F-86 Sabres. The rotation system employed greatly undermined the Soviet fighter pilots' continuity of experience and thus their effectiveness. The Americans inflicted far heavier casualties and were able to dominate the skies, with serious consequences for respective ground support, although the absence of adequate command integration limited the American exploitation of this advantage. The Soviet refusal to heed Chinese pressure for Soviet air support of Chinese ground forces was a major advantage for the Americans and also helped limit the potential extension of the conflict from a limited war into what could have become World War III. U.S. Air Force suggestions in 1950 of the firebombing of the major industrial cities in North Korea were not initially implemented. However, once the Chinese had entered the war, major incendiary attacks were launched on North Korea, resulting over several years of heavy bombing in much devastation and heavy casualties.

During the war, the Chinese made a full transition to a conventional army, with tanks, heavy artillery, and aircraft, continuing the process started during the Chinese Civil War. The UN forces, however, were now a more formidable opponent than

American GIs head to the front as civilians flee the conflict zone, Korea, 1950.

when the war started. The Chinese were fought to a standstill in mid-February and late May 1951, as UN supply lines shortened thanks to the retreat of UN forces and as Chinese human-wave frontal attacks fell victim to American firepower, particularly in the "Wŏnju Shoot" on February 14. Even the Chinese Fifth Offensive, that of April 22–30, 1951, which pushed the UN forces back toward Seoul, suffered heavy casualties. Heavy Chinese and North Korean losses of men (about 160,000 casualties in April and May 1951) and equipment, including the surrender of large numbers of soldiers, as well as the arrival of American reinforcements, led the Chinese commander P'eng The-huai to abandon the attack in late May. The Chinese advance had also greatly increased the logistical burden of supporting China's large commitment of troops. Many of them were Nationalist troops who had defected to the Communists in 1948–1949: Mao was keen to see that they took the brunt of the casualties.

Thereafter, the war became far more static, with the front pushed back by a UN offensive between May 20 and June 24 to near the 38th Parallel. The attritional conflict that MacArthur had sought to avoid by Operation Chromite now prevailed, and he himself had been relieved in March 1951 for insubordination. MacArthur had requested an expansion of the war to include a blockade of China, as well as permission to pursue opposing aircraft into Manchuria and to attack their bases there, to bomb bridges along the Yalu River hitting Chinese logistics, and to employ Nationalist Chinese troops against the Chinese coast (as a second front) or in Korea. These proposals were rejected by the Joint Chiefs of Staff as likely to lead to an escalation of the war, with the possibility of direct Soviet entry.

Truman's patience with MacArthur was exhausted, and he was also under pressure from his allies, including Britain, about the general's views, although on the whole the Americans tended to make decisions without much, or any, consultation. Soviet entry into the war was seen as a threat to Western Europe, which was regarded as particularly vulnerable. Had the Soviets attacked there, there would indeed have been no American reinforcements to spare for Korea. American restraint therefore helped ensure that the conflict did not become World War III or a nuclear war, and the Korean War served as an important introduction for American policy makers and politicians to the complexities of limited warfare. Korea was an education in strategy. In turn, Stalin, with his marked preference for taking advantages rather than risks, did not wish to take the chance of formal Soviet entry into the conflict.

The advantage given to the defense by Korea's mountainous terrain was accentuated by the politics of the conflict. Operational intensity and casualties both decreased, and lengthy negotiations became more important, with offensives tied to their course, a feature also to be seen in other conflicts, for example, the latter stages of the Vietnam War. As trench replaced maneuver warfare in Korea, the role of artillery became more important, and as the defenses on both sides became stronger, the tendency for a more fixed front line was accentuated. With the Americans seeking an exit strategy from the war in the shape of the territorial *status quo* and a cease-fire, there was no attempt to move forward from stalemate. On July 10, 1951, cease-fire talks began at Kaesong on the 38th Parallel. The Americans and Chinese no longer felt they could take the casualties and risks of fighting on for unification.

Nevertheless, there were still costly clashes. For example, from July until November 1951, in the last major UN offensive of the war, in a series of assaults that recalled the methods of World War I trench warfare, UN forces suffered 60,000 casualties and their opponents about 234,000. After October 1951, the front line changed little. Casualty rates were too high to justify the continuation of the UN advance. In turn, in the summer of 1953, the Chinese mounted a series of attacks to win an advantage in the closing stages of the war. The Chinese made territorial gains, but only at the cost of heavy casualties. Moreover, as the Americans had helped build up an effective South Korean army, so the possibility of its weaknesses giving them opportunities in further fighting declined.

More positively, containment—both by UN forces of the Communists and by the nature of the war—prevented the risk of escalation. Aside from the decision not to use atomic bombs in Korea, which the British warned in December 1950 would probably lead to a totally unwanted all-out war with China,[3] there was no hot pursuit of Communist aircraft into China. It was difficult, however, to end the conflict, which was the goal of Dwight Eisenhower, who was elected American president in November 1952, although Mao, convinced that his opponents lacked the necessary willpower to persist, felt it appropriate to fight on. However, Mao was weakened by a shift of Soviet policy after Stalin died in March 1953, a shift accentuated by antigovernment riots in Communist-controlled Eastern Europe—in East Germany and Poland—and by the serious strain the war was placing on the Chinese military. Moreover, Eisenhower threatened to use atomic weaponry to bring the war to an end, a threat enhanced because the Americans had first tested a hydrogen bomb in November 1952. The eventual armistice, signed on July 27, 1953, left a military demarcation line along the 38th Parallel with an unfortified demilitarized zone 2 kilometers deep on either side. At that stage, the largest UN contingent in Korea was South Korean (509,911), followed by the Americans (302,483), British (14,198), and Canadians (6,146).

By the time the Korean War ended in 1953, with over 3 million dead (of whom 33,741 were classified as American battle deaths, with 2,827 nonbattle deaths), the pattern of the Communist–Western confrontation known as the Cold War was set. The majority of casualties were Korean, prefiguring the situation with the Vietnam War, and for Korea the war was far from limited, with the South Korean military alone losing 415,000 killed. The war closed with the partition of the peninsula between two hostile states well entrenched and with this hostility unlanced. Indeed, the conflict had seen many of the symptoms of civil war, not least with the harsh treatment of civilians regarded as opponents by advancing Korean forces, both North and South Korean. The year 1953 provided an armistice

---

[3] *Foreign Relations of the United States 1950*, Vol. VII (Washington, D.C., U.S. Government Printing Office, 1976), pp. 1296–1297.

agreement, not a peace treaty, and tensions exacerbated by the war remained high in Korea. Although Chinese forces were withdrawn from North Korea, a process completed in 1958, the United States built up the South Korean army and in November 2013 still retained a 28,000-strong military presence in South Korea and offered a guarantee of protection to deter the heavily armed North Korea from invading.

THE IMPACT OF THE KOREAN WAR

Outside Korea, there was a process of radicalization in the early 1950s that further helped entrench ideological and political differences. Thus, Mao used conflict with the United States to consolidate the position of the Communist Party within China and to push through land seizure, killing large numbers labeled as counterrevolutionaries, probably several million, in the process. This radicalization was accompanied by a markedly hostile Chinese stance toward the United States, which greatly furthered Stalin's goals. There had been little chance of a *rapprochement* between Mao and the United States, but Stalin was well used to abrupt changes of policy, and Chinese entry into the war made such a chance highly unlikely. Indeed, it was postponed for more than two decades, which provided the Soviet Union a key element of strength for much of the Cold War. Before the Chinese Civil War ended, Stalin had been concerned about Mao becoming too strong and had taken unsuccessful steps to probe the possibility of dividing China, with a Nationalist rump state remaining in southern China.

Moreover, the Korean War left the United States engaged in an area that was of scant strategic concern to the Soviet Union. Conversely, however, the conflict gave Mao a stronger sense of China's importance, which was to pose problems for the Soviet Union and also involved heavy costs for the Soviets as they provided support for China and North Korea during it while also having, in a developing arms race, to meet the consequences of greater military expenditure by the United States and its allies.

Indeed, the war led to a process of militarization and a major increase in military expenditure, especially in the West. For example, in the United States it increased, as a percentage of total government expenditure, from 30.4 percent in 1950 to 65.7 percent in 1954, and a military–industrial complex came to play a greater role in the American economy and governmental structure. "Peacetime" America became a state that was mobilized for conflict. Conscription was revived, and the size of the armed forces greatly expanded, with the American army increasing to 3.5 million men. A Cold War culture developed intensity in the United States, encouraging an emphasis on a conservative cast of American values. The Americans also put pressure on their allies to build up their military and, more clearly, called for West German rearmament, a policy criticized by Soviet propaganda.

The Korean War helped ensure that NATO (established in 1949) was transformed into an effective alliance. Created as a way to anchor the United States in the defense of Western Europe against possible Soviet expansion, NATO became part of the diplomatic and military architecture of America's global power. In Canada, which played an active role in NATO and also sent troops to Korea, defense spending increased from $196 million in 1947 to $1.5 billion in 1951. Under American pressure because it needed allies, Britain embarked in 1950 on a costly rearmament program, which undid recent economic gains and strengthened the military commitment that was to be such a heavy postwar economic burden. At the same time, the war encouraged the expenditure of American wealth and use of American credit, which led to a boom in economic demand that helped economic growth in Japan and Western Europe.

Similarly, the war ensured that Stalin pushed harder for industrial growth, which ensured that even less of an effort was made to meet Eastern bloc demand for consumer goods. Unrest in East Germany, Bulgaria, and Czechoslovakia, especially in the first, led to violence in 1953, and once the workers rose up in rebellion, this created a serious problem for the Communist bloc. To argue that therefore the Soviet Union would have been better off had there been no Korean War is, however, to miss the point that this war was in accordance with Communist notions of world revolution.

The Korean War also greatly increased American sensitivity to developments and threats in East Asia, leading to an extension of the containment policy toward the Communist powers, the maintenance of American army, navy, and air power in Japan (where important bases were preserved after the occupation was ended with peace and security treaties in 1952), and a growing commitment to the Nationalist Chinese in Taiwan, a marked shift from the position prior to the war when President Truman had considered accepting a Communist invasion of the island. The outbreak of the war and China's subsequent intervention instead led to a marked increase in aid to the Nationalists and, in June 1950, to the move of the powerful American Seventh Fleet into the Taiwan Strait, providing protection against possible invasion. The American military presence in the region was fostered precisely because it could serve a variety of purposes, countering North Korea, China, and the Soviet Union, but also providing an important element in relations with Japan. Concern about China also led to greater American interest in India as offering a democratic Asian ally, a view outlined by the secretary of state John Foster Dulles in June 1953,[4] one that was to be repeated in the 2010s. In Tibet, occupied by Chinese forces from 1950, the CIA backed rebellion, notably by Khampa rebels.

More generally, a sense that the situation might slip out of control through a "domino effect," as the fall of one country to Communism led to that of others, encouraged the American government to take a greater interest in the course and consequences of the Western retreat from empire, especially in IndoChina where the French were under great pressure in Vietnam. From 1950, assistance to the

---

[4]*Executive Sessions of the Senate Foreign Relations Committee*, Vol. 5: 1953 (Washington, D.C., U. S. Government Printing Office, 1977), p. 450.

French in IndoChina was increased, and by 1953 the United States was support-ing most of the financial burden of the war there.

This commitment to the European colonial powers, however, was unwise from the perspective of America's wish to win Third World support. Nationalist movements throughout the Third World were to be increasingly viewed by the Americans in their perspective of the struggle with Communism. The *realpolitik* of international relations was perceived in ideological terms by both the United States and its Communist opponents, helping to ensure that tensions remained high and encouraging the development of covert operations. In 1953, Operation Ajax, a CIA-instigated coup, led to the fall of the Iranian nationalist President Mohammed Mosaddeq, securing power for Reza Pahlavi, the Shah, who had gone into exile in 1951. However, in the long term, the coup encouraged Iranian hostility to the West. In 1954, there was similar action in Guatemala, with the Americans backing a military coup that overthrew Jacobo Arbenz Guzinán, a president who had backed land reform.

COLD WAR CONFRONTATION

Western policy was militarized, America had become a national security state, and the division of Europe had been cemented, but such remarks pay insuffi-cient attention to the threatening character of Stalin's policy and to the extent to which Western preparedness as a result of the Korean War may well have lim-ited the possibility that the Soviet Union would subsequently risk war by aggres-sive action. In other words, containment worked, although it also meant that Communist control was entrenched. This was a clear consequence of the parti-tion of Korea, and the latter suggested that the partition of Germany would be a lasting one. NATO powers did not intervene when opposition in the Commu-nist bloc was suppressed by force: in Hungary (1956), Czechoslovakia (1968), and Poland (1981). The policy established in the first case was that there would be no "rollback" of Soviet power in Europe. It was feared that any such attempt by NATO would lead to large-scale conflict. Thus, deterrence, the development of strength to discourage attack, a situation usually discussed in terms of deter-ring the Soviets from attacking Western Europe, actually operated in a number of directions.

The threat from other powers was also crucial to the development of intelligence agencies, the practice of surveillance against both domestic and foreign opponents, and a culture of novels and films in which secret agents, espionage, and subversion all played central roles. In the United States, the CIA was created under the National Security Act of 1947 to organize foreign intelligence through the executive office of the president. Covert operations became a major theme in the 1950s. In November 1962, Harold Macmillan, the British prime minister from 1957 to 1963, told the House of Commons that "hostile [Soviet] intrigue and espionage are being relent-lessly maintained on a very large scale." Intelligence operations involved conflict, as with attempts to intercept aerial reconnaissance missions, which included the

Soviet shooting down near Sverdlovsk of the American U-2 high-altitude photoreconnaissance spy plane flown by Gary Powers on May 1, 1960.

There had been major differences among American policy makers and politicians in the late 1940s over the strategy that should be followed, not least the degree to which there would be a policy of foreign commitment and global containment of Communism and a reliance on nuclear weaponry. There had also been a powerful Republican lobby pressing for intervention against the Communists in the Chinese Civil War. By the early 1950s, however, the requirement and strategy for atomic defense and war were in place: the American forces in Western Europe had to be protected, and the same was true for South Korea and

Before the uprising against Soviet rule was crushed, large parts of the Hungarian army went over to the insurgents; here revolutionaries ride in an armored car.

Japan. Whereas initially the American Joint Chiefs of Staff had assumed that the defense of Western Europe would be the responsibility of the Europeans, with the Americans providing help from the Strategic Air Command, and being most concerned about its air bases in Britain, where atomic-capable aircraft were deployed from 1950 alongside bomb components, membership in NATO led to a full-scale American ground commitment to the defense of Western Europe.

On December 18, 1950, the NATO Council agreed to a strategy of forward defense, which meant holding West Germany. This affected American, British, and French planning and force requirements. Particularly after the Communist takeover in Czechoslovakia in 1948, which considerably extended the frontier between Communism and West Germany, the linear defense of the latter was a formidable and costly task across a broad front. NATO, conversely, did not cover European colonies, and despite French arguments, the exclusion extended to Algeria, which legally was part of metropolitan France.

A clear front line was also in place across Europe as a whole. The Communists had been defeated in Greece in 1946–1949, and thanks to its anti-Communism, Franco's Spain, a Fascist dictatorship, was brought into the Western alliance.

In 1953, the United States and Spain signed an agreement giving the Americans rights to establish air bases, although Spain did not join NATO until 1983, by which time it was a democracy. Behind the front line, the Americans encouraged political, economic, and cultural measures across Western Europe to limit support for Communism and saw this as a crucial aspect of defense. The period of the Korean War was an important one for the consolidation of NATO, one in which positive NATO policies combined with aggressive Soviet ones.

Cold War confrontation shaped the politics of Europe. The threat of Soviet attack in Europe while the Americans were committed in Korea led, from 1950, to American pressure for West German rearmament. West Germany was finally admitted to NATO in 1955, laying the basis for West German rearmament within an alliance system, a rearmament that was seen as necessary to provide the forces required to defend Western Europe, not least because of the heavy imperial commitments of Britain and France in protecting their empires. This rearmament was a key step in West Germany's integration into the Western alliance, although that integration did not extend to supporting the acquisition of nuclear arms. West German accession to NATO, in turn, created a new political requirement for the alliance, that of a forward defense designed to protect all of West Germany from any Soviet offensive.

The rival Soviet-dominated Warsaw Pact, based on the Warsaw Treaty of Friendship, Cooperation, and Mutual Assistance, was formed 10 days after West Germany joined NATO, and the inclusion of the East German National People's Army in the Warsaw Pact forces sealed the international division of Germany. Soviet fears of NATO were a mirror image of Western fears of the Soviet Union. Each side's fears were encouraged by intelligence reports suggesting the aggressive intentions of the other.

MISSILE RACE

The United States and the Soviet Union built up their nuclear arsenals such that the Cuban crisis of 1962 focused on the deployment of nuclear missiles, in this case Soviet ones in Cuba. Nuclear weaponry played a role in planning how best to respond to attack. To counter the Soviet superiority in ground forces, the United States put the emphasis on strategic airpower, initially with aircraft armed with atom bombs. The B-52 heavy bombers deployed from 1955 gave the United States an advantage in strategic airpower, providing substance to President Dwight Eisenhower's policy of massive retaliation and explaining why the air force received close to half of the American defense budget in the late 1950s.

Alongside the development of strategic nuclear weaponry, there was a commitment to tactical nuclear weaponry. Assuming that the best form of defense was attack, the Soviets planned to use tactical nuclear weapons to maintain the pace of their assault. American tactical nuclear weapons were treated as a form of field artillery. In 1957, the situation changed when the Soviet Union launched

Sputnik I, the first satellite, into orbit, revealing a capability for intercontinental rockets that brought the entire world within striking range. The advantage the United States appeared to have in strategic airpower as a result of the deployment of B-52 heavy bombers in 1955 now seemed countered. In May 1957, Charles Bohlen, who had been ambassador to Moscow, told the Senate Foreign Relations Committee that "the Soviet rulers have become very acutely aware of what is involved in nuclear warfare, and I think they would have to have a very high margin of certain victory before they would be disposed consciously and as a matter of cold policy to unleash a nuclear war." On January 18, 1960, Allen Dulles, the director of the CIA, told the Senate Foreign Relations Committee that "one of the key factors behind Soviet diplomacy lies in their view of their increasing power in the military field, particularly missiles."

Meanwhile, the American army and air force (somewhat separately) had been developing long-range ballistic missiles since World War II using captured German V-2 scientists. In 1958, the Americans fired their first intercontinental ballistic missile. As a result, the "missile gap" much discussed in the United States in 1959–1960 reflected more on domestic American politics than on the true situation. Indeed, John F. Kennedy fought the 1960 presidential election in part on the platform of a more vigorous prosecution of the Cold War. Expenditure on missiles increased both before and after the election. In response to the enhanced Soviet capability, the United States developed an effective retaliatory second-strike capability to make it dangerous to risk attack on the United States. The availability of submarines equipped with ballistic missiles was important to this capability. In July 1960, the submarine USS *George Washington* was responsible for the first successful underwater firing of a Polaris missile. The American navy argued that its submarines could launch carefully controlled strikes. By 1962, the United States had a nuclear stockpile of over 27,000 weapons.

READING LIST

Ian Beckett, *Modern Insurgencies and Counter-Insurgencies*, London, Routledge, 2001.
Anthony Clayton, *The Wars of French Decolonisation*, Harlow, Longman, 1994.
Jonathan Haslam, *Russia's Cold War: From the October Revolution to the Fall of the Wall*, New Haven, Conn., Yale University Press, 2011.
Alan Millett, *The War for Korea, 1950–1951: They Came From the North*, Lawrence, University Press of Kansas, 2010.

SIX

THE COLD WAR: THE MIDDLE
YEARS, 1960–1975

Fidel Castro and Nikita Krushchev surrounded by police officers and journalists during
the annual meeting of the U.N. General Assembly, September 1960.

These years were dominated in military history by the confrontation of the Cold War, but conflict in the shape of the Vietnam War dominates attention. It was both important in its own right, notably for the powers directly engaged, and significant in that it became a touchstone in subsequent debate over power projection and military capability.

THE CUBAN MISSILE CRISIS

Prior to American intervention in the Vietnam War, tension between the United States and the Communist bloc had risen to a new height during the presidency of John F. Kennedy (1961–1963). In part, this was a matter of Soviet pressure on Western interests, which became more frequent under Nikita Khrushchev (who dominated Soviet power from 1957 to 1964) in the early 1960s. This pressure reflected in part his misplaced determination, while preserving peace, to gain success by pushing the West. Tensions rose.

The building of the Berlin Wall from August 11, 1961, provided an apt symbol of the lack of freedom that the Communist government gave rise to, but was also a breach of the agreements among the Soviet Union, the United States, Britain, and France over the status of Berlin. This challenge to the Western powers, which was part of a Soviet plan for the signing of a peace treaty with East Germany designed to end Allied rights in Berlin, indicated the extent to which Eastern bloc "stabilization" of interests was destabilizing at the international level. The crisis escalated when the Soviet Union resumed nuclear testing on September 1, 1961, and, secretly, with Soviet preparations for a military exercise designed to counter any Western response over Berlin.

In any event, there was no war, and the Soviet Union backed away from the idea of a German peace treaty. Khrushchev's caution may have reflected his concern about the American response and thus been an instance of deterrence working, but the extent to which his bitter dispute with Mao Zedong came into the open in March 1960 may also have been a factor. The Cold War rarely involved developments only on one front, but the consequences of broader interactions were, and are, frequently difficult to gauge. Away from the tense front line in Europe, there was more widespread volatility.

On January 6, 1961, while stating that "wars of liberation" against Western colonial control must not become wars between states, Khrushchev praised the former. The Soviets actively sought to strengthen their position in the Third World. Thus, in 1961–1962, the Soviet Union pursued plans for a naval base in Egypt, sought to profit from the civil war in the Congo (Zaire), and decided to help Fidel Castro counter American pressure, including the use of covert force.

Initially, Kennedy badly mishandled the situation by backing an invasion of Cuba in April 1961 by 1,300 CIA-trained anti-Communist exiles and then refusing to provide the necessary air support. The total failure of this poorly planned invasion in the face of stiff opposition at the Bay of Pigs on April 17, 1961, was followed by the authorization of Operation Mongoose, which involved covert operations including sabotage. The Americans feared that Cuba would serve as the base for subversion across Latin America, which was more accurate as an account of the intentions of Castro's ally, Che Guevara, than of the realities on the ground there. Che's attempt to launch a revolution in Bolivia in 1967 failed totally.

Khrushchev believed reports that an American invasion in Cuba was imminent in 1962. Indeed, it is possible that some such action was intended, not least to help produce a show of force before the American midterm elections. Khrushchev decided to send nuclear missiles to Cuba. The plans entailed secretly dispatching 230,000 tons of *matériel* and sending 42,000 military personnel, but secrecy was lost because of American aerial surveillance, and on September 4, the Americans warned the Soviets against deploying any significant offensive capability in Cuba. Far from dropping his plans, Khrushchev continued. He planned to install strategic missiles that brought Washington within range, as well as tactical nuclear weapons, and he hoped that these missiles would not only protect Cuba but also strengthen the overall Soviet position. The latter was at issue not only as far as the West was concerned but also with regard to China, which had criticized Khrushchev for failing to stand up to the West.

On October 14, 1962, as an instance of the significance of intelligence in the Cold War, a U-2 spy plane obtained proof that medium-range nuclear missile sites were under construction in Cuba. This was a breach of Khrushchev's

U-2 reconnaissance photo identifying Soviet nuclear missiles in Cuba.

assurance that he would not send offensive or nuclear weapons there. American decision makers agreed on the need for a response to get the missiles out, but were divided as to how best to do so, not least over whether to launch a preemptive military strike. This policy was advocated by General Curtis LeMay, the bellicose air force chief of staff, who in 1944–1945 had taken a leading role in the strategic air offensive against Japan. Kennedy determined on a blockade of Cuba designed to stop the shipment of missiles. He was understandably concerned that an actual attack on Cuba might not be completely successful and would lead to a damaging Soviet reaction from Cuba or elsewhere, such as an attack on Berlin.

Tension meanwhile rose when, in response to an Indian attempt to seize a border area, China launched an offensive on October 20, 1962, defeating and driving the Indians back. This defeat led to the supply of American weaponry and airlift support to India. The Soviet Union, in contrast, refused to back India. Having revealed that the Indians would be unable to defend the frontier province of Assam, the Chinese declared a unilateral cease-fire on November 21 and withdrew their troops.

On October 22, 1962, Kennedy addressed the American people and proclaimed the blockade, using the argument that 1930s appeasement must not be repeated. He also made clear that Cuba could prove the trigger for Armageddon because any nuclear attack from Cuba would be seen as requiring a full-scale nuclear attack on the Soviet Union. The threat led to military preparations by both sides. Khrushchev threatened "catastrophic consequences" if the American blockade took effect but turned down the idea of ordering a Soviet blockade around Berlin. On October 24 at 10 AM, the blockade took effect, and instead of pressing on, the Soviet ships stopped. Having decided not to escalate the crisis, Khrushchev sought to settle the matter so as to protect Cuba from invasion. In return for such an assurance, he was willing not only not to test the blockade but also to dismantle the missile sites on Cuba. In contrast, the Cuban leaders, Castro and Guevara, wanted a nuclear war, which they saw as a way to forward world socialism.

On the American side, there was continued interest in an invasion of Cuba, not least because Soviet approaches were inconsistent and included the demand that any withdrawal of missiles from Cuba be matched by that of American missiles from Turkey. Kennedy, however, urged caution, not least when a Soviet ground-to-air missile brought down a U-2 over Cuba, killing the pilot. Concerned about the risk that Cuba would lead to war, either by an American invasion or because of Castro's irresponsible belligerence, Khrushchev agreed to remove the offensive arms in return for a promise not to invade. Kennedy's secret concession over the missiles in Turkey did not sway Khrushchev. Despite Castro blocking on-site inspections, the blockade ended on November 20, and the nuclear weapons were removed by the Soviets.

The crisis had revealed the importance of restraint by the leaders, Kennedy and Khrushchev, but also suggested the risk that conflict could have resulted from unforeseen circumstances, notably clashes between armed units. Failures to obey orders, either because of breakdowns in communications or as a result of deliberate action, were a contributory risk. The problems of maintaining communications with nuclear-armed submarines posed a particular difficulty during the crisis.

Kennedy came out of the crisis with his reputation enhanced. Khrushchev, in contrast, was compromised, being perceived as erratic by his Politburo colleagues. In addition, the deal between the two powers was criticized by Castro and Mao, who saw it as a "Soviet Munich." This response helped explain the difficulties the Americans encountered later in the decade: whereas American–Soviet relations were eased by the restraint Khrushchev learned, the Americans proved mistaken in their conviction that they could use similar pressure to force other Communist powers to back down. Indeed, Ho Chi Minh, the North Vietnamese leader, was not to do so. Thus, the Cuba crisis was followed by stability in Europe, but not elsewhere.

Khrushchev tried to build up the Cuban settlement to reach a broader agreement with the United States, suggesting talks on arms limitations and disarmament, but all that was achieved was the 1963 nuclear test-ban treaty. This (relative) failure compromised Khrushchev's position, as did the absence of progress in attempts that year to settle the dispute with China and the disappointing grain harvest that obliged the Soviet Union to import grain from the West. When Khrushchev was removed from office by the Central Committee on October 14, 1964, accused of risking war over Berlin and Cuba, collective leadership took power, but the main figure, until his death in 1982, was Leonid Brezhnev. The first general secretary of the Communist Party, Brezhnev was determined to avoid war, in part because of his own experience of World War II.

VIETNAM

Alongside a determination to show that America was robust militarily and able to resist any Soviet attack, the American government was determined to resist the Communist advance in the Third World. Although nationalism was crucial to anticolonial "liberation struggles," the struggles were also characterized by Communist exploitation as the Soviet Union and China sought to challenge the United States indirectly by encouraging supporters to attack U.S. allies. These attacks brought together notions of popular warfare, nationalism, and revolutionary Communism in a program of revolutionary struggle in which success was believed to be inevitable.

Conversely, Western governments feared that Third World anticolonial movements and nationalism would be exploited by the Communist powers, and this fear encouraged a view that the West's front line ran round the world and that Communism had to be contained. In March 1955, John Foster Dulles, the American secretary of state from 1953 to 1959 and a keen anti-Communist, told the Senate Foreign Relations Committee that in Southeast Asia he regarded "the subversive problem . . . [as] . . . a greater menace than the open military menace of the activities of the Communists."[1] The United States was determined to keep the front line not only away from the Western hemisphere, but also as close to the Communist bloc as possible.

This policy brought the Americans to Vietnam, which had been partitioned as part of the withdrawal of the French in 1954. The Communist Viet Minh were left in control of North Vietnam, and an American-supported government was established in South Vietnam, where, from 1957, it faced a Communist rebellion by the Viet Cong that resulted in more overt and widespread American intervention. The South Vietnamese government, led from 1954 to 1963 by Ngo Dinh Diem, was corrupt and unpopular. It had won the 1956 election using fraud, and it represented best the landowning elite that composed it. The Catholic identity of the regime further compromised its popularity in what was a largely Buddhist country. The Viet Cong offered an attractive program of socioeconomic transformation, including land reform, and won considerable support, providing a basis for military action.

From 1959, forces from North Vietnam were infiltrated into South Vietnam in support of the Viet Cong. The Americans were concerned that a failure to support South Vietnam would lead to the further spread of Communism in Southeast Asia. In response, the commitment of American "advisers" to South Vietnam, including the foundation in February 1962 of Military Assistance Command, Vietnam, encouraged pressure for increased support as the Americans, although not the colonial power, in effect increasingly adopted the role of the French. By 1963, when Diem was assassinated by the military with American connivance, there were 16,000 American advisers. American intervention helped limit Viet Cong advances in 1962, but the combination of the lack of fighting quality of much of the South Vietnamese army (which grew in size from 150,000 men in 1960 to 250,000 in 1964) and flawed advice from the Americans, in particular an emphasis on firepower (as had been used in Korea), failed to win victory.

Meanwhile, invalidating notions supported by France in particular that conflict in, and over, South Vietnam could have been neutralized through negotiation, the North Vietnamese were determined to maintain the struggle. Meeting in December 1963, the ninth plenary session of their Communist Party's Central Committee criticized the Soviet notion of "peaceful existence" with non-Communist powers, decided to step up the war in South Vietnam, and pushed forward more militant politicians.

An attack on the USS *Maddox* by the North Vietnamese in the Gulf of Tonkin off Vietnam on August 2, 1964, followed by an alleged attack on August 4, both provoked by American support for South Vietnamese commando raids, led Congress to pass a resolution permitting President Johnson "to take all necessary measures to repel any armed attack against the forces of the United States and to

---

[1]*Executive Sessions of the Senate Foreign Relations Committee*, vol. 7, 1955 (Washington, D.C., U.S. Government Printing Office, 1978), p. 390.

prevent further aggression," in short to wage war without proclaiming it. This was the preferred American option because Johnson wanted to avoid an explicit choice between war and disengagement and to apply more easily the strategic concept of graduated pressure, which appeared to offer a low-risk means to success. Already, under Kennedy, the abandonment of Eisenhower's policy of massive retaliation, with its emphasis on nuclear warfare, and the switch instead to a policy of flexible response encouraged a commitment to Vietnam as a way to fight and win a nonnuclear conflict.

In a general sense, the credibility and means of American power seemed at issue in Vietnam by 1964, notably to Johnson who, as he put it in July 1965, did not want to "be the architect of surrender." There was a belief in Washington that the line against further Communist expansion had to be drawn somewhere, and that this was it; this policy differed from France's retention of empire against Communist-led nationalism, but similarly focused on Vietnam.

The Americans were concerned about the impact of developments in South Vietnam for those elsewhere in Southeast Asia, especially Laos, where Communist moves greatly concerned its neighbor, Thailand, and where Kennedy had sought to oppose Communist expansion. The Americans were also concerned about the more general implications of developments in Southeast Asia for the situation throughout South Asia and the West Pacific. Thus, the Vietnam struggle could be put alongside China's successful 1962 war with India and also Indonesian attacks on Malaysia (from 1963, Sukarno, the president of Indonesia, was close to China) to indicate a widespread threat as part of a crisis that America could respond to, and affect, by acting in South Vietnam. The United States provided India with arms in 1962. The power in the United States of the "China Lobby," that is, the supporters of Taiwan, was also significant in encouraging an active military stance in South Vietnam.

Whereas the Soviet Union appeared to threaten expansionism in Europe, Communist expansionism actually seemed to be in progress in East Asia. These anxieties conflated American concern about the ideological challenge from Communism with the longstanding instability of the region that looked back to the 1890s. The domino theory of incremental Communist advance, a concept that enjoyed powerful traction, not least because it could be readily explained in public, appeared to require a vigorous containment in South Vietnam.

At the same time, the easing of the issues that had brought the United States and the Soviet Union close to war over Berlin and Cuba in 1961–1962 provided an opportunity for the Americans to focus on South Vietnam. This was not the priority Johnson had sought, but it came to dominate his administration (1963–1969), and with toxic effects. Johnson would have preferred to concentrate on his Great Society reform program at home, but he believed it necessary to display firmness over Vietnam to show determination, both to the American people and to the rest of the world. The personal dimension was important to Johnson, but so was his conviction that America had a worthwhile purpose in the world and must heed its calling. To Johnson, this global mission was linked to his policies at home.

In late 1964, regular units of the North Vietnamese army were sent south in strength, and by 1965, the South Vietnamese army was on the verge of collapse. The American response was encouraged by Johnson's wish to appear tough on Communism and thus thwart criticism by the Republican presidential candidate in 1964, Barry Goldwater, whom he defeated with a landslide win. Similarly, in 1960, Kennedy had exploited the idea of a "missile gap" with the Soviet Union to appear tougher than his Republican rival, Richard Nixon.

By the end of 1964, American forces in South Vietnam had reached 23,000; the number shot up to 181,000 in 1965, with the first combat battalions landing on March 8, to 385,000 in 1966, and to a peak at 541,000 in January 1969. Aside from the important contribution by the South Vietnamese, massive American involvement was supplemented by troops from South Korea, the second largest international contingent with 48,000 troops, and from Australia, New Zealand, Thailand, and the Philippines. The South Koreans were largely paid for by the United States, which regarded them as good troops who cost less than Americans. Although the war effort was less international than the Americans had wished and than had been the case in the Korean War, with Harold Wilson, the prime minister of Britain, preferring to get involved as a would-be (and unsuccessful) negotiator rather than as a combatant, the effort reflected a widespread concern about the strategic position in Southeast Asia and the Communist advance, as well as a need to support the United States. Thus, Australia, which kept troops in Vietnam until 1972, was anxious to secure American support in the event of confrontation with Indonesia, although the risk of that was lessened after President Sukarno lost power in 1966 to Indonesian generals, notably Hadji Suharto, encouraged by the CIA.

In North Vietnam, the Communists were well led and organized, and their political system and culture enabled them to mobilize and direct resources and to maintain a persistent effort. American involvement permitted the North to promote the war as a national crusade against Western imperialism. Military struggle and political indoctrination were seen to act in symbiosis, and the North Vietnamese and Viet Cong were more willing to suffer losses than the Americans. Limited War theory was (and is) a Western concept that was not shared by the Vietnamese, and American strategy was wrongly based on the assumption that unacceptable losses could be inflicted on the North Vietnamese in the way that they could be on the Americans. A similar contrast was later to be seen with first Soviet and then American operations in Afghanistan.

In the face of North Vietnamese and Viet Cong determination, morale, and intolerance of all dissent, the Americans cracked first, after attrition had led to military and political stalemate. Looked at differently, the Americans came to appreciate the consequences of limited war, that it could lead to failure, and they did so rapidly once their initial hopes for success had been thwarted. Subsequent debate as to whether total war, which with the technology of the period would have encompassed nuclear weapons, as was considered in 1965–1966, would have led to American victory can only go so far because the intention was not to fight such a war.

The Americans, moreover, did not have the possibility of a radical change in North Vietnamese policy comparable to that in Indonesia, after the failed coup there in October 1965 that was blamed on the Communists led the army to slaughter the Communists as well as to gain effective power by the following March. This outcome permitted in August 1966 a settlement of the confrontation that had begun in 1963, a border struggle between Indonesia and Malaysia, the latter of which was supported by Britain and other Commonwealth states. This settlement was not the result of British military operations; indeed, it had proved difficult to turn successes in the field into political outcomes.

The international political context had a more direct impact on American grand strategy in the Vietnam War. Concern that China might intervene, as in the Korean War in 1950, discouraged any American invasion of North Vietnam and thus dramatically reduced the options available to the Americans. It can be debated whether the risk was exaggerated, but Chinese intervention in Korea encouraged caution, as did the volatility of China under Mao Zedong during the radical politicization of the "Cultural Revolution," which began in 1966 and remained acute until the army restored order from 1968, reflecting a pattern that was common with revolutionaries. The Chinese anyway provided North Vietnam with large quantities of *matériel* and substantial numbers (eventually 320,000 men) of support troops, while the Soviet Union, competing for influence, also provided aid. Soviet-supplied SAM surface-to-air missiles were particularly important in increasing the cost of using American airpower.

Despite an initial thaw after Khrushchev's fall in 1964, Sino-Soviet relations, which had markedly deteriorated at the end of the 1950s and the start of the 1960s, remained poor, with serious ideological and geopolitical tensions at play. The Chinese, who saw themselves as the more rigorous Communists, were particularly intransigent toward efforts to negotiate an agreement over Vietnam, notably in May 1965, when the Soviets were initially more accommodating. Similarly, in 1967–1971, the Chinese pressed the North Vietnamese not to accept a compromise solution suggested by the "revisionist" Soviets. Thus, the Vietnam War served China and the Soviet Union as an opportunity to pursue their rivalry alongside their goal of weakening the United States.

The role of the Communist great powers in the Vietnam War led American policy makers to conclude that it was necessary to demonstrate that these powers could not succeed by means of such a proxy war. Thus, Vietnam became the place to show that America could, and would, act, and because it was this place, it became the place where America must act. This issue took precedence over the political possibilities for an acceptable settlement in Vietnam because, in practice, the Americans were committed to an unpopular, corrupt, and unimpressive government. Moreover, the quest to demonstrate the credibility of American power helped lead to a failure to understand the military situation in Vietnam. Looked at more harshly, there was an unwillingness on the part of Johnson and his advisers to admit that they might be wrong.

Despite a major commitment of force, the Americans failed, as so many militaries did when engaged in counterinsurgency operations, to translate output into outcome because Viet Cong and North Vietnamese morale was sustained despite heavy casualties. This morale, which owed much to coercion and indoctrination, extended throughout the army: the soldiers who built the Ho Chi Minh Trail, down which supplies moved from North Vietnam to Communist forces in the South, were inferior troops in military terms, but they believed that they could attain status by doing these menial tasks. They were also taught to believe that if they died—as most did—their descendants would be rewarded, for instance, in the distribution of land. In contrast, American morale suffered once success proved elusive, and as a result, serious drug use and indiscipline grew, affecting unit cohesion and operations.

When the Americans intervened in force in 1965, their opponents were already operating in sizeable units, which led, in 1965–1968, to battles that were won by the Americans. Initially, the Americans focused on defending coastal areas that were the centers of South Vietnamese population and power and the areas of American deployment, but having prevented South Vietnam from being defeated in 1965, they then moved into the interior, aiming to force battle on the Viet Cong. The Americans were able to advance into parts of South Vietnam, which had been outside the control of Saigon, and to inflict serious blows on the Viet Cong in the Mekong Delta. In addition, direct mass Viet Cong attacks on American positions were generally repulsed with heavy casualties, such as at the siege of Plei Me in the Central Highlands in 1965. Under General William Westmoreland, commander of the U.S. Military Assistance Command, Vietnam, the Americans sought to attack throughout South Vietnam, establishing bases from which operations would be mounted to inflict casualties on their opponents and wear down their strength. Helicopters played a major role in this extension of activity, particularly with the use of the new 1st Cavalry Division (Airmobile).

Yet, the activity only brought so much advantage, in part because the situation was very different from that during the Korean War, which provided the Americans with an inappropriate model of how best to fight Communist forces in Asia. Although heavy casualties were inflicted, opposing numbers increased as North Vietnam responded to the American buildup by sending troops down the Ho Chi Minh Trail, thus vitiating American attempts to win by escalation and instead consigning them to stalemate. The Americans had to mass troops to prevent them from being overwhelmed by Viet Cong and North Vietnamese attacks, but there was no concentration of opposing power that could be rapidly fixed and readily destroyed by them as the Israelis were to do, in very different circumstances, against Egypt, Jordan, and Syria in 1967 and the Indians against the Pakistanis in 1965 and 1971. American advances concealed the extent to which they shared the initiative with their opponents, and the need to devote so much strength to building up forces, logistics, and security limited American combat

U.S. helicopters arriving to airlift South Vietnamese soldiers into battle against the Viet Cong, 1965.

strength, a problem faced in other counterinsurgency struggles. By the end of 1967, the situation nevertheless appeared promising, and Westmoreland felt that he was winning. With the Viet Cong's momentum stopped, there appeared to be an opportunity for pacification. Under the aegis of Civil Operations and Revolutionary Development Support, the Americans sought to win popular backing for the South Vietnamese government, a version of nation building.

However, the Tet offensive of 1968, which involved large-scale Viet Cong and North Vietnamese attacks on cities and military bases across South Vietnam, indicated the resilience of the opposition and also, however misleadingly, contributed greatly to a sense of crisis in the American world order, a crisis that suggested that the United States was losing the Cold War. The North Vietnamese and Viet Cong attacks, mounted under cover of the Lunar New Year celebrations of Tet, were launched in the belief that they would engender a popular uprising against the South Vietnamese government, but, as an instance of the degree to which all sides could misjudge a situation, none followed. Instead, the assaults were beaten off with heavy losses, hitting Viet Cong morale.

The United States benefited from a pre-Tet decision to move some combat units back from near the North Vietnamese border, where they had been concentrated. This decision, made on January 10, 1968, was in response to indications that Viet Cong and North Vietnamese forces were being built up near the cities. However, the Americans failed to anticipate the timing and, more particularly, the scale and character of the attack: overoptimistic assumptions about enemy casualties in the border battles of late 1967 were matched by an inability to believe that a full-scale attack on the cities would be mounted.

About 85,000 Viet Cong and North Vietnamese forces attacked from January 30, 1968, with 36 of the 44 provincial capitals and 5 of the 6 autonomous cities among the targets. Assaults also on 23 airfields were one testimony to the role of American airpower. More than two divisions were used for the attacks in and close to Saigon, but these attacks were largely contained and overcome within several days. The most serious and longest battle was waged for control of the city of Hué, the former imperial capital, which was close to North Vietnam; much of the city fell to the Viet Cong on January 31. The city was not regained until February 25, after both difficult house-to-house struggles within its walls and an eventually successful cutting off of supply routes into the city. The Americans lost 216 dead, the South Vietnamese forces 384 dead, and their opponents over 5,000. Part of the nature of the conflict, as well as its brutality, was shown by the slaughter, or "disappearance," of about 5,000 South Vietnamese civilians by the Viet Cong during their occupation: their crime was that they came from social categories judged unacceptable in the Maoist society the Communists were trying to create. The massive use of American air and artillery power during the recapture of Hué destroyed about half of the city, making over 100,000 people homeless. This was an instance of the wider devastation brought by American power to those it was trying to protect, a process that greatly compromised support for the South Vietnamese government and for the Americans and that was to be seen on other occasions, notably in Iraq and Afghanistan in the 2000s.

By the end of February 1968, it was clear that the North Vietnamese/Viet Cong offensive had failed to achieve its goals. There was no popular uprising in South Vietnam, and the Americans and South Vietnamese had not been defeated, although their losses were heavier than in earlier battles. However, although the Americans could repel mass attacks on their strong points and could drop thousands of bombs from a great height, their will for the war was worn down by its continuation, and they could not deny control of the countryside to their opponents. This point about the limitation of conventional forces in counterinsurgency struggles in support of weak foreign allies was more generally true: there was no American exceptionalism in this case. Thus, the Egyptian intervention from 1962 to 1967 in a civil war in North Yemen, on behalf of a radical republic resisting tribal insurgents supported by neighboring Saudi Arabia, became a costly and embarrassing commitment that weakened Egypt internationally.

General Vo Nguyen Giap, the North Vietnamese commander, was an effective leader who developed logistical capability to give effect to his strategy of denying his opponents (first France and then South Vietnam and the United States) control over territory while maintaining operational pressure on them. Giap was less successful when he turned to positional warfare and to mass attacks against opposing forces in reasonable defensive positions, as in 1951 against the French and in 1968 and 1972 against the South Vietnamese and Americans, but his military strategy and, crucially, the political determination of the North Vietnamese government did not depend on continual success.

The jungle nature of the Vietnamese terrain limited the options for American airpower, which was applied for strategic, operational, and tactical goals and, in the last case, played an important role in helping army and marine units under attack, as at Khe Sanh in 1968, complementing artillery support in this valuable role. Over half of the $200 billion the United States spent on the war, a sum far greater than that expended by other Western powers on decolonization struggles, went to air operations, and nearly 8 million tons of bombs were dropped on Vietnam, Laos, and Cambodia; South Vietnam, indeed, became the most heavily bombed country in the history of warfare. There were also major American bombing offensives against North Vietnam, which were designed both to limit Northern support for the war in the South and to affect policy in the North by driving the North Vietnamese to negotiate. These attacks faced serious opposition from SAM-7 Soviet surface-to-air missiles, supplied from April 1965, as well as from Soviet MIG-17 and MIG-21 aircraft. American use of electronic jamming to limit attacks by missiles and radar-controlled guns had considerable success, but the North Vietnamese learned in part to counter this by aiming at the jamming signals. Prisoners taken from American planes that were shot down gave the North Vietnamese a valuable negotiating card that they could also use in their struggle to influence American domestic opinion.

As an instance of the difficulty of assessing military history, controversy continues over the extent to which, among other options, a more determined (and less reluctant and restricted) and persistent air campaign would have ensured American victory. American policy makers, seeking to contain the struggle, were reluctant to use an all-out nonnuclear air attack with unrestricted targeting and were influenced instead by the idea that, by means of gradual escalation, they could send appropriate messages and affect their opponents' decisions, a view that was not vindicated by the Vietnam War. Indeed, the impact of air power was questioned. Writing to an American correspondent in July 1965, the British military theorist J. F. C. Fuller argued, "Today your government and its military advisors appear to have accepted the concept that the way to defeat Communism in Vietnam is by bombing when clearly the precepts garnered from World War II should have told them that ideas cannot be dislodged by bombs."[2]

Conversely, the proponents of airpower claim that had Operation Rolling Thunder (the unrestricted bombing of the North) continued, instead of ending in 1968, it would have led the North to yield, but it had certainly not stopped the Tet offensive. A drive west of the Demilitarized Zone to cut the Ho Chi Minh Trail, a policy rejected during the war, has also been hotly debated subsequently, as has a "northern" hook landing (similar to Inchon in the Korean War in 1950) around the port of Vinh and west into the entrances to the Trail.

---

[2]London, King's College, Liddell Hart Archive, Fuller Papers 4/6/24/2.

A U.S. Air Force A-1E Skyraider bombs a Viet Cong hideout near Cantho, South Vietnam, 1967.

Airpower also played a major role in the unsuccessful attempt to block Viet Cong supply routes, as well as the more successful endeavor to provide tactical and supply support for American troops on the ground. Tactical support led to the use of slow-flying gunships able to apply massive firepower, although the Viet Cong were proficient in entrenching to minimize their losses. Helicopters were extensively used, not least in supplying positions and in applying the doctrine of air mobility: airlifted troops brought mobility and helped take the war to the enemy. As an instance of the scale of conflict, the Americans flew about 36,125,000 helicopter sorties during the war, including 7,547,000 assault sorties, in which machine guns and rockets were used, as well as 3,932,000 attack sorties. More than 2,000 helicopters were lost to hostile causes (and many others to accidents), but heavier losses had been anticipated. Helicopters had become more reliable, more powerful, and faster than in the 1950s, and their use helped to overcome guerrilla challenges to land supply and communication routes.

The Americans had to adapt to fight in a variety of unfamiliar terrains in Vietnam, including dense jungle and rice paddies. The jungle nature of much of the terrain gave the Viet Cong ideal cover and ensured that superior American technology had little to aim at. Partly as a result, both Westmoreland's quest for battle, in which American firepower could be applied to ensure successful attrition, and the search-and-destroy operations, pursued until 1968 to build up a "body count" of dead Viet Cong, were each of limited effectiveness, not least because it was difficult to "fix" the Viet Cong. The Americans lacked adequate intelligence of their opponents' moves, and instead, the Viet Cong tended to control the tempo of much of the fighting, mounting ambushes that caused heavy casualties and then ambushing relief units in their turn. Discussing the difficulties of defeating guerrillas by conventional means, Allen Dulles, the director of the CIA, had explained to the Senate Foreign Relations Committee in 1959 that in Cuba "what you need against guerillas are guerillas . . . It is rough country, and there is no use sending tanks and heavy artillery up there."[3]

As with the air offensive against supply lines, the Americans displayed a preference for seeing the Viet Cong as a regular force that could be beaten by conventional means, rather than developing an understanding of their doctrine and operational methods. Furthermore, the creation of a political organization by the Viet Cong ensured that more than the defeat of the guerrillas was required. The American army, however, lacking a reliable political base in South Vietnam, preferred to seek a military solution and to emphasize big-unit operations over pacification, but without the latter its operations were of limited value and instead alienated civilian support. Prefiguring the difficulties Israel was to encounter when confronting Palestinian opposition in the *Intifidah* (shaking off) from 1987, many Americans found it difficult to try to understand the nature of the war they were engaged in and to appreciate the extent to which their opponents, by refusing to fight on American terms, nullified American advantages and thus multiplied the difficulties that the terrain posed for the Americans. The Americans failed to grasp that although they had more firepower and mobility than the French had had in Vietnam in 1946–1954 and were not the colonial power, they were still faced with the same problems of Communist determination; even if it was achieved, victory in battle would not change this. Westmoreland responded to problems by asking for even more troops.

Domestic financial and economic problems, as well as political opposition and his own disillusionment at continued signs of North Vietnamese vitality, led Johnson, his views confirmed by a policy review by a group of senior outside advisers, the "Wise Men," to reject, in March 1968, Westmoreland's request for an additional 206,000 men in Vietnam. Instead, he authorized only 13,500 more troops. Military difficulties, combined with political pressures within the United States, resulted in an attempt to shift more of the burden back on the South Vietnamese army by improving its capability, and some success was achieved in this. Indeed, Vietnamese units had fought better in response to the Tet offensive than had been anticipated. Yet, the context was very different from the successful use of large

---

[3]*Executive Sessions of the Senate Foreign Relations Committee*, vol. 11, 1959 (Washington, D.C., U.S. Government Printing Office, 1982), p. 125.

numbers of native troops in European imperial forces earlier in the century, for example, the contribution by Indian troops to British hegemony in South Asia.

Creighton Abrams, who replaced Westmoreland as American commander (of Military Assistance Command, Vietnam) in June 1968, preferred to rely on small-scale patrols and ambushes, which, he argued, provided less of a target for his opponents than large-scale sweeps. Westmoreland had used conventional, operational tactics to fight an unconventional enemy. In contrast, Abrams put into practice a counterinsurgency doctrine that centered on protecting the population. At the same time, it is important to note that some recent scholarship has queried this conventional contrast between Westmoreland and Abrams and has argued instead that the former had a more subtle approach than one based largely on firepower. Indeed, it has been suggested that although both Westmoreland and Abrams believed in the use of American firepower to defeat Communist main force units, equally both men understood the need for the pacification of the countryside and building up the South Vietnamese military. In this account, Westmoreland had to employ tactics to confront an opposing field army that was backing a popular insurgency. Abrams appears to follow a different generalship, but in practice that was largely because of a switch in Viet Cong strategy after the Tet offensive toward guerrilla warfare.

As a further reminder that scholarly interpretations in part reflect present concerns, this debate over Vietnam in part reflected and reflects disagreements in the 2000s and 2010s over the possibilities of counterinsurgency warfare, specifically American policy in Iraq and Afghanistan. Some of the recent criticism of Westmoreland is linked to the idea that American success in Vietnam and elsewhere could have been/can be obtained by better leadership. Conversely, there is the view that the wars were unwinnable, in large part because of political circumstances, both in the United States and in the other country. Indeed, it may well have been the case that the political objectives were unattainable by military force, notably in light of the political parameters of the time. The difficulty of transforming foreign societies tends to be underplayed because belief in counterinsurgency encourages a sense that foreign intervention can work and that the military has a role accordingly. In the end, the view that hearts and minds could be won at gunpoint faces serious problems, notably if linked to nation building on the Western model.

An impressive commander and a veteran of the Battle of the Bulge (1944) and of Korea (1950–1953), Abrams set out to contest the village-level support the Viet Cong enjoyed and to counter the impact of the Tet offensive, which had led to a regrouping of American and South Vietnamese troops as units were pulled back to defend the cities. The Americans also tried to lure the Communists onto killing grounds by establishing "fire bases": positions supported by artillery and infantry. In 1969, the Americans inflicted serious blows on the Viet Cong, whose capability had already been badly compromised by the failure of Tet in which the Viet Cong and the North Vietnamese had lost close to half the troops used. Viet Cong attacks in 1969 suffered heavy casualties and achieved little.

American and South Vietnamese counterinsurgency policies worked in some parts of Vietnam, but they were generally unsuccessful, although, conversely, support for the Viet Cong should not be exaggerated. The pacification program entailed a "battle for hearts and minds" involving American-backed economic and political reforms, but these were difficult to implement, not only because of Viet Cong opposition and intimidation and the effectiveness of their guerrilla and small-unit operations, but also because the South Vietnamese government, prefiguring its Afghan counterpart in the 2000s and 2010s, was half-hearted, corrupt, and weak and thus unable to take advantage of military success. The Americans could not find or create a popular alternative to the Viet Cong, a problem that was also to face them in the 2000s–2010s, in part in Iraq and even more so in Afghanistan. As the Americans also brought much disruption to South Vietnam, including high inflation and devastation through the use of firepower, pacification faced additional problems, and the culture clash between the Americans and their South Vietnamese allies hindered cooperation, again prefiguring the situation in Afghanistan.

Conversely, the Communists came to rely in the 1970s more heavily on conventional operations mounted by the North Vietnamese. This was a consequence not only of the casualties and damage that Tet had inflicted on the Viet Cong, but also of the failure of Rolling Thunder, the American bombing of North Vietnam launched in March 1965 to destroy the war-supporting capability of North Vietnam, as well as the failure of the air offensives launched against the Ho Chi Minh Trail. The latter was crucial to North Vietnamese logistics, and the inability to cut it on the ground was a major limitation in American war making. On March 30, 1972, encouraged by increased Soviet military shipments inspired by a desire to limit Chinese influence, the North Vietnamese launched the Nguyen Hue campaign (to the Americans, the Easter Offensive). After initial success, this conventional invasion of South Vietnam was blocked by South Vietnamese defenders supported by American air attacks.

Meanwhile, in what was described as the "First Television War," domestic opposition in America to involvement in Vietnam had risen. This was because of the duration of the conflict, because the goals seemed ill-defined, and increasingly as an aspect of the countercultural movement of these years, notably from 1968, which proved particularly attractive to the young. The latter opposition has attracted most attention in retrospect, but it is important to remember also the wider-ranging basis of criticism of the war. With their leadership divided on policy, the Americans had lost the strategic initiative, but there was already a lack of deep commitment.

By denying the Americans victory in the field and instead continuing to inflict casualties, the North Vietnamese and Viet Cong helped to create political pressures within America and sap the will to fight, although their objectives were focused on success in South Vietnam: affecting American public opinion was only a side issue. In the United States, the absence of victory resulted in many seeing the continuing casualties as futile, especially when the Tet offensive in

Antiwar protesters in front of the White House, January 1968.

early 1968 led to questioning of optimistic Pentagon pronouncements about the course of the conflict. In contrast, North Vietnamese military strategy and the political determination of its government did not depend on popular support.

The conscription necessary to sustain a large-scale American presence in an increasingly unpopular war played a major role in the growth of disenchantment. A majority of the Americans who went to Vietnam were volunteers, not draftees, but in 1965–1973, about 2 million Americans were drafted, and draftees accounted for a third of American deaths in Vietnam by 1969. The draft led to a massive increase in antiwar sentiment. Opposition was widely voiced and "draft dodging" common, with many Americans taking refuge in Canada. The war was fought with soldiers who were, on average, younger and less educated than those who had taken part in World War II. The education exemption and family 9 (fatherhood) exempted many citizens from the draft, and the army was dispro-portionately made up of the poor.

Johnson abandoned his reelection bid on March 31, 1968, because he had failed to end the war and was facing a challenge from within the Democratic Party. Once elected, his successor, Richard Nixon, the Republican candidate who had promised peace with honor, pressed ahead with substituting Vietnamese for American troops so that he could bring the troops back home, end the draft, and reduce the political cost of the war while, he hoped, securing an acceptable out-come. Initially, the war was expanded with American and South Vietnamese invasion forces, respectively, attacking Communist bases in neighboring Cambodia and Laos. Nevertheless, already by the end of 1971 there were only 156,000 American troops in South Vietnam. The defeat of the North Vietnamese

Easter Offensive in 1972 provided the opportunity for a negotiated American withdrawal in 1973, although the South Vietnamese were left vulnerable and were ultimately overrun in April 1975 in the Ho Chi Minh campaign. Communist forces also prevailed that year in Cambodia and Laos.

THE EARLY 1970s

The early 1970s were pivotal to the Cold War, as well as for the international order that lasted until the 2000s. The early 1970s also appeared to demonstrate changes in military capability, in conflicts very different to those of World War II and the Korean War. The focus for military commentators was on America's failure in Vietnam, but there was a more general sense of military crisis for the West, notably with the collapse of Portugal's African empire in 1974–1975, and also with the ability of Soviet-supplied Egypt and Syria to mount a more dangerous opposition to Israel in the Yom Kippur War of 1973 than had been the case with the Six-Day War of 1967.

The impression was of the failure of an entire military system, that of the United States, which, despite its great resources, seemed unable to do better than the former European imperial powers. This interpretation, however, led too readily from the operational failures and difficulties of counter-insurrectionary warfare that were the case to assume a basic strategic weakness that was less clearly the case. Instead, the roots of the eventual American success in the Cold War owed something to strategic and other developments in this period.

American failure in Vietnam encouraged hostile forces elsewhere. In the Yom Kippur War in 1973, Egypt and Syria ultimately failed in their surprise attack launched on October 6, but the conflict was a serious blow to Israeli prestige and to the Israeli reputation for invulnerability, cemented in the Six-Day War in 1967. In a surprise assault, the Israeli Bar Lev line on the eastern bank of the Suez Canal was successfully stormed by the Egyptians and initial Israeli counterattacks failed. In a demonstration of the vulnerability of advanced technology, Israeli jets were shot down by relatively inexpensive Soviet heat-seeking missiles. The Egyptians were only defeated when they advanced beyond their missile cover into the Sinai Peninsula. In a striking illustration of the continuing difficulties of assessing relative capability, claims varied (and still vary) over the effectiveness of tanks and missiles in that conflict. The Israelis claimed that their tank losses were overwhelmingly to other tanks, whereas the Egyptians stressed the role of their missiles.

This conflict was very much located in the superpower confrontation of the Cold War. In response to the Soviet airlift of weaponry to the Egyptians, the United States rushed supplies to the Israelis by air during the war via their air base in the (Portuguese) Azores. As the conflict turned against the Egyptians, with the Israelis advancing west across the Suez Canal from the night of October 15–16, 1973, the Soviet Union faced the threat that the crisis would lead to pressure for intervention; to avoid this, the Soviets pressed the Americans for joint mediation. Talks in Moscow led to agreement for a UN Security Council Resolution for an immediate cease-fire followed by peace negotiations, but whereas Egypt agreed, Israel fought on to pursue its battlefield advantages as it had successfully done in 1949. Certain they had been cheated, the Soviet government on October 24 threatened unilateral action, which led the Americans the next morning to issue a DEFCON III alert, ordering military readiness just short of war. American pressure forced Israel to stop fighting. Like the Cuban Missile Crisis of 1962, this serious confrontation showed the capacity of Third World crises to cause superpower conflict.

The sense of Western weakness in the Third World was to be exacerbated by the collapse of the Portuguese empire in Africa: Angola, Mozambique, and Guinea-Bissau. Portugal faced a left-wing revolution in April 1974, a revolution that owed much to growing military and civilian opposition in Portugal to the war, an intractable struggle to which the Portuguese could not bring a military solution. The new government gave independence to the colonies the following year, and the consequences became a key instance of the southward move of the Cold War, one that provided the Communist powers with opportunities. Civil war in Angola saw Cuba and the Soviet Union back the MPLA, one of the two leading independence movements, which seized control of the government in 1975, while South Africa and, indirectly, the United States backed its rival, UNITA. The South African advance on the Angolan capital, Luanda, in 1975 was blocked by the Cubans and left in the lurch by the United States. The South Africans had to withdraw, but their support for UNITA continued.

In Europe, the rival blocs tried in 1975 to pursue coexistence and lessen tension through a process known by contemporaries as *détente*, which led to the Helsinki Agreements, a recognition of the existing situation; but Angola was scarcely *détente* in action. Instead, the Soviet Union successfully pursued a unilateral advantage in Angola and, more generally, in sub-Saharan Africa to counter what it saw as the one gained by the United States in the Middle East through negotiating easier relations between Egypt and Israel by means of the Camp David Accords of 1978. Confrontation in Africa and the Middle East suggested that, as far as the Soviet Union and the United States were concerned, *détente* was only a truce between rivals.

Détente, indeed, arose from the particular circumstances of the mid-1970s in Europe and also from the military stalemate in Europe that was the product of the nuclear standoff. The enhancement and deployment of intercontinental missiles meant that war was likely to lead to mutually assured destruction because both sides appeared to have a secure second-strike capability, so that however effective one power's first strike missile attack was, the other power would be able to hit back. Enhanced capability in rocketry, notably the deployment of multiple independently targetable reentry vehicles (MIRVs) from individual missiles, was matched by attempts to lessen the possibility of nuclear war, with parity in strength and the horrific prospects of any nuclear conflict encouraging *détente*.

The American-Soviet Anti–Ballistic Missile Treaty of 1972, the Strategic Arms Limitation Talks (SALT) I agreement, which Nixon, seeking reputation as a peacemaker and keen to contain the Soviets, felt able to conclude thanks to the MIRV program, limited the construction of defensive shields against missile attack. These shields were restricted to two anti–ballistic missile complexes, one around a concentration of intercontinental missiles and the other around the capital. By leaving the United States and the Soviet Union vulnerable, the treaty was designed to discourage a first strike because there would be no effective defense against a counterstrike. Thus, atomic weaponry was to be used to prevent, not to further, war. Nuclear *détente* through the SALT negotiations played an important role in a reduction of tension in the mid- and late-1970s, although ultimately SALT II fell victim to the subsequent heating up of the Cold War.

The West appeared to be in a parlous situation in the mid-1970s, with its military position compromised by American failure in Vietnam, but also by broader political and economic developments. The American decision to pay for the Vietnam War (and much else) by borrowing rather than taxation, a policy that was to be repeated with the Iraq and Afghanistan commitments of the 2000s and 2010s, helped build up inflationary pressures in the United States. These led, from 1971, to the collapse of the Bretton Woods fixed currency exchange system, the basis of the Western economic order. The situation was exacerbated by the oil price hike after the Yom Kippur War, as the Organization of Petroleum-Exporting Countries sought to put pressure on the Western supporters of Israel. This rise hit oil importers and fueled inflation, damaging economic confidence.

There was also a crisis of confidence in American leadership because of the Watergate scandal, which led to the fall of President Nixon in 1974. The Watergate hearings were scrutinized carefully by North Vietnam as it planned its final assault on the South. Congress's refusal in 1975 to provide the money required to help South Vietnam continue to resist was a blunt warning to America's allies and contributed greatly to the fall of South Vietnam. Moreover, Western disunity was seen in growing French alienation from the United States, and Britain was faced from 1974 by a political upheaval stemming from a coalminers' strike and then by a more general crisis as high inflation and trade union power contributed to an acute sense of malaise and weakness. In addition, West Germany and Italy were affected by violent radical movements that embraced terrorism, the Baddar-Meinhof group and the Red Brigades, creating an impression of instability.

These years, the pivot of the Cold War, were understood differently at the time and subsequently. At the time, Western weakness seemed clear and varied. Apparent nuclear parity between the United States and the Soviet Union left the Soviet superiority in conventional forces a threat to Western Europe, and in the United States presidential prestige and power were compromised by the Watergate affair. The War Powers resolution passed in November 1973 by a Democrat-dominated Congress over Nixon's veto stipulated consultation with Congress before American forces were sent into conflict and a system of regular presidential report and congressional authorization thereafter. This law was to be evaded by successive presidents and was not to be enforced by Congress, but it symbolized a post-Vietnam restraint that discouraged military interventionism in the 1970s. American annual inflation rose at a rate of 15 percent in early 1974, the economy went into recession, and stagflation posed a threat to the social fabric, notably with rising crime rates in the cities.

The international strategic situation appeared threatening for the West. Either this situation was essentially static while, within its sphere, Western societies were facing increasing problems that would weaken them fatally or the very front line of the Cold War was moving against the West, notably in Southeast Asia and southern Africa. The attempt by the United States to resist this process in Southeast Asia by intervening in Vietnam had failed and, in doing so, had exposed stresses in American society and the weaknesses of its conventional military.

Western commentators proved eager to accept the views of left-wing writers who argued that peoples' warfare was invincible. This (partly misleading) interpretation of the Vietnam War was joined to that of the Chinese Civil War and of national liberation struggles. The emphasis was on guerrilla warfare, popular mobilization, and political radicalism and not on conventional operations and professionalism, including the essentially conventional strategy and operational means employed by the Communists in 1948–1949 to bring victory in the

A Peruvian youth—part of a peasant self-defense force—trains with a wooden rifle, 1975.

Chinese Civil War. In 1965, Lin Piao, a Communist marshal and Mao's heir apparent, published *Long Live the Victory of the People's War*, a proclamation of the invincible nature of the People's War, as a means to defeat imperialism and the West. This conflict also offered Mao a model for the use of force to overcome domestic opponents, notably with the Great Proletarian Cultural Revolution from 1966. Organized as the Red Guard, Mao's supporters were encouraged to overcome the forces of conservatism within China, creating a chaos that only finally ended when the army was used to restore order.

From the present perspective, a different situation and outcome from that envisaged by many commentators in the early 1970s is apparent. The Communist economies were also hit by the economic downturn of the mid-1970s, and the Soviet government lacked an effective response. Heavy investment in armaments was distorting for these economies, but more generally, they suffered from the role of Soviet state planning, particularly by Gosplan, the State Planning Commission, and from the failure to develop the consumer spending that was so important to economic activity and growth in the United States and Western Europe. In addition, with its lack of flexibility and support for initiative and enterprise, the Soviet Union was not laying the foundations for the development of computer technology that was to be so important to American economic and military improvements in the 1980s and beyond.

Moreover, whereas previously the United States had had to plan for nuclear war against the Soviets and China, now the American opening to China meant that the Soviet Union had to prepare for war on two fronts. Indeed, in 1969, against a background of frontier clashes on the Ussuri River, the Soviet Union, feeling threatened by Mao Zedong's radicalism and by China's far greater population compared to that of Siberia, had sounded out the United States, first on the idea of joint action against China and then to ask how the United States would view a Soviet nuclear strike against Chinese nuclear facilities. There was no American support for such a move. In response to China's stance, the Soviets redeployed many of their missiles to deter China.

The rivalry between the Soviet Union and China also affected the situation in the Third World, weakening what would otherwise have been an expansion of Soviet influence. Thus, Chinese support for Pakistan and for the Pol Pot regime in Cambodia countered Soviet backing for India and Vietnam, respectively; there was also serious rivalry between the Soviet Union and China in Africa and in Southeast Europe. In 1971, Henry Kissinger, the American National Security Adviser, secretly pressed China to send forces to India's border to deter India from intervening in East Pakistan in support of rebellion there, although he knew that the Soviets might respond forcefully against China. After its defeat by China in 1962, the Indian government had decided to increase the size of its army from 550,000 men to 825,000.

China's effective alliance with the United States, negotiated from 1971 with Nixon visiting China in 1972, was to last until the early 2000s. Nixon's move was an arresting step for such a noted anti-Communist and one he would have bitterly decried had there been a Democratic president. The alliance with China provided a linkage between the second stage of the Cold War and the post–Cold War situation.

Another linkage was that of the revival of American military power and the determination of the American army not to engage in another war like Vietnam. Instead, the focus in the late 1970s and 1980s was to be on developing a conventional capability such that Soviet forces could be successfully fought, notably in Europe, without resorting to nuclear armaments. This process led the army to become the improved warfighting institution that won a dramatic victory over Soviet-armed Iraqi forces in 1991. Thus, the early 1970s were far more of a pivot toward Western success than was apparent at the time.

READING LIST

Ahron Bregman, *Israel's Wars, 1947–93*, London, Routledge, 2000.
Spencer Tucker, *Vietnam*, London, UCL Press, 1999.

SEVEN

The Later Cold War, 1975–1989

Sandinista patrol, Nicaragua, 1983.

The years of the second half of the Cold War were far more years of conflict and confrontation than is generally recalled in the standard American treatment, where the focus instead is on the earlier Cold War, notably the Vietnam War, but also the Korean and Arab–Israeli wars. However, the *détente* of the mid-1970s was followed by revived confrontation between the Soviet Union and the United States, particularly in the early 1980s. Moreover, from the mid-1970s, there was a series of "hot wars," notably in southern Africa, the Horn of Africa (Ethiopia and Somalia), Southeast Asia, and Central America.

Great power intervention played a major role in these struggles and was also exacerbated by them. For example, far from being marginal, success in Africa in the 1970s gave many Soviets a renewed sense of pride in their own achievements and a conviction that the Soviet Union could contribute decisively to breakthroughs for Communism elsewhere. Conflict was linked to assessments of political systems. Although Soviet-supported forces helped Ethiopia against Somalia from 1978, the Soviet willingness to overlook the bloody reign of terror of Haile Mengistu, the dictator of Ethiopia from 1977 to 1991, indicated the degree to which the attitudes associated with Stalinism continued thereafter. As an instance of the longstanding tendency for Soviet commentators to interpret developments elsewhere in terms of Soviet history and ideology, the Soviet envoy, Anatoli Ratanov, saw a similarity between the brutal activities of Mengistu's supporters within the Derg (Coordinating Committee) and the early revolutionary experience in Russia.

There was also an increase in rivalry between states that was not focused on Cold War alignments, notably the Iran–Iraq War of 1980–1988. This was the most large-scale struggle in the post-Vietnam stage of the Cold War world. In contrast, the major powers fought only limited wars. The United States intervened successfully in the Caribbean region, in Grenada (1983) and Panama (1989). French airpower helped Chad defeat Libyan invasions, and Britain defeated Argentina in a limited war over the Falkland Islands (1982). The Soviet Union, however, failed to achieve the same speed or success in its intervention in Afghanistan (1979–1988), and China found Vietnam a difficult opponent in 1979. The maritime and air expeditions against small targets in the Falklands, Grenada, and Panama therefore proved more successful than the Continental-style involvement in Afghanistan and Vietnam.

Along with war, the military was a major source of power in many states, notably in sub-Saharan Africa, Latin America, and parts of Asia. This power was an important aspect of the military history of the period because it involved the seizure of control and the suppression of opposition and was also crucial to what "war and society" meant across much of the world.

If the central theme is therefore conflict and force, there was in fact no war between the major powers, and it is necessary to explain this because the absence of war is also significant to the military history of the period and to the wider issue of war and society. Moreover, it is important to consider why the Cold War, the largest-scale military confrontation of the period, not least in terms of the lethality of the weaponry deployed and the length of the confrontation, ended without conflict among the protagonists, the United States and the Soviet Union.

THE LATE 1970s

The relative American position in the Cold War in the late 1970s was less bleak than it appeared at the time. America benefited from an economic rebound after the crisis of 1974–1975, although problems continued. Moreover, the general revival of world growth helped the American economy, and issues of investment opportunity ensured that much of the money from the Organization of Petroleum-Exporting Countries was recycled back into the United States. This financial link increased American interest in the stability of the Gulf States. As a result of this growth, the economic background and finances necessary for the arms buildup in the 1980s were available.

At the strategic level, the key development was a transition of power in China that did not affect the alignment with the United States. After the death of Mao Zedong in September 1976, the attempt by the radical "Gang of Four," including Mao's widow, to gain power was thwarted. Instead, Deng Xiaoping, who took power in 1978, favored not only this alignment but also a reevaluation of Communism in terms of economic liberalization alongside continued party dominance, rather than a revolution focused on Marxist purity. Deng backed cooperation with the United States and a treaty was signed; so also was one between China and America's leading East Asian ally, Japan. In 1979, the Americans ended the Taiwan Patrol Force, which, from 1950, had policed the waters between China and Taiwan, protecting the latter.

The alignment between the United States and China was linked to war in 1979 between China and Vietnam, an ally of the Soviet Union that had overrun Cambodia, an ally of China, the previous year. This conflict underlined the extent to which the Cold War involved proxy conflicts between the major powers. Moreover, it is mistaken to see the United States as necessarily the initiator of great-power intervention. Last, the war between China and Vietnam offers a possible comparison with the earlier American intervention there. The scale, duration, and context of the two conflicts differed, but both displayed the difficulties of securing outcomes. In 1979, the Chinese sent eventually about 120,000 troops across the frontier to confront an equal number of Vietnamese. Capturing three provincial capitals, the Chinese then lost the initiative when the Vietnamese turned to guerrilla tactics. The Vietnamese benefited from their extensive recent experience of conflict with the United States and South Vietnamese, whereas the Chinese lacked such experience. Bar a brief (and successful) frontier conflict with India in 1962, the Chinese military had had no combat experience since 1953, and both its equipment and its doctrine were dated. Moreover, an emphasis on political compliance and factionalism in securing promotion affected the quality of the command. With poor logistics and failures in coordination affecting operations, the Chinese withdrew, with perhaps 63,000 casualties.

In military terms, Chinese failure in 1979 indicates that in a different political context it was possible for another great power to fail in Vietnam. As a consequence, the tendency on the part of some American commentators, in another version of the "stab-in-the-back" approach, to blame American failure in the Vietnam War on domestic public opinion and social trends must be called into question.

The political consequences of the China–Vietnam 1979 war were instructive and serve as a reminder that the results of conflict can bring benefits and problems to both sides. In one respect, China failed. It was unable to force Vietnamese forces to leave Cambodia; indeed, they did not do so until 1990. Moreover, China retained its strategic dilemma of hostile powers to the north and south (the Soviet Union and Vietnam), a dilemma that underlined China's need for alignment with the United States. On the other hand, China had shown that it would not be deterred by this dilemma, and the invasion underlined the division in the Communist bloc, the diplomatic weakness of the Soviet Union, and the extent to which its alignment with China furthered American geopolitical goals in Southeast Asia. By the end of the 1970s, it is therefore possible to argue that the United States, thanks to a coincidence of diplomatic interests with China as well as the change of regime in Indonesia, had come out of the Vietnam War in a better strategic position than had seemed threatening in the early 1960s. In short, the wider strategic context pointed in a different direction from the operational course of the conflict. As yet, there is no comparable strategic "profit" to serve as a context for discussing the intervention in Iraq and Afghanistan in the 2000s.

China's failure was followed by a "Cold War"—style confrontation in Southeast Asia, notably between China and Vietnam, that has continued with changes in intensity to the present day. The same was true of the consequences of the Iranian Revolution, whereas the Soviet invasion of Afghanistan in 1979 precipitated an instability there that has lasted until the present day. Thus, although the Cold War is presented as ending in 1989, its results remain highly significant, and many of the alignments and tensions have lasted to this day.

The overthrow of the Shah in Iran in January 1979 indicated the weakness of a divided government, however militarily strong, in the face of large-scale popular opposition. The massive popular demonstrations were intimidating, and the Shah suffered from a lack of international support, notably from his traditional ally, the United States. The Americans did not win any gratitude from the revolutionaries, and American military and political prestige was compromised in April 1980 by the miscarriage of an attempt to free the staff of the American embassy in Tehran who were being held prisoners by militants.

This failure indicated the extent to which even quite small-scale military episodes could have a disproportionate political impact, a situation that owed much to the rapid spread of information and opinion by the modern media. The humiliation of this failure was scarcely a second Vietnam, but it combined with other factors to associate President Jimmy Carter with repeated failure. Just as politics under Nixon had shrunk, or at least appeared to shrink to the Watergate case, so it was for Carter and the hostages. On the heels of the Vietnam War, the trauma arising from the hostage crisis and the failed attempt at rescue fueled a sense of decline and desire for rejuvenation that Ronald Reagan, Carter's successful opponent in the 1980 presidential election, understood and exploited.

The Islamic regime that gained power in Iran became a force of regional instability, as it has remained to the present day, while also using large-scale brutality, including the mass slaughter of political prisoners, to consolidate its control and force through its agenda. Moreover, the Islamic regime put religious goals, or at least language and ideology, at the center of policy, so that struggle appeared necessary and continuous. The path from this to extreme methods, such as terrorist bombers, was not direct, but there were significant links, not least because Iran became a major patron of some of the more extreme Islamic movements, notably, in Lebanon, Hezbollah, a bitter opponent of Israel.

THE IRAN-IRAQ WAR

However, the immediate military response to the takeover was not a revolutionary assault on other states by Iran on the pattern of the Soviet invasion of Poland in 1920, as was feared, but instead an attack on Iran by the Iraqi dictator Saddam Hussein. Seeking to gain a favorable settlement of longstanding border disputes and to wield the regional hegemony previously enjoyed by the Shah, Saddam invaded Iran in September 1980, launching a struggle that lasted until 1988 and that involved more combatants and casualties than other conflicts of the period.

As with the Americans and Chinese in Vietnam, comparisons are instructive, not least because the Iraqis planned to use the same method against Iran, a more populous neighbor, as Israel had employed against its similar rival, Egypt, in 1967. The emphasis was on a surprise attack, with the surprise enhanced and focused (as also by Japan against the United States in 1941) by the use of airpower. However, as so often in military matters, it was easier to copy doctrine and strategy than to ensure implementation. The surprise Iraqi attack on 10 air bases on the night of September 22 failed because of a lack of adequate expertise and targeting equipment, a failure that ensured that the Iranian air force survived and was, in turn, able to attack Iraqi oil facilities successfully on September 25, hitting the financial underpinnings of the Iraqi war effort.

Despite having a large number of Soviet-supplied tanks (a product of Iraq's oil wealth and of Cold War alignments), the Iraqis lacked the mobility and tactical flexibility displayed by the Israelis against their Arab opponents in 1967, 1973, and 1982. Instead, the Iraqi advance was slower and their tanks were frequently employed as artillery, downplaying their capacity for maneuver warfare. The relationship between technology and usage was clear. Iraqi failure showed yet again that advanced weaponry in inexpert hands brought few advantages. Iraqi forces also lacked adequate logistics, and, as an aspect of an hierarchical and politicized military, they also suffered from inflexible command systems.

The Iraqis, moreover, displayed another characteristic of failure, one seen also with China in Vietnam in 1979 and the Soviet Union in Afghanistan in 1979–1988: their war aims were misconceived, and there was no clear exit strategy. The nature of Iranian politics had been misread by Saddam because, far from collapsing, the Iranian forces fought back, helped by an upsurge in patriotism. More particularly the Arab-majority population of southwest Iran did not rebel in favor of Iraq, as Saddam had anticipated.

Once Iraq had failed to win success, it did not have the means to disengage, in part because Saddam feared for his own position at the hands of domestic opponents and Iranian invaders if he admitted defeat. As the war became intractable,

Iranian women solemnly march in support of the war effort, early 1980s; note the boy wearing a gas mask.

there was a turn to extreme methods and the international context became more significant. Threatened by the human-wave nature of Iranian assaults, a return to early World War I tactics, the Iraqis used chemical weapons against these attacks; both sides employed missiles, targeting opposing capitals and causing civilian casualties. There was also the first modern "martyrdom operation" by an Islamic group when an Iranian-backed Shia movement was responsible, in 1981, for the suicide bombing of the Iraqi embassy in Beirut.

The Iranians outnumbered the Iraqis, but international isolation made it difficult to keep their equipment maintained, which is always a major problem with the refit, resupply, and maintenance of complex modern weaponry and with foreign sources of supply. These sources are of particular significance for aircraft because they are manufactured by few states and spare parts are difficult to produce. Moreover, the Iraqis benefited from assistance from most other Arab states, as well as from powers fearful of Iran, including the United States. This help was financial, notably from Kuwait and Saudi Arabia, and in the form of the sale of weapons, particularly by France and the Soviets. Having driven the Iraqis back from 1982, the Iranians finally accepted international pressure for peace in 1988 because they could not sustain the costs of the offensive. By the end of the war, the Iraqis had lost approximately 105,000 dead and the Iranians approximately 262,000.

The Iran–Iraq War showed that not all the conflicts of the period can be fitted into an alignment focused on the Cold War. In addition, the Iran–Iraq war helped determine what were to be important strands in politics and policy thereafter.

As in the case of Communist China and the Korean War, war with Iraq helped further to radicalize the Islamic Revolution in Iran, although such a radicalization had already been latent in 1979–1980. The war had also spread to involve Iranian attacks on shipping in the Persian Gulf designed to block the sale of Iraqi oil. These attacks led to a major American-led Western naval commitment to protect shipping and to the destruction of attacking Iranian warships and planes.

This commitment developed the stronger American engagement in the region that followed the Iranian Revolution, notably with the Carter Doctrine in January 1980 and the establishment that March of the Rapid Deployment Task Force, which was to become the basis of Central Command, the organization responsible for implementing American policy in the two Gulf Wars with Iraq (1990–1991, 2003). The commitment was to be greatly enhanced by another consequence of the Iran–Iraq War; its financial strains led Saddam Hussein to seek a quick profit by invading vulnerable and oil-rich Kuwait in 1990, only to find that this led to intervention by an American-led international coalition.

THE SOVIET INTERVENTION IN AFGHANISTAN

The response to the Iran–Iraq War was affected by the rise in international tension following the Soviet intervention in Afghanistan in 1979. This was a response to instability in a different part of the Islamic world and, in turn, contributed greatly to that instability, as well as to regional tensions and to great-power rivalry. This intervention is instructive in comparative terms, both with regard to other conflicts in the period and with reference to the Western intervention in Afghanistan from 2001. Indeed, the latter comparison was frequently to be made to suggest that such intervention was bound to fail.

A major contrast, however, was provided by geography, always a key element in military history, in operational and strategic terms and with reference to the politics of the conflict. Neither Vietnam nor Afghanistan bordered the United States, and this ensured that its intervention in both cases was a "war of choice." In contrast, Afghanistan bordered the Soviet Union. First, this helped to increase Soviet concern about developments there and, second, it ensured that the Soviet government did not feel that it had an easy exit strategy once the war went badly. From its outset, the Soviet Union had backed Afghanistan, against first Britain and then the U.S.-backed Pakistan, as an aspect of the Cold War.

In April 1978, in the Saur (April) Revolution, the Soviet-backed People's Democratic Party of Afghanistan seized power in a military coup, replacing a non-Communist authoritarian strongman, Mohammed Daoud Khan, who in turn had seized power in 1973 from the last king, Zahir Shah, his cousin and brother-in-law. Daoud, a former lieutenant-general and prime minister, had been backed by a group of Soviet-trained officers, and the coup was seen as an extension of Soviet influence, although Daoud himself was a firm nationalist. In 1978, the presidential palace fell to a rebel tank assault assisted by air strikes. The new government rapidly discovered the problems of trying to push through reform in an inherently conservative Islamic society, one, moreover, with no tradition of taking central direction. Equality for women was unacceptable to the bulk of Afghan society, and land reform was unwelcome to those powerful in the tribal clans that dominated rural societies. Rebellions from late 1978 were met with brutal repression, not conciliation, and notably, for example, with the city of Herat, with the colonial-era remedy of "pacification" by bombing, which, despite the improved specifications of aircraft, was little more effective than it had been in the 1920s and 1930s.

A coup in September 1979 from within the murderously divided regime did nothing to stem the tide of chaos, and the Soviets intervened on December 27, overthrowing the government and installing their client, Babrak Karmal, as president. Soviet intervention was designed for defensive and aggressive purposes. In defensive terms, it helped prevent the spread of Muslim influence into Soviet, Central Asia and to prevent Afghanistan from turning to China, the United States, and Pakistan. The KGB feared that the Afghan government, which was run by a Communist faction, the Khalq (which was not the one favored by the Soviets), was threatening Afghan stability and posing the risk of a move toward the West. In aggressive terms, intervention was intended to weaken Pakistan, which looked to China and the United States, encircle China, and take Soviet power closer to the Gulf. Indeed, the Soviets expanded and fortified the airbase at Shindand in southwest Pakistan.

It was easy for the Soviets to seize the cities, in part by the use of airborne troops, but the weakness of the new government led the Soviets to a wider commitment. Guerrilla resistance in the countryside by the *mujahideen* proved very different from engaging with the concentrated target of cities. As with the

Soviet soldiers rest on a tank during a lull in combat, Afghanistan, early 1980s.

Western intervention in Afghanistan from 2001, and more particularly 2006, in part this intractability was a matter of the nature of Afghan society and politics, at once bellicose and fragmented, and in part the limitations shown in counter-insurgency warfare in a very difficult military environment. Linking the two was the difficulty of translating operational success into lasting advantage. As with later Western intervention, the Soviets exaggerated the strength and popularity of their local allies and failed to appreciate those of opponents stigmatized as reactionary, but seeing themselves as motivated by *jihad* or religious war. For example, in each case, there was a hostile reaction to governmental policies in favor of women.

There were also operational and tactical parallels between the Soviets in the 1980s and later Western forces in Afghanistan. The difficulty of distinguishing opponents from the rest of civil society was a problem, as was the linked ability of the guerrillas to avoid having battle forced on them. Soviet advances therefore tended to have only short-term benefit and were followed either by leaving vulnerable outposts or by a return to base that created a sense of futility. Technology was useful, notably with aerial resupply and airborne special forces, but, as with the Western forces in the 2000s and 2010s, it could not bring lasting victory. Moreover, the problems of operating in Afghanistan ensured that, as again later for Western forces, convoy escort tied down many troops. In another similarity, there was a lack of enough troops to provide both sufficient security for controlled areas and the ability to launch large-scale campaigns into areas that were not under control. The Soviet emphasis on conventional doctrine, tactics, and operations matched what was designed for conducting war against NATO in Europe. However, motorized columns were prone to ambushes, although with time the Soviets proved better at using air support. Designed to weaken the *mujahideen*, the targeting of noncombatants did not win the Soviets any friends. Moreover, the Soviets treated Afghanistan as a tangential sphere. Even when the pace of offensives increased, in 1984 and far more in 1985, the number of troops only increased to 108,000, of whom only 73,000 were combatants. This was far fewer than the American numbers in Vietnam, as were Soviet casualties and expenditure. The Soviet forces in Afghanistan suffered from disease, notably hepatitis, typhoid, and dysentery, as well as from drug and alcohol abuse and poor morale.

The conflict in Afghanistan overlapped with the Cold War, a situation that lacked a comparison in the 2000s and 2010s as China, America's rival then, did not support opposition there. The guerrillas who resisted Soviet forces in Afghanistan were supplied through Pakistan by the United States, Britain, China, and Saudi Arabia, not least with, beginning in 1986, ground-to-air missiles, the American Stinger, and the British Blowpipe, which brought down Soviet helicopter gunships, forcing them and aircraft to fly higher, therefore with reduced effectiveness. Some of the guerrillas were later to become part of the al-Qaeda network, whose terrorism was directed against the United States, Britain, and Saudi Arabia. In Afghanistan, Cold War alignments in the 1980s overlapped with

Islamicist anger at the occupation of an Islamic state, which led to Saudi, Iranian, and Pakistani support for the guerrillas, although bitter sectarian, ethnic, and political rivalries within the Islamic world ensured that competing assistance was channeled to rival factions. The impossibility of sealing the frontiers helped in the supply of the *mujahideen*.

THE HEATING UP OF THE COLD WAR

The Afghan war contributed greatly to the heating up of the Cold War from 1979. The Soviet intervention was seen by the United States not as a frontier policing operation designed to ensure a pliant government, but as an act of aggression that needed to be countered, an approach that drew on a tendency to exaggerate Soviet economic resources and military capability. Under Ronald Reagan, the American president in 1981–1989, and Margaret Thatcher, the British prime minister in 1979–1990 who greatly encouraged him, this determination was matched by action. Reagan sought to build up American military strength and political determination so as to be able to negotiate with the Soviets from a position of superiority. The Strategic Defense Initiative ("Star Wars" to critics), outlined by Reagan in a speech in 1983, was designed to enable the Americans to dominate space using space-mounted weapons to destroy Soviet satellites and missiles.

Both the United States and the Soviet Union sought to alter the situation in Europe, the prime area of confrontation, by the deployment of short- and intermediate-range nuclear missiles. These offered tactical and operational alternatives to the strategic capability of the intercontinental arsenals and suggested that there would be a significant bridge between conventional and nuclear warfare, one in which the newly deployed missiles would supplement and, in part, replace artillery and airpower. The significance of this capability was enhanced by the mutual distrust of the superpowers in the early 1980s. Reagan's rhetoric about the "evil empire" was interpreted in the Soviet Union as a challenge, and the Soviet leaders who succeeded Leonid Brezhnev, notably Yuri Andropov (1982–1984), a former head of the KGB, the Soviet spy system, were heavily influenced by KGB analyses that presented the United States as threatening. In 1983, tensions rose to a height with the KGB reporting that NATO exercises would be a cover for attack, and the Soviets in turn made preparations for an attack of their own. The likely consequences of such hostilities remain unclear, but they underline the risks involved in the Cold War, as well as the reasons why both sides prepared for war. In 1983, however, such preparations accentuated the concerns of the other power, making preemptive war a danger.

Ultimately, there was to be no conflict between the United States and the Soviet Union and no use of nuclear weaponry. This outcome can be seen as a successful use of deterrence and also, indirectly, as a vindication of the airpower enthusiasts of the 1920s; it can also be employed as an argument to support the view that peace can be maintained through deterrence if many states have nuclear weapons. However, as an instance of the limitations of arguing from historical

Soviet tactical short-range nuclear missiles on display, Moscow, 1985.

examples, there were additional factors involved in the avoidance of war in the late 1970s and 1980s, notably the caution of the elderly Soviet leadership and the extent to which Reagan's rhetoric was not, in effect, matched by any policy of "rollback" in Europe. However, relations were not to ease until after Mikhail Gorbachev succeeded as Soviet leader in 1985. In the meantime, tensions remained high.

There has been considerable controversy over whether Reagan had a grand strategy of confronting and weakening Communism or whether there was no such strategy but, rather, a set of beliefs. These focused on the clashing aspirations of destroying Communism and ending the risk of war: a "crusade for freedom" alongside "peace through strength." Although the policy was unclear, the means were not. Far from being cowed by Soviet military advances, not least the creation of a major navy and the deployment of intermediate range missiles, the American government and military responded with higher expenditure and with a vigorous determination to develop new weapons, tactics, and operational means. Keen not to be involved in another conflict like Vietnam, the American military focused on preparations for conflict with the Soviet Union and for bringing forward weapons systems, planning, and training accordingly. Heavy forces characterized the army, and it lost the counterinsurgency expertise developed during the Vietnam War.

Like hot wars, the Cold War exemplified the significance of war and society. The Republican presidencies of 1981–1993 benefited from considerable domestic political support and also from a combination of economic growth and "easy money," such that it was possible to cut taxes and increase military expenditure on the basis of massive government borrowing. In contrast, the Communist order, at least in the Soviet Union and Eastern Europe, but also in Mongolia and to a degree in China and Vietnam, sat increasingly uneasily on societies where individualism, consumerism, and demands for change and freedom could not be accommodated by inherently inefficient command economies and by Communist ideology.

Reagan was also anxious to halt the spread of Soviet influence around the world, especially but not only in Central America. His presidency witnessed a development of covert operations outside formal military structures and (related) support for anti-Communist insurgents in Afghanistan, Nicaragua, and Angola, the latter thanks to a repeal of the congressional ban on involvement. Nicaragua, a state in Central America where the left-wing Sandinista guerrilla movement had gained power from the Somoza dictatorship in 1979, faced American pressure, including the mining of its harbors and the secret arming, beginning in 1981, of a counterrevolutionary movement, the Contras, who were based in Honduras. The illicit financing of the Contras revealed in the "Iran-Contra" affair in 1986 was a direct defiance of congressional authority. In 1983, with regular forces, the Americans successfully invaded the Caribbean island of Grenada in response to the possibility that a left-wing coup would lead to a Soviet military presence.

OTHER CONFLICTS IN 1975–1989

As with other periods, there were conflicts that were difficult to fit in with the master narrative, in this case the Cold War. Again, struggles between and within states were significant; so also were struggles between states and opponents who were not recognized as such, as with the pattern for the Soviets in Afghanistan and for the Israelis in Lebanon.

The range of conflict helped ensure that no one factor was significant in leading to success. The struggles of the 1980s demonstrated the significance of airpower, but also the extent to which it did not determine outcomes: it was possible to project power, but not to end opposition. On the ground, established issues, notably unit coherence, morale, tactical ability, and leadership qualities, proved more significant than weaponry in creating capability gaps and related outcomes as seen with the British defeat of Argentinean units in the fighting on the Falkland Islands in 1982. That war was made easier for Britain because it was not fought to gain control of a hostile population. That the situation was different for the Soviets in Afghanistan or for the Israelis in southern Lebanon in 1982 helped ensure that these issues had to be worked through in conflict in a wider and more complex social environment that proved impossible to direct.

The Israelis were militarily successful in 1982, invading Lebanon and gaining the advantage over the rival Syrians and the Palestine Liberation Organization, both of which were established there. The Syrians initially fought well, but once their missile batteries in Lebanon had been knocked out and their air force badly pummeled by Israeli aircraft and armed with American Sidewinder missiles and supported by electronic countermeasures, the Syrians proved vulnerable to Israeli attack, now bolstered by clear mastery in the air. The Israelis, however, found it difficult to translate this military success into an ability to dominate southern Lebanon politically. Conversely, Syria's defeat encouraged subsequent caution in confronting Israel.

In addition to international conflicts, there were others within states. The attempt to suppress regional separatism (protonationalism in another light) played a significant role and linked, for example, the Pakistani army fighting rebellion in the western province of Balochistan in the 1970s to the British army fighting Catholic Republican separatists in Northern Ireland throughout this period. In each case, the maintenance of control did not mean the end of opposition. Coups continued to play a role in changes in government, as in Uganda in 1985.

GORBACHEV AND THE END OF THE SOVIET BLOC

The rise to power in the Soviet Union in 1985 of Mikhail Gorbachev, a leader committed to reform at home and good relations abroad, greatly defused Cold War tension. Convinced, against the advice of the KGB, that American policy on arms control was not motivated by a hidden agenda of weakening the Soviet Union, Gorbachev in 1987 accepted the Intermediate Nuclear Forces Treaty, which, by ending land-based missiles with ranges between 500 and 5,000 kilometers, forced heavier cuts on the Soviets while also setting up a system of verification through on-site inspection. In addition, Gorbachev saw the Soviet commitment in Afghanistan as an intractable struggle that was detrimental to the Soviet Union's international position, particularly his wish to improve relations with the West, and domestically unpopular. The Geneva Accords of April 1988 led to a Soviet withdrawal that was completed by February 1989, although Soviet military and financial aid to the Afghan government continued. Moreover, Soviet disengagement from supporting the government played a role in the ceasefire in Angola in 1988.

The hot conflicts of the Cold War continued in a number of countries, notably El Salvador until 1992, but there was a winding down in the late 1980s that changed the pattern of military activity across the world. It became less focused on interventions by the great powers or, indeed, directed by their alignments. Instead, the patterns and causes of local rivalries, both between and within states, came to the fore.

At the same time, the Cold War understood as the ideologically based rivalry between the United States and the Soviet Union came to a close, with both politics and society determining in this case the outcome of the war. Gorbachev unintentionally ended the struggle because his reform drive and policies, which sought to modernize Soviet Communism, instead unraveled its precarious domestic basis and at the same time failed to provide sufficient food, let alone reasonable economic growth. Furthermore, his pressure on Soviet satellite states in Eastern Europe for reform led instead to their collapse because Gorbachev was unwilling to use the Soviet military to maintain their governments in power when they faced pent-up popular pressure for change.

The change from the situation in 1981 was instructive. Then, in the face of large-scale popular agitation for reform in Poland from the Solidarity movement, the Polish army, under pressure from the Soviet Union (which was not willing to act itself), had intervened to introduce martial law and suppress this movement. In 1989, when popular opposition against the Communist governments developed, initially in East Germany and Hungary, there was no comparable steer from the Soviet Union. Moreover, the local Communist regimes felt destabilized by a lack of support from the Soviet Union. Only in Romania, where the regime of Nicolae Ceaușescu had cultivated detachment from the Soviet Union since the 1960s, was an attempt made by the secret police to resist popular pressure. This attempt failed, in part because the army did not back the regime. Indeed, the army was responsible for the execution of Ceaușescu. Thus, yet again, the relationship between society and force helped determine political outcomes and was thereby redefined by them.

In contrast to Eastern Europe, on June 3–4, 1989, the Chinese government successfully used force to suppress popular pressure for reform, sending tanks against demonstrators in Beijing. Thousands were killed. Deng, who had played a significant role in the Chinese Civil War and had been active in the slaughter of supposed counterrevolutionaries in the early 1950s, was ready to send in the

The aftermath of Tiananmen Square, June 1989.

army against what was inaccurately described as a "counterrevolutionary rebellion." In part as a consequence of this use of force, a reformed Communism that embraced capitalism survived in China, whereas that in the Soviet bloc, on more precarious foundations, collapsed.

The latter outcome, however, was still unclear at the close of the 1980s. The consequences for the Soviet Union of the rapid collapse of Communist governments in Eastern Europe in late 1989 were uncertain, not least as the Red Army remained a major force in the Soviet Union. What was clear from the 1980s was that, in the right circumstances, popular pressure could counteract and even overawe the availability of military force. The consequences of that were to play through thereafter, as also would the example and implications of the success of the Afghan opposition.

The role of force in the outcome of the Cold War had a number of dimensions. America's military buildup in the 1980s, a qualitative as well as a quantitative change, drove a process of attempted modernization in the Communist bloc that unraveled both the bloc and Communist rule. As an aspect of this modernization, the decision not to use the military to suppress opposition in 1989 (unlike in 1956, 1968, and 1981) was very important to the process of change, and once that had begun in one state, it proved impossible to stop the process. The wider geographical context was another dimension: the confrontation between the United States and the Soviet Union had spread, or at least refocused, war or tension around the world, but events in Africa, Latin America, and Southern Asia had only limited impact on developments in the United States, the Soviet Union, or Europe. In particular, although military confidence and prestige and domestic morale were also affected, the Afghan War did not have the impact on the Soviet Union that the Vietnam War had on the United States. However, because central direction was more important in the Soviet system, the political crisis in the Communist bloc in 1989–1991 proved far more transformative, in both the short and the long term, than that in the United States in 1973–1975.

READING LIST

John Gaddis, *We Now Know: Rethinking the Cold War*, Oxford, Clarendon Press, 1997.
David Gates, *Sky Wars: A History of Military Aerospace Power*, London, Reaktion, 2005.
D. Hiro, *The Longest War: The Iran–Iraq Military Conflict*, London, Grafton Books, 1989.
William Maley, *The Afghanistan Wars*, Basingstoke, Palgrave, 2002.

EIGHT

From the Cold War to the War on Terror, 1989–2001

American soldier standing atop a destroyed Iraqi tank, March 1991.

As ever, a number of themes vied for attention in the 1990s, the decade in which the collapse of the Soviet Union meant that there was only one superpower, the United States. The themes included the impact and changing character of "high-specifications" conflict seen in the American defeat of Iraq in 1991 and in the Revolution in Military Affairs (RMA) that analysts discerned and applauded in the 1990s. At the same time, there was a failure in the West to understand how best to overcome the problems posed by the very different nature of conflict in countries lacking such forms of warfare or, indeed, developed and centralized state forms, notably Somalia. This issue overlapped with the intractable nature of instability in a number of states, especially Afghanistan and Sudan. In turn, certain of these states, particularly Afghanistan but also Angola and El Salvador, were affected by continuations of the conflicts of the last stages of the Cold War. There were also the "post–Cold War" conflicts, notably in Yugoslavia and the Caucasus, as areas that had had stability under the rule of Cold War states lost it with their collapse. This pattern matched that seen at the close of World War I (see pp. 52–58). Separate from these rivalries, there was the more constant feature of the military as the guarantor of government control, as an aspect of the government itself, or as the means by which control over the government was contested. Although it is possible to separate out these factors, there was also a considerable degree of overlap between them.

THE GULF WAR OF 1990–1991

The development of American military capability in the 1980s was displayed in action in the Gulf War of 1990–1991. On August 2, 1990, oil-rich Kuwait swiftly fell when attacked by its neighbor Iraq and was annexed as Iraq's 19th province. The Americans responded rapidly, displaying an impressive ability to move troops and *matériel*. In response to Saudi concern that Iraqi forces would press on into Saudi Arabia, the Americans deployed ground troops, providing the protection that helped ensure that there was no such attack.

The deterrent use of force was a significant factor in the military history of the period, even if it did not always lead to conflict. After negotiations had failed to lead to an Iraqi withdrawal from Kuwait, an air offensive was launched on January 17, 1991, followed by a ground attack on February 24. Each revealed the sophistication of American weaponry and military methods, as well as the development since the last major American military operation, in the Vietnam War in 1972. There was continuity with the Vietnam War, as with equipment brought into service in the later stages of that war, notably guided bombs, but the range of new weaponry, the integration of air and land operations, and the tempo of campaigning were all new. Earlier, on a smaller scale, improvement had been shown in the differences between American intervention in Grenada (1983) and Panama (1989).

The air offensive saw an overcoming of the sophisticated Iraqi antiaircraft system that was far more complete and rapid than the comparable operations in the Vietnam War. This left the Iraqi forces already in part defeated, certainly vulnerable to American attack, and disoriented, ensuring that the initiative in the subsequent campaigning rested with the American-led coalition forces throughout.

The Iraqis were outflanked and pummeled, losing more than 50,000 dead as well as 81,000 prisoners and nearly 4,000 tanks in 100 hours of nonstop conflict. As with the Israelis against the Egyptians in 1956 and 1967, the Americans benefited from the Iraqi reliance on a static defense, which, in practice, could not provide both protection and killing power.

In the land assault, the Iraqis were defeated not only by better technology but also by Allied fighting skills at the tactical and operational levels. There was a clear contrast, for example, in the use of tanks. The Iraqi tanks were both technically inferior and poorly used. The Iraqis dug them in, believing that this would protect them from air and tank attack, but they failed to understand the capabilities of both precision munitions and up-to-date tank gun technologies that could ensure a high first-shot kill capability even when only part of the turret was visible.

In this conflict, the Americans used their post-Vietnam weapon systems, including the Blackhawk helicopter introduced in 1979; the M1A1 Abrams tank, deployed from 1980; the Bradley Fighting Vehicle, designed to carry a squad of infantry and armed with a TOW (tube-launched, optically tracked, wire command data link) missile system, introduced in 1981; and the Apache attack helicopter, equipped with radar and Hellfire missiles, introduced in 1986. The Americans also used airplane stealth technology. The use of Cold War assets involved the new grasp and use of the operational dimension of war, a grasp that had developed with the doctrine, planning, and training of the 1980s as the Americans developed their capability to fight the Soviets without having to make an automatic resort to atomic weaponry.

Apache helicopters.

Approximately half of the Iraqi army was destroyed, but the campaign did not lead to the overthrow of Saddam because it ended too rapidly. Instead of pressing on into populated areas of Iraq, the coalition ceased its advance, and Saddam was able to retain control. Indeed, he turned his military against a rebellion by the country's Shia majority, using the firepower of helicopters, tanks, and artillery with great effectiveness to suppress the rebellion.

The speed and completeness of Iraq's defeat encouraged a belief in America that a revolutionary change in military capability had occurred. In practice, a range of factors was responsible for the linked (but differently caused) events of Iraqi defeat and Allied victory, not least Iraqi planning and doctrine, notably command and control. After the war, sanctions prevented the rearming and development of the Iraqi military. Moreover, airstrikes launched in 1998 drove home this constraint.

THE REVOLUTION IN MILITARY AFFAIRS

Despite the role of a range of factors in Iraqi defeat, the 1991 campaign became the evidence for what was claimed as an RMA, a process, goal, and event now usually termed transformation. More widely cited than defined and often meaning different things, the RMA had a number of meanings and associations that, in combination, suggested its usefulness to its advocates. The RMA was a military term, analysis, and ideology of the time, one that was symptomatic of cultural and political assumptions that spoke more to the aspirations of the 1990s and early 2000s than they do about any objective assessment of military capabilities. At one level, the RMA was an aspect of cheap hawkery, in this case the desire for unquestioned military potency without any matching need to accept conscription, a war economy, or many casualties. As a result, the RMA was a reflection of the decline of the warrior ethos and a response to the growing gap between society and the military.

The RMA also reflected the assertion of Western, more particularly American, superiority, as well as the ideology of mechanization that had long been important to American military thought and the influence of the vision of future war developed in the wake of World War II. This was war by magic bullet, most obviously with stealth technology, but without the horrific moral dilemmas posed by atomic weaponry.

This ideology and vision were crucial because capability, if not worth, was defined in a machine age—especially but not only in the United States—in terms of machines, particularly aircraft, which were then used to assert and demonstrate superiority. The machine was almost the proof of value. Reflecting the norms of American society, there was a preference for seeking technological solutions to military challenges. This process was encouraged by suggestions that machines would acquire an ability to substitute for human decision making. Automatic firing mechanisms provided an apparent example. A focus on machines also appeared to offer a ready measure for assessing the strength and prospects of different states and, indeed, civilizations. It was also apparently possible to shape the cutting edges of equations of military strength by investing in new capability at the cutting edge of technological progress. Thus, the RMA was an expression of the modern secular technological belief system that is prevalent in the West and that easily meshes with theories of modernization that rest on the diffusion and adoption of new technology and related concepts. Moreover, it was particularly crucial to Americans that the RMA was an American-led military revolution: the RMA. It appeared to guarantee continued superpower status in the 1990s at the same time that there was a determination to gain a peace dividend by reducing the size of the American military after the Cold War.

However, the assumptions underlying the RMA faced serious intellectual challenges. If change was to be understood in terms of movement along a line in a graph, then it appeared important to be at the head of the line, as well as to determine the axes of the graph, but this approach derived from an inadequate understanding of technological change, which does not occur as a linear progression. In addition, the concept of the RMA was based on the notion that order and pattern can be found in all things, whereas in fact chaos is the natural state. In addition, although some degree of order is necessary for matters of whatever hue to be described and discussed in a meaningful way, that does not mean the order or pattern actually exists. In particular, perceptions vary, and in military terms, this variation is directly linked to the situation whereby the definition of victory by one side, usually in terms of territory captured and casualties inflicted, is not shared by the other. This contrast was to affect American forces in Iraq and Afghanistan in the 2000s. Moreover, only a small portion of the army had been trained in the American Military Center established in 1988 to provide training in counterinsurgency warfare.

Thus, in accordance with a long-held tendency in American military and political thinking, the RMA met the American need to believe in the possibility of high-intensity conflict and total victory, with opponents shocked and awed into accepting defeat, rather than offering an engagement with the ambiguous and qualified nature of modern victory. For Americans, the victory that was fit for discussion was provided by a discussion that ran together confident analysis with rhetoric. A survey of American officers in 2000–2001 indicated confidence in America's ability to control the terms of an engagement against a competent adversary, along with a lack of knowledge about future threats outside their tactical specialties. The latter point was also true of other militaries.

The RMA sat alongside other concepts and slogans of the decade, including the "new world order" and the "end of history." These claims rested on the belief that the fall of the Soviet Union represented a triumph for American-led democratic capitalism and that there would be no future clash of ideologies to destabilize the world. The anchoring of East Asia to the American economy and the major rise in American foreign trade from 1993 to 2000 appeared to vindicate this. Global politics were certainly widely reshaped in the 1990s. An imploding Soviet Union did not challenge American hegemony, and unlike the political transformations in Russia in 1917–1920 and Germany in 1933–1939, Russia in the 1990s did not swing from revolution to dangerous war maker.

However, across much of the world, identity and conflict were shaped and expressed in terms of ethnicity, a practice that did not provide opportunities for American leadership. The upsurge of ethnic violence in Yugoslavia, the Caucasus, and much of sub-Saharan Africa indicated the persistence of deep-seated tensions and tarnished confidence about a new international order. Furthermore, the internationalism that had greatest impact was that of religion, particularly Islam. In many countries, hostility to globalization meant opposition to modernism and modernization and thus could draw on powerful interests and deep fears. The hostile focus was frequently on the alleged standard bearers of globalization, particularly the United States and multinational companies.

SOMALIA

The limitations of new-model weaponry, warfighting, and theory had been demonstrated within the two years of the success over Iraq in 1991 because intervention in Somalia proved a total failure. Following Somalia's defeat in the Ogaden War with Ethiopia in 1977–1979, the government had faced growing opposition from the clans that were the key unit in social organization. After a full-scale civil war in 1989–1990 that involved the fall of the government, Somalia was split into areas controlled by the heavily armed clans. The UN intervened in 1992 to bring humanitarian relief, although also, if necessary, to disarm the factions. The UN forces, however, were inadequate to the latter task. The Americans, who in Operation Restore Hope initially provided 28,000 of the 37,000-strong UN force, were determined to remove Mohamed Farah Aidid, whose faction dominated the capital, Mogadishu. On October 3, 1993, an American task force failed to capture Aidid and met opposition in the difficult urban terrain, with two helicopters shot down and 16 Rangers dead.

In reaction to their losses, the Americans abandoned aggressive operations in Somalia. This decision was used by Osama bin Laden, leader of the Islamic terrorist movement al-Qaeda, to argue that the Americans could be forced to retreat. This conviction helped inspire bin Laden's "Declaration of War against the Americans Occupying the Land of the Two Holy Places," issued in August 1996, that called for the expulsion of American forces from Saudi Arabia (a legacy of the Gulf War of 1990–1991) and for the overthrow of what was seen as the pro-American Saudi government.

In March 1994, with the United States no longer willing to bear a share, the UN forces withdrew from Somalia, which continued to descend into chaos, a situation still essentially true today. Moreover, the failure of the intervention in Somalia helped ensure that no American troops thereafter were sent on peacekeeping missions to Africa. Partly as a result, nothing effective was done to prevent the genocide in Rwanda later that spring as extremist Hutus slaughtered about 800,000 Tutsi.

BOSNIA

In contrast, in the less difficult environment of Haiti, the Americans successfully intervened in 1994 to restore order, whereas in the former Yugoslavia there was eventually successful Western intervention, both in 1995 and in 1999. The collapse of Yugoslavia, a Communist federal state, had been part of the wider transformation of Eastern Europe and the Soviet Union with and after the fall of Communism. Yugoslavia was divided between ethnic groups, notably Serbs and Croats, and, as the state collapsed, they both sought independence for the areas they dominated and pursued the widest possible definition of the latter. Croatia under Franjo Tudjman and Serbia under Slobodan Milošěvic, both authoritarian populists, used nationalism to provide both identity and justification. The Serb-dominated Yugoslav army made a major effort to resist neighboring Croatia's drive for independence, not least because Croatia contained a large Serb minority. Croatia was able to win independence in 1992, but the war spilled over into Bosnia, a part of Yugoslavia bordering both Croatia and Serbia that was ethnically mixed with large Croat, Serb, and Bosnian Muslim minorities. Bosnian Croat and Bosnian Serb forces cooperated with the armies of Croatia and Serb in a complex mix of politics and harsh atavistic violence.

The Bosnian Serbs conquered much of Bosnia but lost the struggle for international support. Instability in the Balkans appeared to threaten a more general regional conflagration, but was also judged unacceptable because of the nature of the conflict. The brutal slaughter of civilians by the Serbs (and, to a lesser extent,

A private moment in front of a wall of photographs of the Bosnian victims of the massacre at Srebenica in July 1995.

by their opponents) was an all-too-familiar feature of conflict in much of the modern world, reflecting the extent to which, in an age of nationalism, ethnic groups were seen as the units of political strength and thus as targets. Most prominently, but with many other examples at a different scale, in July 1995 the Bosnian Serbs slaughtered about 4,000 unarmed Muslim males in Srebrenica, which had been designated a safe zone by UN's representatives whose peacekeeping force lacked the strength and determination to act. Rape was also used as a form of collective punishment. Possibly 50,000 Bosnian women were subjected to sexual violence.

"Ethnic cleansing," the expulsion with considerable, often murderous, violence of members of an ethnic group, was even more common. It looked back to longstanding patterns of ethnic rivalry and violence, but more specifically to the emphasis after each world war, notably in Eastern Europe, on national self-determination and related population moves. By 1995, there were nearly 350,000 Bosnian refugees in Germany alone, and this refugee flow increased political pressure for a settlement of the conflict.

In some respects, the ethnic cleansing seen in former Yugoslavia (and indeed in the Caucasus in the 1990s, especially in the conflict between Armenia and Azerbaijan) was an instance in the post–Cold War world of an already-established practice, one that had been incorporated into the rivalries of the Cold War as well as into other struggles. However, humanitarian assumptions were now different. Moreover, the clear political and military dominance that had facilitated such a process after World War II, notably with the expulsion of Germans from Eastern Europe but also with the movement of Poles from areas annexed by the Soviet Union to those cleared of Germans, was not a factor in the 1990s. Instead, ethnic cleansing led to pressure on outside powers, particularly in the West, to intervene to protect civilians. This process led to the reinterpretation of peacekeeping as peace enforcement but, more generally, to a sense of the need to act forcibly that lasted until policy changed in 2013 with the decision not to use military means against the murderous Syrian government.

In Bosnia, direct Western military intervention in 1995, in what was NATO's first offensive military mission, took the form of bombing and the use of cruise missiles. The latter were unmanned missiles that could deliver precise firepower without the risks, costs, and limitations associated with airpower. In their planning for conflict with the Soviet Union in the 1980s, the United States had intended to respond to any attack using cruise missiles to inflict heavy damage on Soviet armor advancing across West Germany. They had been used in the Gulf War in 1991.

Valuable as the technology was, operations on the ground were also highly significant. In the autumn of 1995, the Croats and the Bosnian Muslims, brought together in large part by American pressure, were able to mount successful offensives against the Serbs, with the Croats overrunning first western Slavonia and then the Krajina. The substantial forces deployed reflected the overlap between conventional and irregular warfare and units, the lack of particular skill and professionalism required for the weaponry and conflict in question, and the ability to draw on local sources of manpower and supplies.

The impact of NATO pressure was increased by the weakness of Serbia's traditional ally, Russia, and by the extent to which, unlike in the case of Syria in 2013, Russia was then under a government that was willing to accommodate Western interest. In November 1994, Boris Yeltsin, president of Russia from 1991 to 1999, delivered a menacing "Cold Peace" speech in Budapest, employing threats to try to prevent the expansion of NATO membership into the former Communist bloc. Subsequently, the Russians adopted an aggressive stance toward Ukraine. However, this approach was not sustained by Yeltsin, in part because of a lack of regional support and in part because of severe economic problems in Russia in 1998. Indeed, in 1999 there was a wave of Eastern European accessions to NATO, the result of a shift in American policy in 1994–1995 from initial reluctance to support for NATO's expansion. As a result of this expansion, a major strategic transformation occurred without conflict.

KOSOVO

The Bosnian crisis was not to be the last in former Yugoslavia. Later in the decade, there was a similar crisis in Kosovo, an autonomous area in southern Serbia with a majority ethnic-Albanian and Muslim population. Ethnic cleansing by the Serbs, intended to suppress separatist demands and to destroy support for the Kosovo Liberation Army, led to the flight of about 800,000 Kosovans, mostly to Albania. The crisis resulted in Western pressure in the form of diplomacy supported in 1999 by an air assault. This was another instance of external intervention into a longstanding local dispute with a narrative of its own, one in which ethnic identity and revenge interacted with the quest for land and position. Criminality, in the shape of drug trafficking and smuggling, also played a role on both sides, as did atrocities.

The extent to which this air assault inflicted destruction on Serb forces and, differently, led to a change in Serb policy is a matter of controversy. In the former case, there is the contrast between the actual amount of damage inflicted, which seems to have been relatively modest, and the potential for damage threatened by clear NATO air superiority. This contrast is always significant when assessing military capability, operational success, and strategic options. Damage to bridges, factories, and electrical power plants was important, not least because it affected the financial interests of the Serbian elite, as well as their morale and the functioning of the economy.

A number of factors were responsible for the change in Serb policy, including a Russian refusal to follow up on threats to intervene on behalf of the Serbs. This wider geopolitical context was crucial. In effect, the Kosovo crisis was the last stage by which the Balkans were transferred from the Russian to the Western sphere of interest. Indeed, the entire Yugoslav crisis was consequent upon, but also marked stages in, a transfer of power to the West and, more particularly, to the United

States and Germany. The United States was responsible for most of the air sorties. Germany was a key ally of Croatia, in part for cultural reasons, and Britain pressed hard in the Kosovo crisis to support the concept of humanitarian or liberal interventionism advocated by the prime minister Tony Blair from 1997 to 2007 and to show Muslims that the Western powers could and would defend their interests.

Western intervention, however, revealed major differences between the NATO powers, notably over the feasibility of intervention, differences that were to be more pronounced over Iraq (2003) and that indicated the difficulties of giving NATO an offensive mission. More specifically, there was a failure to draw due attention to the difficulties of ensuring that the "shock and awe" of the Allied air assault led to a change in policy on the part of the shocked and awed. This problem did not attract the attention of military planners who, as usual, underplayed the political context, nor did it attract that of politicians who preferred to remain confident that the use of force would deliver an assured output. The limitations of the RMA were an aspect of this wider problem, as was a degree of naivety about the possibilities for peacemaking and peacekeeping.

By 2000, as a result of the flight of Serbs from Croatia, Bosnia, and Kosovo, Serbia had the largest refugee population in Europe. The individual and collective disruption this represented was a grim legacy of war. So was the use of rape as a deliberate weapon. After the Serbian withdrawal from Kosovo, the continuing isolation of Serbia as a result of economic and financial warfare in the form of sanctions helped cause serious problems, an erosion of support for Milosěvic, and this all in the face of Serbian popular action in 2000, which led to the electoral victory of pro-Western parties. He was arrested in 2001 and sent to stand charges of genocide, the first head of state to be tried in this fashion. Linked to this process, Eastern European militaries were transformed into bodies under the control of democratic governments and with their structures, tasking, doctrine, and weaponry no longer determined by membership of the Warsaw Pact.

RUSSIA

It is all too easy to focus on the deficiencies of the Western military as in the Kosovo crisis, but the limitations, yet also potential, of a military response were also clearly indicated elsewhere. This was notably so with Russia, which in the Caucasus confronted problems similar to those faced by the Serbs in Kosovo. In the Caucasus, Islamic independence movements were able to rely on considerable local popular support, in part because of a tradition of ethnic strife, as well as the difficult mountainous terrain. These movements tried to extend the breakup of the Soviet Union in 1991 to Russia, but the Russian leader, Boris Yeltsin, was unwilling to accept such separatism. This political choice, which was to have military consequences, reflected the fear that such separatism would be contagious and that it would root radical Muslims near southern Russia, as well as an awareness that concessions would discredit the new non-Communist political order with Russian nationalists.

Chechen women mourn the destruction of their homes in Grozny, October 1999.

In the winter of 1994–1995, the Russians invaded the rebellious region of Chechnya, launching a campaign that continued until they withdrew in 1996. In this, the Russians revealed a campaigning ethos and style similar to that shown by the Red Army in Afghanistan in 1979–1988. This indicated the extent to which there was a "cultural" character to war making, with differing national practices at least as presented in particular militaries. In the capture of the Chechen capital, Grozny, in January 1995, the Russians employed devastating firepower, causing a level of destruction that was no longer acceptable to Western commentators. Russian brutality fostered a guerrilla resistance that the Russians were unable then to crush. The limitations of counterinsurgency policies were fully apparent. In 1999–2000, there was a repetition with an assertion of Russian control seen in the capture of Grozny in January 2000, but continued guerrilla opposition. This campaign was presented as a defense of Russian national greatness.

THIRD WORLD

Insurrectionary conflict in a number of countries overlapped with both civil wars and a politics of force. The common currency was the use of violence to secure political outcomes. "Failed states" provided the clearest examples, in that levels of continuous violence were high, and the use of force there did not produce a degree of stability. In Afghanistan, Soviet military and financial aid to the government of President Najibullah, put in power in 1986, continued after the 1988–1989 Soviet withdrawal. The government was initially more successful than had been predicted, in part because the guerrillas found it difficult to translate their capability to achieve offensive goals; they were also very divided. However, the government was greatly weakened by the fall of the Soviet Union in 1991, which meant no more money to pay the army, and by the defection of its strongman, Abdul Rashid Dostum.

The Afghan government was overthrown in 1992 as already strong ethnic–regional tensions escalated in what was not a vacuum of power, but rather a collapse of central power matched by the competition of an unstable array of sectional warlords. The basic rivalry was between the non-Pushtun Northerners, notably Dostum, and the Pushtuns of the south, who were readier to adopt radical Islamic policies, notably those of the Taliban movement, and to align with neighboring Pakistan, where there was a large Pushtun minority. Afghan Pushtuns rallied round the Taliban, which overran much of the country, including the capital Kabul in 1996, only for serious resistance to continue in the north. The international context was different to that which was to be seen in the 2000s with the War on Terror. In the 1990s, the equivalent to the American role in the Afghan conflict was that of the rivalry between India and Pakistan. The latter sought strategic depth against India and regarded Afghanistan as an area of natural interest, while in response, the Indians aligned with the Afghan Northerners.

Ethnic tension and wider geopolitical tensions also played key roles in the civil wars in Central Africa: in Rwanda, Burundi, and Zaire (Congo). In the first two, ethnic tension between Tutsi and Hutus played a role, with a civil war in Rwanda in 1990–1993. In April 1994, an extremist group of Hutus seized power in Rwanda, touching off the slaughter of about 800,000 Tutsi. The inability of the UN or United States to stop this genocide led to serious questions about the effectiveness, purpose, and means of international norms. In turn, the overthrow of the Hutu militias that staged the genocide helped lead the new Rwanda government to intervene in Zaire (Congo), the government of which allowed them refuge. In 1997, Mobutu Sese Soko, the dictator of Zaire since 1965, fell as a result of the Rwandan invasion. Other neighboring powers, such as Angola, intervened in Zaire in a pursuit of influence and mineral wealth and to prevent unwelcome outcomes. Ethnic tension also played a major role in Sudan, not only in the rivalry between the Arab north and the non-Arab south, but also in the latter, with tribes there fighting each other as the Dinka and Nuer did.

External intervention was also a highly significant factor in West Africa, where in Liberia from 1989 and Sierra Leone from 1991, civil warfare helped lead to a breakdown of social order. The combatants can be presented as warlords, both in and outside government, but that suggests a degree of organization and coherence that is somewhat misleading in the case of what were often large criminal gangs, relying on looting and extortion and often using drug-taking teenagers. This gangland chaos led to intervention, both by neighbors and by the regional power, Nigeria, which found it difficult to enforce peace in a society where it was difficult to identify opponents. Nevertheless, a measure of order was restored in Sierra Leone by 2002 and in Liberia by 2003.

Children soldiers undergoing military training, Congo, 1997.

In Liberia, the guerrilla campaign launched in 1989 by Revolutionary United Front rebels of Charles Taylor was financed by diamonds mined by slave laborers as well as by Libya. Taylor became in effect a warlord and then president in 1997, a post he held until 2003. The warfare of the period led to possibly 120,000 fatalities, the forced conscription of children, more than two thirds of the population becoming refugees, and an estimated 400,000 amputees: the Revolutionary United Front repeatedly cut off the limbs, noses, and lips of those it wished to punish. In 2008, the population was about 3.9 million.

In addition to the brutalization of civilians, not least by and in ethnic cleansing, there were also conflicts in which there was a degree of more regular conflict. This was true in the former Soviet Union in the war between the newly independent republics of Armenia and Azerbaijan over control of the region of Nagorno-Karabakh, a largely Armenian-populated autonomous enclave inside Azerbaijan. This struggle was won by Armenia, with the enclave's size doubled and linked to Armenia in 1994. A more narrowly defined frontier dispute that was also a conflict over hegemony was waged by Ethiopia and Eritrea in 2000. The Ethiopians benefited from superior airpower, better armor (Russian T-72 tanks), and greater numbers although the Eritreans fought well, taking advantage of the terrain.

Many conflicts in the 1990s reflected the Cold War, either its last stages or its aftermath. Thus, in El Salvador, the Farabundo Martí National Liberation Front insurrection continued until a settlement was negotiated in 1992, under which the front was able to enter civilian politics. So it was also with Mozambique in 1992, when Renamo, a South African–backed guerrilla organization, negotiated an agreement with the Communist government. It did not prove possible to make such a lasting transition in Angola, where the UNITA insurrection continued until its leader, Jonas Savimbi, was killed in 2002.

Equally, there was conflict with other causes, some of which reflected tensions that preceded the Cold War. In Indonesia, ethnic and religious rivalries were exacerbated by the Asian financial crisis of 1997, which led to a marked downturn that also spawned food riots. Demonstrations by radical students and factory workers were met by the use of force by the army in May 1998. In the face of the resulting chaos, the dictator, Suharto, resigned.

There were also unsuccessful insurrections. Sikh separatism had been a significant problem in India in the early 1980s, but by 1997 the insurgency in the Punjab had come to an end, in part because of the more cautious stance of the central government in the handling of Punjabi politics, but also thanks to the strength and methods of Indian counterinsurgency. The ratio of troops to area was greater than with the Americans in Iraq in the 2000s, in part because the cost of using paramilitaries in India was far lower. In addition, the Punjab Police recruited local auxiliaries who were paid and armed to kill militants, deny them recruits, and take the initiative from the insurgency.

CONCLUSIONS

The agenda and narrative of military history in the 1990s looks different depending on which country is the focus of attention. In "advanced" liberal societies democratization, disenchantment with violence and glory, individualism, and different concepts of national interests had all contributed to a reaction against war that was deeper rooted and more sustained than other negative responses over the previous half millennium. There were indications that developments were making a number of human societies less keen to embark on wars, more reluctant to inflict casualties, and more unwilling to accept losses. This was readily apparent in the increasingly negative response of governments and populations to the commitment of resources abroad, as with the Americans in Somalia. It was unlikely, however, that a similar response would arise if these societies were attacked. Indeed, it was reasonable at the close of the twentieth century to suggest that, in such an eventuality, the position might repeat that of the beginning of the century when, despite their internationalism, the overwhelming majority of Socialist leaders supported their countries' participation in World War I. Nevertheless, the situation with regard to conflicts that were not wars of national survival was very different from the situation a century earlier, and there was a readily apparent contrast between the American response to the Korean War in 1950–1953 and the more qualified involvement in Somalia, Haiti, or Bosnia in the 1990s.

A reluctance to embark on aggressive, or indeed, any wars did not extend to all powers and did not prevent an assertive global or regional interventionism, as with the American invasion of Panama in 1989 or the dispatch of Indian troops to Sri Lanka in 1987. Nevertheless, however much such episodes might reveal the heavy-handedness and assertiveness of global or regional powers, they were presented not as aggressive, but as designed to maintain legality: war by peacekeeping. In short, armies were to serve as the police force of a benign global or regional order. This was dramatized in the response to the Iraqi conquest of Kuwait in 1990. The Americans went to great pains to ensure that their response was part of a wideranging reaction, one far more akin to the UN-supported American-led response to the North Korean invasion of South Korea in 1950 than to American participation in the Vietnam War. Vindication in these terms was seen by the governments of the United States and its allies as necessary for domestic as well as international reasons. America went to war in reaction to the Iraqi invasion, but this war had to be acceptable, in form as much as content, to domestic suppositions.

This set of ideas, assumptions, and practices was clearly not the case in control societies, such as Iraq, Syria, China, Burma, or Indonesia, societies where the military determined policy or where politics did not involve much of a dialog between government and populace. In some modern control societies, governments chose to use military aggression as an aspect of politics; indeed, military aggression could become politics. This policy could be presented in terms of "rationality," with the argument that such wars were commenced to bolster domestic positions, but the wars can equally be seen as stemming from cultural suppositions about the role of force and the forces, and the rationality can be presented as constructed in those terms. Thus the Argentinian invasion of the Falklands/Malvinas in 1982 was an exercise in which the use of force was a means as much as a goal for Argentina's military junta. The islands would possibly have ended up under Argentinian suzerainty, eventually, by peaceful means, but such a success would have been less desirable than a military victory. In certain societies and political cultures the latter is far more glorious than peaceful diplomacy, and the definition of glory, as well as many aspects of the practice of politics, had shifted singularly little from that of the nineteenth century.

This was also the case with the ethnic and religious identities and demands that contributed greatly to much of the fighting in the Balkans, the Caucasus, and Central Africa in the 1990s. In each case, it was possible to draw attention to frontiers that ignored such divisions, thus apparently explaining or excusing the resort to violence, but elsewhere in the world, such ethnic and religious divisions did not necessarily lead to conflict. However, in the Balkans and the Caucasus in the 1990s, the collapse of a former political order created the very situation of flux, opportunity, and fear that most encouraged and encourages a distrust of negotiation and a resort to violence in bellicist cultures. In the former Yugoslavia, a belief in the value of violence rapidly surfaced, and force became the crucial means of demographics, economics, and politics.

For the United States and Britain, there were "wars of choice" in the 1990s, as decisions were made as to where to intervene and how best to define goals and means. In Peru, in contrast, the army was used both against *Sendero Luminoso* (Shining Path), a radical left-wing guerrilla movement that relied on drug trafficking, and in 1992 to shut down Congress and the courts as the president,

Alberto Fujimori, sought to consolidate his power. The Peruvian experience of *Sendero Luminoso* inspired the Communist insurgency that began in Nepal in 1996. The *Janayuddha* (People's War) launched by the People's Liberation Army of Nepal and the vigorous, often brutal, response by the security forces were responsible for more than 13,000 dead and more than 200,000 displaced by the time a peace agreement was signed in 2006. The insurgents had many women and children among their forces but were greatly outnumbered by the army and police. In Haiti, where military coups in 1988 and 1991 cut short democratization, American intervention in 1994 was followed by the abolition of the army in 1995.

The use of force, both in external warfare and to confront domestic opponents, could appear successful in the 1990s but also faced problems in securing consent and in confronting the realities of international power: foreign states could intervene against this use. Such intervention was more serious than the general diplomatic attempt to enforce norms about appropriate behavior. No state was going to intervene to dissuade the Chinese government from employing force to maintain its position in Tibet or to deter the Russians from operations in Chechnya.

However, in East Timor, which Indonesia had invaded and annexed in 1975 as Portuguese imperial power ended, the brutal suppression of popular separatist pressure led in 1999 to the intervention of Australian forces under UN auspices, and independence was secured. Without such UN auspices, there was also intervention in support of separatism, by Pakistan, for example, in neighboring Indian-ruled Kashmir, but such intervention was generally covert.

The 1990s is a difficult period to characterize, falling as it does between the Cold War and the War on Terror. In practice, albeit without the nuclear confrontation that had characterized the former as well as the large-scale American expeditionary warfare seen in the latter, many of the features of conflict in the 1980s and 2000s were apparent in the 1990s. This was particularly true in Africa and Latin America and also if the focus is on the use of force in internal politics. However, the more general geopolitical context was very different after the end of the Cold War, and this difference affected strategic planning, notably for the great powers and particularly the United States.

READING LIST

R. H. Scales, *Certain Victory: The US Army in the Gulf War*, Fort Leavenworth, Kan., Office of the Chief of Staff, 1993.

Anatol Lieven, *Chechnya: Tombstone of Russian Power*, New Haven, Conn., 1999.

NINE

THE 2000S

A young soldier, Darfur, 2004.

TERRORISM'S ATTEMPTED REVOLUTION
IN MILITARY AFFAIRS, 2001

The suicide attacks launched on New York and Washington, D.C., on September 11, 2001, by Osama bin Laden's al-Qaeda (the Base), a virulently anti-American Islamic terrorist organization, represented a major contrast in means from those employed by terrorist movements in the 1910s. Hijacked planes employed as weapons to slaughter large numbers of civilians (both passengers and on the ground) were very different from the assassin's pistol or knife, such as the shots fired in Sarajevo in 1914 that killed Archduke Franz Ferdinand and his wife and helped precipitate World War I.

Yet, there was also a common element: the use of unexpected violence to inflict great damage and have a disproportionate political effect. Thus, al-Qaeda sought to employ terrorist methods to strategic end by crippling, or at least symbolically dethroning, American financial and political power. Al-Qaeda did not have the success anticipated, not least because it rested on a greatly flawed assumption about the concentrated and top-down nature of American power and society, an assumption linked to the usual totalitarian position that democracy is weak and pliable. Indeed, al-Qaeda, like other terrorist movements and totalitarian adversaries, failed to understand the unwillingness of people to give in to terrorism and attack. More particularly, attacking the population, as opposed to military targets, can help harden opinion against terrorists and thus can enable governments to take action the public might not otherwise endorse.

INTERVENTION IN AFGHANISTAN, 2001–2002

The terrorist attacks focused on and accentuated American concerns about developments in the Islamic world and their own vulnerability. The optimism that had followed the fall of the Berlin Wall in 1989 and success in the Gulf War in 1991 was finally shattered. The newly revealed vulnerability led to a determination to employ American order to transform the situation and end the threat. As a result, the administration took a more determined position in warfare in the early 2000s than had been the case in the Balkans in the 1990s. The replacement of President Bill Clinton by George W. Bush in January 2001 was also significant. There were domestic policy consequences, as with the Patriot Act of 2001, which authorized the government to gather information to scrutinize the population and identify potential terrorists. Moreover, in what was proclaimed a War on Terror, the Bush administration, seeking to protect America by preemptive action aimed at destroying the terrorist threat, attacked what were identified as terrorist bases and supporters. The National Security Strategy issued in September 2002 pressed the need for preemptive strikes in response to what were presented as the dual threats of terrorism and "rogue states" possessing or developing weapons of mass destruction and sought to transform the global political order so as to lessen the chance of these threats developing. There was a major buildup in military spending, from $276 billion in 1998 to $310 billion by 2001, with the latter greater than the next nine largest national military budgets. For 2002, the sum was about 40 percent of the world's total military spending.

Hitting back at terrorists is not easy because the target is difficult to identify, but if they have a base, and notably in a "failed state," then action is possible. In the case of al-Qaeda, the Taliban regime in Afghanistan had provided shelter. Already, in 1998, the Americans had bombarded al-Qaeda bases in Afghanistan with cruise missiles. In 2001, the Taliban had refused to yield to pressure to hand over

the al-Qaeda leaders who financed the regime. In response, the Americans intervened, launching Operation Enduring Freedom to crush al-Qaeda and remove the
Taliban. They undertook a formidable air assault by allying with the Taliban's
local opponents, the Northern Alliance, notably Abdul Rashid Dostum, the leader
of the Uzbek minority. A different impression is provided depending on which is
emphasized. Thus, the successful American air assault seemed to justify earlier
talk of an RMA, notably in the shape of providing precise firepower. This was
deployed in the form of air attack, a form that did not involve the commitment or
casualties of troops on the ground. The range in American air capabilities reflected
the development of airpower in recent decades. In 2001, the Americans used long-
range B-52 and B-1 (stealth) bombers, extensive aerial refueling enabling planes to
fly very long missions, intermediate-range airpower in the shape of aircraft and
Tomahawk cruise missiles from carriers and warships in the Arabian Sea more
than 400 miles away, air bases in Central Asia and Pakistan, unpiloted drones
providing reconnaissance or firing missiles, and CBU-130 "combined-effects
munitions," which spread cluster bombs. The availability of dual-mode, laser, and
GPS guidance for bombs increased the range of precision available, and cameras
on planes provided the public with a sense of inevitable power.

The airpower, however, was significant not in itself but as part of a
combined-arms strategy, a standard pattern in a subnuclear conflict. The
Northern Alliance, which deployed perhaps 15,000 troops, benefited in its
attacks on the Taliban from American airpower, but also from the more traditional porosity of alignments in Afghanistan, a situation accentuated by the
lack of coherence of the Taliban regime and by the availability of American
bribes. The Americans assisted the Northern Alliance with CIA operatives
and Special Operations Forces, as well as with air attack guided by Special
Operations Forces teams using portable laser designation and offering precise
targeting data; they also provided the Alliance with crucial capabilities as well
as additional combat power. The fighting experience and willpower of the
Northern alliance were also important. Moreover, as the Taliban position collapsed in November–December 2001, the international context was also significant, notably the willingness of President Musharraf of Pakistan to permit
American overflying and to cut support for the Taliban.

A pro-Western government was installed in Kabul in late 2001, but bin Laden
was not captured and opposition by the Taliban continued. The Americans found
Afghanistan very difficult, both militarily and politically. The first major
American land operation in Afghanistan, Operation Anaconda in March 2002,
saw poor planning and logistics and a lack of effective air and artillery support.
In addition, the opportunity to consolidate success was thrown away as the
Americans turned to focus on Iraq. Having overthrown Taliban rule, the Western
forces did not establish support at the regional, let alone local, level across
Afghanistan and, crucially, did not acquire key knowledge about tribal relationships. The new constitution led to a degree of centralization that fell foul of traditional regional and ethnic loyalties and could not be sustained by Hamid Karzai,

Taliban fighters outside Kabul, early 2000s.

the chairman of the Afghan Transitional Administration from 2002 to 2004 and president from 2004 to 2014. Moreover, making no effort to win over the Taliban left them an alienated and rebellious force.

THE IRAQ WAR

Although committing special forces against Islamic terrorist movements linked to al-Qaeda, such as in Georgia and the Philippines in 2003, the United States also sought to deal with Iraq, a rogue state that was regarded as a supporter of terrorism in the Middle East and also as a challenge because of its apparent or at least alleged determination to develop weapons of mass destruction and related delivery systems. There was also a sense that the removal of Saddam Hussein would ensure regional stability by safeguarding Saudi Arabia, the Gulf States, and Israel, all targets of Iraqi subversion, and thus would strengthen America's alliance system.

Within a few weeks of the overthrow of the Taliban, Bush decided to invade Iraq, a definite target with regular armed forces, rather than the more intangible struggle with terrorism. The Joint Chiefs of Staff wanted delay so that al-Qaeda could be completely crushed in Afghanistan, but in a major failure of planning, the administration argued that both could be achieved and insisted on an invasion of Iraq by the spring of 2003, presumably to have it settled before the 2004 presidential campaign. As a result, American priority shifted radically from Afghanistan, ensuring a lack of resources there that hindered the development of an appropriate strategy and, indeed, of a response to growing disorder.

The preparation for the invasion of Iraq in 2003 and the contrasts between the plans in 2002–2003 and the deployment of troops to the Gulf in 1990–1991 reflected changes in assumptions about capabilities and the nature of warfare. The Americans sent far fewer troops to the Gulf in 2003, in large part because there was a conviction that the RMA offered a new potential. There was tension between civilian policy makers and the generals over this issue, and each was to be correct, although for different reasons. The numbers required to secure the rapid conquest of Iraq in 2003 were far fewer than those needed to defeat the Iraqis in 1991, but there were too few troops to ensure that control could be readily maintained once terrorism and insurrection rapidly followed the conquest.

In assessing the Iraq War, the balance of scholarly emphasis is therefore at issue, and this is linked to the more general approach to military history. If the focus is on battle and conquest, then attention focuses on the successful operation in 2003, but if it is on war in a wider strategic context, then the Iraq operation is seen more as a failure. It led the United States into a major and lengthy commitment that proved very costly and greatly harmed America's international position. Both of these dimensions must be borne in mind when considering the Iraq War and were exacerbated by the fact that, from 2003 to 2011, the United States was simultaneously waging war in two theaters (Afghanistan and Iraq), which it had not done since 1949.

The conquest of an entire country and the replacement of its government was an unusual task for a Western military by the 2000s. The Americans had last done so in 1989 at Panama, but the Noriega regime there was far weaker militarily than that of Saddam Hussein and more exposed to American military power. Moreover, there was no grounding of the dictatorial regime in Panamanian society, and the Americans were rapidly able to hand over authority to local politicians. Guillermo Endara, whose victory in the presidential election in May 1989 had been annulled by Noriega, was installed as president. Endara faced serious economic problems and declining popularity, but there was no collapse into disorder. The reconquest of Kuwait from Iraqi occupation in 1991 was no indication of the task that would be faced in Iraq in 2003 because this reconquest was a more limited task, both militarily and politically: indeed, the Kuwaiti population welcomed liberation from a harsh occupation.

In 2003, as in 1991, Iraqi air defenses were rapidly suppressed. The Iraqi air defenses were already weakened by sanctions and then by the no-fly-zone operations of late 2002. The Americans used their air superiority to destroy Iraqi forces, notably tanks. On the ground, the Americans, who played the overwhelming role in the invasion although they were assisted by allies, notably the British in the south, concentrated on disrupting the Iraqi defense so that they were able to maintain the initiative. This operational dynamic was linked to repeated success in taking the initiative at the tactical level. Moreover, American tanks benefited from real-time (instantaneous) communication with aerial reconnaissance, notably by satellites, and this communication proved effective in target acquisition and engagement. Combined arms took on a new meaning and effectiveness.

As in 1991, although in different circumstances, the Iraqis were outthought and outfought. Developed from 2001, Iraq's defensive strategy differed from the 1991 reliance on static positions. Instead, alongside an attempt to resist American units in the open, there was a reliance on engaging the Americans in Iraq's cities, where their tanks would be less effective. Influenced by the defeat experienced by the Americans in Mogadishu in Somalia in 1993, Saddam Hussein saw the urban terrain as an Iraqi force multiplier. The pace and flexibility of the American advance and the extent to which the cohesion and morale of the Iraqi regime had already collapsed in the initial fighting led to the failure of this strategy. American "thunder runs" into Baghdad completed this process and this major city fell with only limited resistance. Soon after, the rest of Iraq was overrun, and much of the Iraqi military, unwilling to die for Saddam, disbanded and went home.

The effectiveness of American logistics was important to the speed of the advance, and both benefited from there being only 125,000 American combat troops on the ground. The use of airborne assault forces was significant. As with Afghanistan in 2001, the Americans benefited from local allies, in this case the Kurds, who had successfully rebelled in northern Iraq; however, unlike in 2001, the key fighting on land was done by the Americans.

The rapid fall of Iraq led to renewed talk of the RMA and an unwarranted degree of triumphalism. The techniques of the former had definitely been important in the conquest stage. The American military was better equipped than in 1991, not least with far more smart munitions such as directed bombs. The use of nighttime thermal imaging, which proved highly important to the effectiveness of tank combat, helped the United States maintain the tempo of its advance.

However, the difficulty in securing domestic support in Iraq had been underrated. In a serious failure of planning, a frequent element in the military history of this and other periods, the anticipated mass welcome of liberators did not materialize. Nor was there support for the American choice as leader, Ahmed Chalabi. There was also inadequate preparation for postwar disorder and division, not least Saddam's release of all the criminals, general lawlessness, widespread looting, and the breakdown of public services. A conviction of America's success in occupation and reconstruction in Germany and Japan after World War II was linked not only to American confidence that it could control the situation in Iraq after the invasion, but also to particular policies, notably the disbandment of the Iraqi army and the policy of de-Baathification. In practice, these disastrous policies rallied support for Sunni insurrection.

The Department of Defense, which was appointed lead agency in postwar reconstruction, ignored the advice and preliminary work of the State Department. There was a failure to understand the specific character of the individual societies and a misleading readiness to read between examples. In particular, sectarian divides, both ethnic and religious, were far greater in Iraq than in Germany or Japan. Moreover, under Saddam Hussein, there had been a politicization of government, a destruction of Iraqi intermediate institutions, and a hollowing out of civil society. These processes, along with other factors, ensured that American occupation lacked institutional and social anchors and levers of cooperation.

The overthrow of Saddam also exacerbated the divisions between (and within) the Shia and Sunni communities. The Americans and their Iraqi allies found themselves under wide-ranging attack beginning in 2004 from important elements in both, but more particularly from Shia militias that looked to Iran for help. The "stability and support" phase envisaged by the Americans turned out to be very different. Looked at differently, the American attempt at nation building cut across the realignments of political and economic interests and power that followed Saddam's fall.

To a degree, the insurrection fulfilled the prewar hopes of Saddam, although he was soon captured. For six months prior to the invasion, he had been establishing safe houses and secreting weapons and funds for opposition to an occupying force. The American invasion had been more successful than he anticipated, limiting the original Iraqi plans for an urban battleground and fatally fracturing the Saddam regime, but Saddam's idea of decentralized opposition within Iraq was indeed an element of the subsequent disorder, although this was true of the Sunnis and not of opposition from the Shia population, which had been hostile to Saddam. Supporters of the regime played a major role in the Sunni insurgency, providing it with a manpower most insurgencies lack. Now unemployed, members of the army also played a major role.

The failure to command the expected response helped cause the disorientation that affected the occupation forces as opposition increased, and the attempt to dictate such a response contributed greatly to the mounting chaos that engulfed Iraq. The initial American response was a reliance on force that was greatly weakened by a lack of targetable information. House-to-house searches alienated local opinion, and Humvee patrols accomplished little. With a preference for a short war followed by turning security over to newly trained Iraqi security forces, the American lack of a coherent strategy to defeat the insurgency became readily apparent in 2004, despite successes in particular operations such as the storming of the insurgent-held town of Fallujah in 2004. The American government emphasized a narrative of success, notably with the 2005 elections in Iraq, from which the Sunnis had in fact largely stayed out. The Americans claimed that the Iraqi security forces were capable of taking over, but this hope was challenged in 2006 when al-Qaeda and the Sunni insurgents succeeded, through vicious attacks, in provoking Shia opposition and a high level of violence in Baghdad. In 2006, the Americans conducted two operations, Together Forward One and Together Forward Two, but they failed because although the Americans could clear areas, they lacked the manpower to hold them. The Iraqi military did not provide the requested help. By August 3, 2007, a total of 3,648 American soldiers had died in action since the end of the conquests of Iraq in 2003 (with more than 27,000 wounded), whereas 367 had been killed in the conquest itself. The cost to America of the war and occupation by March 2007 was about $500 billion. By 2007 it was estimated that 650,000 Iraqi civilians had been killed, although all

The U.S. 1st Tank Battalion fires a 120-mm gun as it engages enemy insurgents during the Battle of Fallujah, 2004.

figures for civilian casualties are controversial. By 2013, more than 3 million of a population of 32 million Iraqis were refugees or internally displaced.

Faced by apparently intractable opposition that American military and political leaders had not anticipated, the Bush government was unsure whether to withdraw or send more troops. Against considerable political and military opposition, Bush decided on the latter, which was made possible by a lack of troubling commitments elsewhere; and in 2007, a total of 30,000 additional combat troops were sent in what was, in effect, a counteroffensive. Designed to provide the opportunity to create an effective relationship between the Iraqi public and government, this "surge" enabled the Americans to regain the initiative, but that only worked because the availability of more force was linked to an appropriate forward stance, notably platoon Combat Outposts among the people, and to an adroit political strategy in which the Americans sponsored the formation of neighborhood militias committed to stability while also negotiating with former insurgent groups.

This was an aspect, as part of a rediscovery of counterinsurgency ideas, of a more perceptive response to Iraq's sectarian divides, notably by creating a shared political and military constituency with the Sunnis (the basis of Saddam's position) while giving the Shias more reason to compromise. Differentiating among opponents worked because it was information driven, and the latter also became more characteristic of military operations. As a result, raids on the insurgents became more successful, with these aggressive campaigns linked to the more defensive stance within Baghdad. The American military showed intellectual flexibility and operational adaptability. The Americans also benefited from more support from the Iraqi military. Moreover, the extremism of the al-Qaeda fighters and the extent to which they were not Iraqis helped alienate the Sunni insurgents, leading to a vital shift in Anbar province.

Because the context was one in which there was a transfer of authority to the Iraqi government, the stabilization of the situation enabled the Americans to focus instead on the deteriorating position in Afghanistan. At the end of 2011, in response to demands from the Iraqi government, the Americans withdrew their last combat troops from Iraq.

AFGHANISTAN

The trajectory in Afghanistan proved less positive than that in Iraq. A Taliban resurgence from the summer of 2003, which gathered momentum from 2005, led to the collapse of the government position in much of the south and east of the country outside the capital, Kabul. By increasing the level of violence, the Taliban increased its influence over the population and thus lessened the options for the government and its foreign supporters. The Americans responded with a "win in Iraq and hold in Afghanistan" strategy, and as the situation deteriorated in the latter, the Taliban resurgence led to a NATO-led international commitment in the shape of the International Security Assistance Force (ISAF), as well as separate American counterinsurgency operations. America's commitment in Iraq (140,000 troops in 2005) led to an expansion of ISAF responsibilities in 2006, with NATO troops taking responsibility from the Americans in the south. The Afghan security forces were part of the problem because they were smaller than their Iraqi counterparts. However, American and NATO confidence proved misplaced because the Taliban were able to confront the ISAF forces deployed to support the Karzai government. As a result, whereas the United States had had 19,000 troops in Afghanistan in 2004, the Americans by the end of 2008 had greatly increased their forces in the country to about 40,000 men. The election of Barack Obama as president in October 2008 led to a shift in focus from Iraq to Afghanistan, and under a new surge announced in December 2009, a total of 32,000 additional troops were sent in. The challenge, however, was greater than in Afghanistan as well as being different in character. Pakistan provided a base for the Taliban that was even more difficult for the coalition forces than Iran had proved for Shia insurgents in Iraq, although the Pakistani diplomatic position changed from 2011. Moreover, within Afghanistan, the safe havens for the Afghan opposition were largely outside the cities and therefore constituted a different political and military context than the essentially urban focus in Iraq. This situation contributed to the asymmetrical nature of the problems facing ISAF forces.

Although there was a major effort to learn lessons, the surge in Afghanistan proved less successful than that in Iraq, which was a reflection not only of very different military and political factors and operational and cultural environments, but also of the near relationship of success and failure. It was all too easy to talk about Afghanistan's long history of resisting central control and foreign invasion. The country indeed has a low density of population and a mountainous terrain that has acted against the idea of national identity. However, there had been a degree of national cohesion from the late nineteenth century. It is more helpful to focus on the particular factors in the 2000s and 2010s because they help explain why the traditional practices of compromise did not work. In part, there was the crucial element, in a society in which respect and personal links were significant, of a lack of respect for Hamid Karzai, the president from 2004 to 2014; he won reelection in a fraudulent election in 2009. Moreover, the unpopularity of his corrupt and unsuccessful government ensured that there was a weak basis for the efforts of the Afghan military and police and the ISAF forces to maintain order. The extent to which the government, and with it the military and police, was divided on tribal lines was a serious factor. Relying on the Karzai government for much of the civilian dimension of counterinsurgency proved foolish. So also did the attempt to overcome the patronage element in local tribal politics.

The revival of the resistance was significant. Far from its being a case of recalcitrant warlords (although these remained a factor, notably in the north), the key opposition came from the Taliban. Their determination, resilience, and grounding in local society were all important, as was the degree to which, across a frontier that could not be controlled by the ISAF forces, they drew support from bases in Pakistan, as well as from the determination of Pakistan's powerful Inter-Services Intelligence Agency to keep the Karzai government weak. At the same time, as a reminder of the complexity of the international contexts of conflict, there was also action by the Pakistani army against the Taliban and their local allies. This action reflected the extent to which it proved difficult to direct policy and monopolize armed force and foreign policy at the state level, which is the practice of developed states.

Taliban resistance in Afghanistan continued, most prominently in the Taliban heartlands of Helmand and Kandahar, but also in other provinces. There was both a series of local struggles and one overall war. Each of the local struggles involved a different combination of combatants, and the political and environmental challenge had operational consequences. Thus, in Helmand the British were put under heavy pressure by the Taliban. In neighboring Kandahar province, the situation was less difficult for the Canadians, but they also lacked sufficient forces to hold enough positions to provide backing and security for their local allies. The difficulties in these provinces ensured that they were the destination of most of the American troops sent in under the surge of 2010.

At the beginning of 2012, the American-dominated, NATO-led ISAF had 130,000 combat troops (90,000 of them American) deployed, as well as a large number of support troops. However, by then, war-weariness was setting in among the ISAF powers. Their activity as a coalition had always been affected by differing operational priorities. The Taliban, by denying ISAF success in the late 2000s, had prevented a closure to the conflict. This underlined the problem of translating capability into success. To sustain a major Western expeditionary force in Afghanistan for a number of years would have seemed remarkable prior to the end of the Cold War; even when Britain was the world's strongest empire, it had been difficult to sustain a major military presence in Afghanistan. Yet, this greater capability in the 2000s also created expectations of success, notably those encouraged by talk of the RMA. That the surge in Afghanistan did not fulfill this expectation was an aspect of how the perception of success was now shaped, for both domestic and international audiences, by a complex set of assumptions and moods. Western war-weariness became a key parameter by the late 2000s. There was a disjuncture between governmental and military accounts of (partial) success in Afghanistan and a public weary of war. Ultimately, the inability to end the struggle made it appear a failure.

ISRAEL AND LEBANON

A sense of Western military limitations, if not failure, was accentuated by the serious difficulties Israel encountered in the 2000s, notably in conflict with the Hezbollah (Party of Allah), an Islamic fundamentalist party and guerrilla organization. Again, in part, this sense reflected the general assumption that Israel would prevail. It also neglected the extent to which Israel continued to be the most impressive military power in the region, despite being heavily outnumbered by its Arab neighbors. Yet, as with American power, the reality of power in large part depended on the perception of power. This element proved particularly important for Israel because it wished to be able to deter and defeat attack, a situation comparable to that of the South Koreans and their American allies with regard to the possibility of North Korean attack.

Israel's strategic environment had markedly improved in the 1970s as a result of the American-mentored peace with Egypt, a diplomatic realignment as radical as America's with China. This peace gave Israel a strategic depth and focus because the sole neighbor of threat was now Syria, and there was no risk of a two-front war. By the 2000s, however, the situation was more threatening. The key issue was not relations with other states, which could be beaten or deterred, but rather the instability within both Palestine and Lebanon. Moreover, foreign intervention made this instability more challenging. Saddam Hussein's support for Palestinian terrorism was cut short by his overthrow in 2003, but the Iranian–Syrian alignment was a threat, not least because it proved a way to build up the rocket arsenal of Hezbollah, the radical Islamic guerrilla organization and fundamentalist party that dominated southern Lebanon. This security threat, and more particularly the Hezbollah ambush in July 2006 of an Israeli unit patrolling the frontier to capture Israeli soldiers who could be exchanged for Hezbollah prisoners in Israel, led Israel to launch a large-scale invasion of southern Lebanon that month.

This offensive, however, proved strategically misconceived and operationally and tactically poorly executed. Several of the Israeli Merkava heavy tanks fell victim to Hezbollah's use of antitank missiles and large roadside explosive devices, a problem that American-led coalition forces also faced in Iraq and Afghanistan. As a result, the Israeli desire for movement and speed was thwarted by a defense that combined positional strength with guerrilla attacks.

Moreover, although Hezbollah did not have a comparable counter to Israeli air superiority and air assault, the latter failed to crush or overawe resistance. Instead, the effect of the air assault became an aspect of a war and society interface that has been so important to the military history of the past century, namely the struggle to influence international public opinion. The air assault wreaked a degree of devastation on Lebanon's civilian population that challenged Israel's international reputation and helped ensure that Israel suffered in the propaganda war, notably in Europe. In turn, Israel drew attention to the Hezbollah rocket assault on Israel. Nearly 1 million Israelis moved south away from the rockets or took refuge in air-raid shelters, providing television images that rivaled those from Lebanon. Although each side competed in the public arena, Israel also suffered from the extent to which the war apparently moved toward a degree of equality between what was a major military power and a territorially based guerrilla movement. This development reflected the extent to which Hezbollah's launching of about 5,000 rockets dramatically demonstrated the reduction in Israel's capacity for deterrence. Although a large percentage of Hezbollah's stock of long-range rockets was destroyed in the attack, Israeli air power proved unable to end the rocket attacks.

This brief war, which ended with Hezbollah undaunted, reset the terms of conflict, rather as developments in Iraq and Afghanistan were doing. A failure to appreciate Hezbollah's effectiveness had led to unrealistic expectations in Israel about success at the tactical, operational, and strategic levels. Public criticism in Israel led to the postwar Winograd Commission. This found poor Israeli preparation and inappropriate strategy, but wider difficulties were demonstrated by the willingness of Syria and Iran to rearm Hezbollah in breach of a UN arms embargo.

If the emphasis here is on the difficulties facing cutting-edge Western militaries, it is important to note that this was also true for other forces, including those operating within cultural norms in which there was a greater willingness to inflict as well as suffer casualties. This point is pertinent both for other states and for nonstate forces. Thus, if terrorist and guerrilla movements might deny their opponents victory, a traditional long-term guerrilla strategy, this did not mean that they necessarily prevailed in the sense of achieving more positive goals. In the 2000s, the Taliban prevented the Karzai government from consolidating control of Afghanistan, but did not overthrow it. Hezbollah could thwart Israel, but was not in a position to control more than a tranche of Lebanon.

Similar contrasts can be found elsewhere, indicating the extent to which, throughout, there is the question of where to emphasize the significance of the use of force in so many different circumstances, both social and political. The assessment of capability can be difficult. In invading Georgia in 2008 to end its forcible attempt to suppress secessionism in the region of South Ossetia, an instance of the more general problem of stability in the Caucasus, the Russians rapidly defeated

Georgian soldiers carry a wounded boy after a Russian bomb attack on Gori, August 2008.

the Georgian army. At the same time, the invasion revealed problems with the Russian military, not least in achieving air superiority and in night fighting, but all militaries have limitations and encounter problems when operating.

SUDAN

The significance of force was apparent in conflict not only between states, but also within them. At a scale far greater in terms of social disruption compared to what was experienced in Lebanon, there was a level of civil warfare in Sudan and, in a different context, Congo that indicated the folly of assuming that warfare had become obsolescent. In Sudan, the key element was conflict between the government under Omar Hassan al-Bashir and its rivals, whereas in Congo the central government played a relatively smaller role, so that a key element was conflict between nongovernment forces.

In Sudan, conflict focused not on politics but on cultural animosity, culture being understood in terms of ethnicity and religion. The nature of the Sudanese government did not allow for conventional politics, and its autocratic character ensured that opposition was dealt with harshly. The Sudanese regime reflected traditional hostilities, notably between the Arabic Muslim north and non-Arab Sudanese, especially if they were non-Muslim. The Arabic Muslim north had long oppressed the south, particularly with slave raiding, and this pattern remained important once Sudan became independent. In the 2000s, a new sphere of conflict developed in the west, especially in the province of Darfur. The resistance there, beginning in 2003, to the exactions of the central government was countered by a harsh military response, one that involved much violence against civilians. Furthermore, in west Sudan, as had been the practice in south Sudan, the regime sought to exploit local rivalries by means of arming and encouraging tribal militias to attack those tribes that were rebelling. In doing so, the regime was exploiting the extent to which environmental strain was exacerbating ethnic tensions. Habitually rival tribes and clans found that population pressure and a drier climate meant greater competition for grazing land and water, a problem across the sub-Saharan *sahel* and one linked to conflict from Somalia to Mali.

As a result, the rebellious tribes were exposed to vicious attacks that involved the slaughter, rape, and enslavement of civilians, the seizure of animals, and the contamination of wells, usually by throwing bodies down them. This was total war, and it led to large numbers of casualties (approximately 300,000 dead by 2007), as well as to significant refugee flows into neighboring Chad. The social impact was even more disruptive than with contemporaneous conflict in Afghanistan and Iraq, in part because civilians were more exposed in semidesert environments. International pressure on Sudan proved largely ineffective, in part because the regime was oil rich and also had the backing of China, which could block critical action in the UN. Moreover, Western commitment in Afghanistan and Iraq left few opportunities to intimidate Sudan, and this was well understood by the Sudanese regime.

The fighting in Darfur saw a variety of military techniques. The Sudanese government employed airpower, bombing villages, but relied on the Janjaweed, a local Arab militia it encouraged that made many of its attacks on horseback. Open trucks equipped with machine guns were also important, as they had been in Chad in the 1980s and were to be in the Libyan civil war in 2011. The war not only lacked front lines, but also was short of foci for operations.

The environment was different in the forested south of Sudan, but the higher population density was more significant; it provided more troops, a greater longevity of the insurrection, which gave it an institutional structure, and the extent to which the insurrection benefited from support across Sudan's extensive frontiers in the region. Indeed, the insurrection was part of a wider geopolitics in which, for example, the Sudanese government backed the rebellion by the Lord's Resistance Army in Uganda (an Islamic government supporting an extreme Christian sect in its rebellion), whereas the Ugandan government supported the rebels in southern Sudan. Although, as in western Sudan, the Sudanese government exploited tribal divisions to find local allies, such that there was a civil war within southern Sudan as part of the civil war in Sudan, the traction enjoyed by the resistance movement, its ability to deny victory to the regime, and the cost of the struggle ensured that the government was increasingly willing to consider the eventual outcome: the recognition of South Sudan as a sovereign state in 2011 after a referendum for independence had been held.

CONGO

In Congo, the situation was more chaotic. The degree of coherence offered in the 1990s by the overthrow of Mobutu Sese Seko, his replacement by Laurent Kabila in 1997, and the operations of foreign forces, notably the Rwandans, was not present in the 2000s. Instead, armed bands pursuing scant agendas outside survival and extortion were a cause of large-scale lawlessness, notably, but not only, near the eastern frontier. Many of these bands had an ethnic basis, and in turn, the brutalization of civilians from different tribes proved both a means and an objective of conflict. A key form of warfare was attack on a village, slaughter of the men, rape of the women, and looting and destruction of the village. Mutilation and cannibalism were common as part of a process of demonstrating mastery and acquiring occult power. The army proved unable to defend the local population, which instead came, especially in eastern Congo, to rely on village militias and on giving allegiance to particular armed bands. In addition to general chaos, there was also a political agenda, not least in the shape of the determination by the Rwandan government to control nearby border areas. Moreover, there was an economic rationale to much of the conflict, notably in terms of control over the production and movement of valuable raw materials, particularly minerals. This theme matched the important role of diamonds in conflict in West Africa.

SUB-SAHARAN AFRICA

Sub-Saharan Africa was the most violent region in the world in the 2000s, more so than Southwest Asia from Israel/Lebanon/Palestine via Iraq to Afghanistan, the focus of most Western concern; but the situation in Africa did not attract comparable attention, in large part because the United States was far less involved there. However, the War on Terror encouraged American intervention against Islamic movements linked to al-Qaeda, notably in Somalia, and even more American-sponsored intervention there by Ethiopian and Kenyan forces. The civil wars in sub-Saharan Africa indicated the weakness of state forms, in part because of the difficulty of sharing power and authority between different ethnic and religious groups. That was a major problem in Ivory Coast, where longstanding tension between the Muslim north and the Christian south developed, beginning in 2002, into civil war.

The significance of ethnicity as a cause and indicator of division and conflict helped explain the frequency of attacks on civilians, which were far more insistent and devastating than would have been necessary simply to accompany the extortion, seizures, and looting that were crucial to the supply system of the armed bands. Instead, the brutalization of civilians was a technique not only of intimidation but also of destruction of other tribes. Enslavement was an aspect of the latter, as was the sexual politics involved in killing men and raping women. The extreme violence of much of this sexual politics, which extended to the mutilation and murder of raped women, the vicious killing of pregnant women, and the rape of men, served as a reminder yet again that war was frequently not a struggle of combatants but one in which opponents were considered an entire people.

CONCLUSIONS

The pattern of conflict by, against, and among a people was seen more widely, for example, in conflict between Shia and Sunni in Iraq, and must be considered alongside the tendency to present warfare in terms of a developmental model linked to increasing proficiency in weaponry and its use, for example, the growing use of drones by advanced militaries, notably that of the United States. Indeed, the 2000s showed, notably in Iraq after its conquest in 2003, that when these two types of conflict—high-specification conventional warfare as practiced by the United States and warfare among the people—came into opposition, the more sophisticated military power found that its understanding of capability and the use of force did not produce the anticipated results. This disjuncture was to remain the case in the 2010s and constitutes an important aspect of the nature of modern warfare.

However, this does not mean that counterinsurgency warfare is likely, even bound, to fail. Indeed, the 2000s provided instances of the opposite, notably with the crushing by the Sri Lankan military in 2009 of the insurgency by the Liberation Tigers of Tamil Eelam. At the same time, the insurgency had been difficult to crush and that conflict, which had lasted more than two decades, resulted in at least 60,000 casualties, including approximately 18,000 combatants killed on each side, with over 2 million refugees in addition. As a counterpoint, the Indian Ocean tsunami (earthquake-driven tidal wave) in December 2004 was responsible for more than 30,000 deaths in 20 minutes, and more than 700,000 people were displaced. The contrast between the army's eventual success in Sri Lanka and the ISAF's relative failure in Afghanistan is instructive but also indicates the role of particular factors. The Liberation Tigers of Tamil Eelam suffered from a shift to conventional warfare and also lost support among the Tamil population as a result of the continuation of the war and its own brutal techniques. The Sri Lankan military, however, did not provide a "hearts and minds" policy. Western commentators are apt to put the emphasis on Afghanistan, but Sri Lanka is also instructive.

READING LIST

Stephen Biddle, "Afghanistan and the Future of Warfare," *Foreign Affairs* 82, no. 2 (March–April 2003), pp. 31–46.

A. Giustozzi, *Koran, Kalashnikov and Laptop: The Neo-Taliban Insurgency in Afghanistan*, London, Hurst, 2007.

T. Ricks, *Fiasco: The American Military Adventure in Iraq*, New York, Penguin Press, 2006.

TEN

THE 2010S

Maoist insurgents, eastern India, 2010.

INTRODUCTION

Western public attention to war in the early 2010s remained focused on the Islamic world, but with a major shift in geographical focus from the 2000s. Although sectarian conflict continued to be a factor in Iraq, the withdrawal of American troops at the request of the Iraqi government ensured that Western interest in developments there collapsed. Instead, there was a continuing concern with the conflict in Afghanistan, a brief flurry of interest in Libya in 2011 as civil war sparked Western intervention, a smaller flurry of interest in Mali in similar circumstances in 2013, and a marked escalation of concern with Syria in 2013 as the seemingly intractable civil war briefly appeared the likely site of America intervention and great-power confrontation. Al-Qaeda-linked terrorism remained a factor as with the attack in September 2013 on Westgate in Nairobi, Kenya's most fashionable shopping mall, by jihadists from Shabab, Somalia's version of the movement.

Terrorism is a means rather than a goal, but religious tension is frequently the occasion for it, notably but not only between Muslims and others. Thus, in 2013, Muslim terrorist groups attacked churches in both Nigeria and Pakistan. In addition, there is deadly violence that is more of the nature of mob attacks than terrorism, as with the attacks on Muslims by Buddhist mobs in Myanmar in 2013 and deadly clashes that year between Hindus and Muslims in the Indian state of Uttar Pradesh. The deployment of the army to try to end the violence in the latter case indicated that such clashes are indeed part of the military history of the period.

Such an account, however, leaves no place for confrontation and conflict elsewhere in the world and thereby suggests that the narrative and analysis should be set by conflict in the Islamic world and by the reality and possibility of Western intervention. As this chapter will show, such an account is incomplete. Conflict continued to be important in areas where it had been common in the 2000s, notably sub-Saharan Africa, whereas confrontation in East Asia became of greater concern. In addition, the role of the military in domestic politics remained a significant feature in political history, most clearly in its seizure of power in Egypt on July 3, 2013. The significance of the struggle was not only Egyptian but also international, with the military's overthrow of the Muslim Brothers government a step urged by Saudi Arabia.

If the scope of military history is widened to include the use of organized force, then the numbers of relevant episodes can be expanded. They included not only seizures of power, but also resistance to popular pressure, as with the use of the police in a paramilitary fashion by the (civilian) Turkish government in June 2013 to overcome demonstrations in Istanbul. The large numbers of Kurds and others imprisoned under Turkey's tough antiterror laws represented another form of repression and, in effect, were a part of what the government saw as a counterinsurgency campaign.

A RANGE OF MILITARY CHALLENGES

As a reminder of the range of geographical and thematic concern in military history, it is appropriate to begin with a series of different episodes in the autumn of 2013. In the Central African Republic, rebels known as Seleka had begun attacking government targets in December 2012, moving on in March 2013 to overthrow the president, François Bozizé, a survivor of previous coup attempts. By September 2013, endemic disorder and the degree to which there was a threat of wider regional chaos as a result, in the pattern of Mali in 2012–2013, led the

French president, Francois Hollande, to issue what he termed a "call of alarm" when he spoke to the UN General Assembly. The murder and rape of civilians were symptomatic of a breakdown of order that the government appeared unable to control, and this led to the prospect of a UN peacekeeping force.

The crisis from 2011 in Syria, a more populous country, attracted far more attention. It revealed a degree of superpower concern and rivalry not seen in the Central African Republic, but also an intensity of local struggle with a number of combatants as well as external sponsors. In addition to the conflict between the Assad regime and its rebel opponents, there was fighting between the latter, notably between extremists interested in a wider Islamic struggle, especially the al-Qaeda-linked Islamic State in Iraq and Syria (ISIS) group, and less radical rebels who lacked this agenda, particularly Northern Storm, but also the Democratic Unity Party, a Kurdish movement seeking autonomy. Founded in Iraq in 2006, ISIS was able to deploy thousands of disciplined troops in Syria. In areas from where these rebels had driven Assad forces, ISIS seized control in late 2013, notably in September, with the town of Azaz, an important border crossing into Turkey through which the rebellion had been supplied. Turkey's concern about this development, with the president, Abdullah Gul, warning in September that Syria could become another Afghanistan, led its government to consider armed intervention. At the same time, Turkey's opposition to the Democratic Unity

Corpses of children killed by nerve gas after a suspected chemical weapons attack in Damascus, August 2013.

Party risked causing problems with the Kurdish allies of the latter in Turkey, who have a history of rebellion. The Syria crisis also showed the capacity of conflict within a state to attract international interest and participation. The killing of more than 1,400 people as a result of the regime's use of sarin gas in the Damascus suburb of Ghouta on August 21, 2013, excited widespread outrage.

An international element was also significant for tension between China and Japan over competing territorial claims to the Senkaku Islands in the East China Sea. This tension led in October 2013 to a closer security relationship between Japan and its principal ally, the United States, with the latter agreeing to base surveillance drones and reconnaissance planes in Japan so as to patrol waters in the region. The two powers announced an agreement to be ready to deal with behavior regarded as coercive and destabilizing, as well as to work on cybersecurity projects and to base a radar system in Japan that could provide protection against North Korea. China's willingness to use the threat of force had already been displayed in 1996. Then, to make its presence felt on the eve of Taiwan's first democratic elections, China fired unarmed missiles into nearby waters.

This range of activities and concerns could be readily extended, but it captures the continuing centrality of military, defense, and force issues in global politics in the 2010s. Yet again, the idea that war had become obsolescent proved highly misleading.

VARYING GOVERNMENTAL RESPONSES

At the same time, there were marked cultural and political contrasts in the responses of states to the situation. The most obvious was the contrast between states that allowed the relative strength of their military to run down, in large part because they preferred to rely on multilateral diplomacy and to spend in other spheres, notably social welfare, and those that sought to maintain or build up their relative strength. Many of the Western European states provided clear instances of the former. Indeed, with its Cold War goals no longer required, Germany, the leading European economy and the fourth largest in the world, took an essentially pacific role. Having not participated in the Gulf Wars and taken only a modest role in Afghanistan, Germany refused to become involved in the NATO intervention in Libya in 2011 and made it clear that it had no intention of playing a role in any conflict with Syria in 2013.

Most states did not adopt a comparable stance, but instead sought to improve their relative military position. The results included arms races, notably in Southeast and East Asia. As a consequence of this contrast, Asian military investment as a percentage of that in the world increased, whereas European investment declined. The United States, however, overwhelmingly maintained its leading position, with a defense budget of $660 billion in 2013, whereas that of China was $99 billion, although accurate details of expenditure are more difficult to establish for what is a totalitarian regime that regards defense expenditure as a state secret. Estimates of Chinese expenditure ranged as high as $160 billion.

The figure for the United States was inflated by the generous nature of salaries and social welfare, notably hospitals, for the American military. As a result, only about one third of the budget was spent on hardware. Moreover, the situation in America was affected by budgetary issues, notably the size of the accumulated debt and the annual deficit, as well as by political preference: the Obama administration was more concerned about welfare expenditure than defense. Alongside the end of the Iraq commitment and the plans to reduce that commitment in Afghanistan, this situation led to plans for cuts in the military, which, to critics, represented a "hollowing out" process. Thus, the army was to be cut from 380,000 troops to 300,000 and the marines from 220,000 to 180,000; most controversially, there were major cuts in the navy, which was reduced to 280 vessels, of which only about 90 were at sea at any one time. The ability of the United States to inflict a rapid defeat on Iran in any conflict arising from moves against Iran's nuclear program and a wide-ranging Iranian response was called into question in 2013.

For all states, there were the related but different issues of the overall size of the defense budget and the allocation of the expenditure. These issues were in a dynamic relationship to the taskings or goals of the moment, to those that seemed likely, and to changes and possible changes in capabilities, both of one's own forces and of others, notably potential opponents. An emphasis on capabilities provided an apparent opportunity to circumvent existing limitations and to confront new challenges, but in practice, for major powers, this emphasis must be seen alongside a degree of uncertainty in the prioritization of tasks.

Thus, for the United States, it was unclear whether the emphasis should be on the Islamic world, as in the 2000s, or on a "pivot" toward Asia, as the Obama administration proposed. There was also a lack of clarity about how far the Greater Caribbean region might lead to commitments, notably in Mexico, Cuba, and Venezuela. Other states did not have the range of the United States, but there was repeated uncertainty over goals. Thus, it was unclear how far Britain or France might become involved in power projection in the Islamic world, whereas in East and South Asia, the likelihood of regional conflict was unclear. In Britain, the government that came to power in 2010 carried out a strategic review that publicly revealed many issues discussed more privately elsewhere. The first priority was a measured review of defense tasks in light of an agreed definition of national interests. Strategy, operations, procurement, and doctrine are all secondary to this process. However, as toxic lobbying made clear, this process did not occur. Instead, there was a confused, if not incoherent, marshaling of pat formulas designed to ensure a predetermined outcome. The standard view was that the Iraq and Afghanistan wars demonstrated the truth of claims about wars among the people, showed that high-spectrum weaponry can only achieve so much, and underlined the need for more boots on the ground. Moreover, because defense against terrorism required control of Afghanistan and Pakistan by friendly governments, the task was long term. Add a large mixture of blame, shame, anger, and guilt about the inadequate equipment of the troops and concern about the terrible human cost, and stir in the view that only those who were there can write about it, and the case was made.

In the context of a degree of strife over resources and priorities that made a mockery of joint command and planning structures, this pro-army case was accompanied by attacks on the navy and air force for costly irrelevance and specific criticism of their flagship procurement projects, notably the aircraft carriers and new jets. In an echo of the longstanding theme of men versus machines, one very much seen in the 1920s and 1930s, these projects were presented as anachronistic throwbacks to an age of machines that offered nothing in terms of hearts and minds.

Far from planning, as the quip goes, for the last war, Britain (like the United States) was planning for the current one, which is one reason for generals stating in public that their armies would be in Afghanistan for decades. In planning, of course, we should be looking to future conflicts, confrontations, and needs; here there is a central flaw in reading from the present to the future. The idea that conflict between states has in some fashion become redundant or less probable or unlikely to involve Britain, directly or indirectly, is misleading. Moreover, it is far from clear that the army has as much to offer in many of the scenarios that might arise as the higher-spectrum force, deterrent or otherwise, of the navy and air force. The need for this was and is underlined by the risk that an America that is more under pressure and relatively weaker might/may well focus increasingly on the geostrategic challenge of China and leave other current missions, notably Mediterranean security, to its allies. In the specific case of the West and the Middle East, it was also unclear how the army proposes to protect trade through the Gulf from Iranian pressure or, indeed, to project power if local bases were lacking. Navies, indeed, provide a flexibility of presence and force and a speed and promptness of delivery that armies lack. There is room for serious debate about how best to configure the navy for the next half century, but to run it down would be folly, particularly if the reliance, instead, is on an army that can achieve far less than it suggests to fulfill the West's long-term needs.

The possibility of domestic disorder entailing the use of force by the government was more significant for most states, notably so in Africa, although there was an overlap in the sense of possible foreign intervention in domestic conflicts. The risk of instability, indeed of the overthrow of government, ensured pressure not for an enhancement of military capability in terms of expenditure on new weapon systems, but for this enhancement in terms of the loyalty of the military. The latter involved policies of command factionalism, notably the appointment and promotion of officers deemed loyal. Thus, in Syria, there was a focus on appointing members of the Alawite sect, that of the ruling Assad family. Conversely, in Turkey, the Islamic-dominated AK party, in power from 2002, sought to lessen the influence of the senior command, many of whom came from a secular Kemalist background. As a result, many generals were imprisoned. In Uganda, Yoweri Museveni, president from 1986, promoted loyal young officers to senior posts to keep long-established officers in their place. Museveni also gave his son an important position in the army.

More generally, a concern with loyalty led to an interest in military pay and conditions. In many states, there was also the maintenance or development of paramilitary forces that were regarded as an alternative to the regular military. The availability of this alternative was seen as giving the regime more options, and the paramilitaries were also regarded as more loyal and more appropriate for the suppression of internal opposition.

From the perspective of domestic strife, the military history of the 2010s so far, despite important overlaps, notably in Libya, Mali, and Syria, looks different from the picture if the emphasis is on international confrontation. For example, the situation in East Asia is significant in the latter case, notably with serious confrontation between North and South Korea and with increasing tension between China and Japan. However, domestic strife is not to the fore in any of these instances. In contrast, domestic strife is more to the fore in sub-Saharan Africa, although the overlap of such strife in neighboring countries is such that, at least at the regional level, domestic strife and international confrontation can be closely linked. In the remainder of this chapter, the focus will first be on those struggles in which Western intervention came to play a role (Libya, Mali) or seemed in prospect (Syria), next on the situation in East Asia, and finally on domestic strife in other states.

WESTERN INTERVENTION AND THE ISLAMIC WORLD

The Afghan intervention continued to be a major drain on the NATO-led ISAF alliance, particularly on American resources. Despite this drain there were not sufficient troops for clearing and holding territory of any scale. The ability of the Taliban to continue to mount major attacks led to a sense among Western public opinion that the war was without much point and was likely to fail anyway. In 2014, ISAF is due to withdraw its combat troops.

The situation in Libya appeared very different because the Gaddafi regime was rapidly overthrown following Western intervention in the civil war that began in February 2011 when the Islamist militia rebelled in Benghazi. The rebellion gathered momentum because Abdel Fatah Younis, the interior minister who was sent to suppress it, instead decided to try to lead it, a key aspect of the divisions within the regime that helped weaken it. The anti-Gaddafi insurgents made plentiful use of unarmored vehicles, both to transport themselves and to mount weapons, especially antiaircraft guns; these vehicles provided a mobility that helped explain rapid changes of fortune in the campaigning. The heavier conventional units of the Libyan army, both tanks and artillery, were more deadly, but they were countered and then seriously damaged by NATO air attacks despite the major problems the latter faced because of a lack of reliable reconnaissance information. The key role in the air was played by Britain and France, although American stealth bombers were central to the original assault on the Libyan air force and the Americans also play a vital role in air-to-air refueling and intelligence provision.

Smoke rises from Tripoli after a NATO air strike, June 2011.

An air umbrella provided crucial support for the insurgents. The provision of NATO advisers and arms, notably firearms, night-warfare optics, and communication equipment, as well as money from Qatar, also helped the generally poorly organized insurgents who captured the capital, Tripoli, that August, overthrowing the Gaddafi regime. Continuing to resist, Gaddafi was captured and killed in October. The Libyan intervention suggested that airpower would be most effective as part of a joint strategy, although in Libya the situation on the ground was more propitious than in Kosovo in 1999.

Foreign intervention in Libya did not bring stability, not least because longstanding regional tensions continued, notably eastern demands for more autonomy. Struggles between rival *thuwwar* (militias) exacerbated these tensions and had a dynamic of their own. Thus, in June 2013, tribesmen protested against the killing of a kin member by a patrol of Libya Shield No. 1, a leading Islamist militia, attacked its base in Benghazi, joined by al-Saiqa, a special force initially established by Gaddafi, but which had abandoned him in 2011. The militia was forced to flee. Sniping and the use of rocket-propelled grenades were key elements in the conflict. The role of the al-Saiqa reflected the extent to which, in many revolutionary and postrevolutionary contexts, there was division over the monopolization of military authority. In Libya, the Islamist militias were coopted by the new government into 10 Libya Shields and thereby authorized (and paid) as a form of parallel National Guard, only to be dissolved by order of the new army chief of staff in June 2013. As an instance of more general chaos, many Libyan ports and other positions have been seized by local militiamen who have thereby gained control of trade, notably oil exports. The threat by the central government to use force to regain control has proved fruitless. Unlike in Afghanistan, however, no Western forces were involved in propping up the new government against opposition.

In 2013, there was similar French intervention in Mali, with the stress again on air attack. The Tuareg insurgents who had threatened the overthrow of the government were rapidly pushed back by Malian forces assisted by the French. As an instance of the more general extent to which struggles in one state could lead to conflict elsewhere, the insurrection in Mali owed something to the return home of men who had served Gaddafi, as well as to long-established separatist tendencies.

Also in 2013, there was the possibility of Western intervention in the civil war in Syria. The use of gas against insurgents by the forces of the Assad regime, despite the warning from President Obama the previous year that this would be crossing a "red line," led the United States to prepare a military strike intended to show that such action would lead to retribution. Both Britain and France promised participation in what was intended as an air and cruise missile attack, but in Britain and then the United States there was a vital erosion of political support and the plan was abandoned. There had been considerable criticism of it from the military in Britain on the grounds that it was unclear what the consequences, both military and political, of such action might be. Similarly, Western pressure on Iran not to develop its atomic program did not lead to military action.

However, to put Western intervention first is, as in the earlier cases of Korea, Vietnam, and Afghanistan, to underplay the role of local animosities and the extent to which they helped define the parameters of the struggle. In June 2011, the repression of opposition by the Assad regime led to protesters fighting back, and in July military defectors proclaimed the creation of the Free Syrian Army, dedicated to overthrowing Assad. Because refugees in neighboring countries, notably Turkey, became a prime support, the struggle soon had an international dimension that was not dependent on the West. In addition, the Turkish government provided arms. Having begun in the south of Syria in the governorate of Daraa, fighting spread in Syria in 2012, notably to the major cities of Aleppo, Homs, and Damascus. Sectarian consciousness rose, helping guide the configuration of conflict as well as the refugee flows.

The Syrian conflict was of concern to the West for a number of reasons, each of which shed broader light on the reasons for commitment in the Islamic world and for intervention more broadly. In addition to humanitarian concerns, there was anxiety about the impact on the interests and stability of neighboring states, notably Israel, but also Turkey, a NATO ally, as well as Lebanon, Syria, and Iraq. There was also an awareness that strife in any one state could be exploited by the West's opponents, principally al-Qaeda, but also Iran.

Always with a covert and secretive dimension, the War on Terror had become more so. This involved the use of special forces as well as a program of drone attacks on terrorist leaders. The latter represented another iteration of the type of warrior developed in the missile age, one that faced no individual risk while killing at a distance. This was an aspect of a more general change in the ethos and identity of the military toward professionalism.

EAST ASIA

Rivalries in East Asia came into sharper focus in the 2010s in part because a territorial dispute in the East China Sea directed attention to hostility between China and Japan, and the North Korean regime continued a bellicose hostility that challenged regional stability. These issues involved the United States, the ally and, in effect, guarantor of both South Korea and Japan, and also led to concerns more widely in Asia. The sea trials in 2011 of China's first aircraft carrier intensified speculation about strategic rivalry. In response to the apparent direction of Chinese policy, the United States developed strategic partnerships with Australia, India, and Japan. China's military expenditure helped drive up their spending because it led each of them to perceive vulnerability. In Mach 2012, India's army chief, General V. K. Singh, in a leaked letter to the prime minister described the armed forces as "obsolete" and "woefully short" of weapons.

Meanwhile, the North Korean regime under its new head from December 2011, Kim Jon Un, initially struck a positive note, undertaking in February 2012 to suspend both uranium enrichment and the operation of its Yongbyon plutonium nuclear reactor and further testing of weapons and long-range missiles and to permit inspection by the International Atomic Energy Authority. In return,

North Korean soldiers and missiles, Pyongyang, July 2013.

America agreed to provide food aid. However, North Korea rapidly reverted to threatening gestures with its missile program, successfully launching a satellite in December 2012 and carrying out a nuclear test in February 2013. Bellicose language increasingly characterized North Korea's stance. Limited military action against South Korea in contested waters in 2010 was also a feature of a very tense situation.

Anxiety about Chinese and North Korean plans encouraged India and Japan to develop their defenses against rocket attack. Deterrence proved a defense for India. Its Agni 5 missile tested in April 2012 offered an intercontinental (3,100 miles) capacity and was seen as a way to lessen the military gap with China.

THE THIRD WORLD

Alongside economic progress and democratic government in some states, Africa remained a continent where violence within and, to a far lesser extent, between states was a feature. In the 2010s, this was principally a continuation of the conflicts of the previous decade, notably in Sudan, Congo, and Somalia. In Sudan, violence anew served as the prime political means by which the government addressed regional separatism, thus underlining the theme of oppression. By 2009, fighting in Darfur had eased, but in 2011–2012, it revived with militia attacks directed anew against the Zaghawa, the local tribe that was the principal source of opposition. These attacks were supported in 2011 by the Sudanese use of Russian-supplied aircraft against the Zaghawa base of Shangal Tobay.

The Sudanese government employed similar violence elsewhere. Thus, in the province of Southern Kordofa, in response to a rebellion by the SPLM-North movement in the Nuba mountains, the army sought to starve out the rebels and also used great brutality against civilians, including large-scale killing and rape. The contempt of Arab Sudanese soldiers for darker Nubians was an aspect of the violence. There was also ethnic conflict in South Sudan once it became independent from Sudan in 2011, with many thousands killed, in large part because of competition between tribes for land and cattle and raiding for children, a source of labor.

As elsewhere in Africa, ethnic conflict and rebellions were intertwined with rivalries between neighboring states. Sudan and South Sudan accused each other of backing rebel groups. The two states clashed, with Sudan using ground-support aircraft to repel a South Sudan attack in April 2012. So it was also with both Congo and Somalia: the disorder in each provided a basis for rebels acting against neighboring states. Rebel groups opposed to the governments in Rwanda and Burundi, for example, Burundi's National Liberation Front, were able to find shelter in Congo, where they earned money from criminal activities such as gold trafficking. As elsewhere, for example, in the Central African Republic in 2013–2014, there is a clear gender dimension, with frequent acts of rape and sexual slavery.

The Shabab, the Islamic fundamentalist militia in Somalia, sought to weaken Kenya, launching terrorist attacks there, notably in Nairobi in 2013, in reprisal to the attempts by Kenya, Ethiopia, and the African Mission to Somalia to limit the position of the Shabab within Somalia. Ethiopian and Kenyan forces made significant gains when they attacked the Shabab in 2011–2012 and also backed sympathetic Somali militias. In February 2012, using 20 tanks, the Ethiopians captured the city of Baidoa, a major Shabab center.

In addition to such conflict across borders, there was the use of the military or paramilitary forces to seize and retain power. This was demonstrated on a major scale in Syria where the Assad government deployed approximately 300,000 active military personnel in 2012. This was counterinsurgency conflict using the weapons and methods of conventional warfare, as the Russians had done in Chechnya. The army made destructive use of artillery, shelling rebel-held areas, killing civilians in the process, and leading many others to flee as refugees. Moreover, aircraft, rockets, and tanks were employed in urban fighting. In August 2011, about 270 tanks were used to overcome resistance in the city of Hama, a major center of opposition. Having been deployed to blockade the city, contributing to the dislocation of the opposition, the tanks broke through barricades and their machine guns subsequently proved more effective than the Molotov cocktails and stones thrown at them. Nevertheless, despite destructive bombardment, for example, of the city of Homs in 2012, the Syrian government increasingly lost control of the domestic situation in 2012 and found it difficult to control territory other than where its forces operated or where it had ethnic and sectarian backing. The latter element led the army to give out rifles to Alawites, members of the same Muslim sect as President Assad, and the Alawites drove Sunnis from their homes. This was part of the process by which the Assad regime built up paramilitary support to help the army. Local defense militias were an aspect of this support. The Assad regime also received backing from Iran and from Shia fighters from Lebanon and Iraq, whereas Saudi Arabia helped support its rivals. By November 2013, more than 110,000 Syrians had been killed of a population of about 21 million.

The military proved far more effective at suppressing opposition in Egypt in July 2013, with the government, led by the Muslim Brotherhood, overthrown and popular demonstrations in its favor dispelled. In 2012, another elected government, that in the Maldives, was overthrown in a coup that joined mutinous police to popular protests. Whether or not the military acted was a key element in domestic politics. Thus, in February 2011, the decision by the Egyptian army not to act had helped lead to the fall of the Mubarak government. In July 2013, troops were deployed when President Kiir of South Sudan dismissed his ministerial colleagues. Such a use of the military helped explain why governments were so keen to control military commands. Thus, the same month, Hun Sen, prime minister of Cambodia, named one of his sons, already head of antiterrorism, a lieutenant-general and the other a general.

In many states, the prime purpose of the military was internal control because the military challenge came not from foreign powers but from domestic opposition, variously political, social, religious, criminal, and separatist, and often several of these. The resulting warfare, most of which took a guerrilla or terrorist character on the part of the rebels, was asymmetrical. This warfare could also overlap considerably with struggles against crime, specifically conflicts with the drug trade.

This point served as a reminder about the difficulties of defining war and the military. As the terms War on Terror or war on drugs underlined, the definition of war in use complicated understanding of force and legitimacy. Although such usage represented a misappropriation and misuse of the term "war," in practice, for many states and societies, the effort and violence involved made the terms understandable even if they were misleading. Thus, in Mexico, allegedly more than 70,000 people were killed in drug-linked violence in 2006–2012, and the national statistics institute estimated that there were 105,000 kidnappings in 2012 and about 6 million cases of extortion. The military have been deployed alongside the police against powerful drug gangs such as the Zetas. In November 2013, the army, navy, and federal police took over the port of Lázaro Cárdenas, the second biggest in Mexico, to challenge the power of another drug gang, the deadly Knights Templar. In turn, "self-defense" militias also acted against drug gangs. In February 2014, these vigilante militia cooperated with federal troops and police in driving the Knights Templar from the town of Apatzingán.

Moreover, if the War on Terror is crucial and to be regarded as both war and a type of war, then the Saudi security forces that carried out armed raids against al-Qaeda suspects in which people are killed, or the Indian Border Security Force resisting the United Liberation Front of Asom in Assam, or the Chinese-trained People's Liberation Army of Manipur were as much part of the military in the early 2010s as conventional armed forces. Support from within neighboring Myanmar provided the insurgents with necessary bases. Similarly, India's paramilitary police deployed 71 battalions, supported by sophisticated technology including drones, in eastern India to fight the Maoist insurgents known as *Naxalites*. Troops were also used, in India and elsewhere, for policing duties. India has an army of over 1 million and approximately 1 million paramilitaries under the Home Ministry, with many of the officers provided by the army. There are similar parallel structures in Pakistan, with the Frontier Corps of Pakistan being under the Ministry of the Interior.

Widespread ownership of weaponry could complicate these and other problems. In Yemen, there were estimated to be more than three guns for every Yemeni, which contributed to resistance to the government. This resistance took the form of opposition from al-Qaeda, as well as regional separatism and a level of lawlessness. Similarly, in Haiti, large-scale ownership of guns exacerbated problems stemming from mass unemployment and poverty and drug culture and any drug-smuggling network. This ownership challenged Haiti's political stability, leading to a major role for street gangs or *chimeras*. In far more prosperous Brazil, the drug gangs in the *favelas* (slums) were a threat to the paramilitary police, as in 2007 when police stations were attacked in Rio de Janeiro. In Pakistan, the high rate of lawlessness was more directly linked to the violent relationship between ethnic division and politics. Thus, in Karachi, the leading city, the Sindhi

Muhajir and Pushtun populations took rival positions. In Palestine, the refugee camps pose a challenge to the Palestinian Authority as well as to nearby Israel. The ready availability of guns in the camps makes their angry young men a threat to both.

These issues are far less significant in the West, despite occasional calls, as in Marseille in France in 2013, for the deployment of the army to deal with high rates of crime. In the United States, the high rate of gun ownership, which includes assault weapons and high-capacity ammunition clips, contributed to the violent character of criminality, but has not yet had serious implications for political stability.

At sea, the military challenge set by criminality was demonstrated by the rise of piracy. The center in the late twentieth century had been Indonesian waters, but concerted action by the navies of Singapore, Malaysia, and Indonesia brought this challenge under control. In the 2000s and early 2010s, Somalia, a failed state, became the new center of piracy. Although not all attempts to seize ships were successful, the number of attempts by Somali pirates increased to 219 in 2010 and 237 in 2011. International naval action contained the threat and, by 2013, the new center of piracy was off Nigeria.

The response to Somali piracy reflected the extent to which disorder in an individual state could be internationalized. Somalia was seen, correctly, as a failed state. In most cases, in contrast, the use of force within sovereign areas, that is states, by their own governments was generally accepted. This use of force could be a challenge to the precepts of humanitarian interventionism, but such interventionism was usually held at bay unless it conformed to the goals of great-power diplomacy. As the contrast between intervention in Libya, Mali, and Syria in the 2010s showed, politics therefore was very much to the fore. These political aspects and constraints established difficult parameters within which military planning, capability, and effectiveness had to be considered.

READING LIST

Philip Bobbitt, *Terror and Consent: The Wars for the Twenty-First Century*, London, Knopf, 2008.

ELEVEN

INTO THE FUTURE

Hexacopter drones in flight.

Experience and understanding in part involve the anticipation of the future. The sense of what is likely to happen affects both the political contexts of force and the development of technological capacities, force structures, military doctrine, and strategic planning. For a book that considers the past century of military power, it is necessary, at every point of that century, to consider the futures predicted, hoped for, and feared and also to assess the future as anticipated in the present. Moreover, the priorities involved in the latter play a key role in the scholarly and popular presentation and analysis of the past.

TASKS AND TECHNOLOGIES

The short-term future is readily accessible because of existing military systems, expenditure commitments, and strategic planning. The longer term, in contrast, is more difficult to anticipate. Nevertheless, as is the case throughout this book, the crucial parameters are set by tasking and capabilities, each of which is affected by the interplay of war and society. Tasking will probably reflect and involve a mixture of environmental trends, notably the rise in population and resource pressures, particularly over water and land and both between and within states. The ideological and political character and consequences of this pressure will vary, but the rise in population, to an estimated 10.65 billion by the close of the century, will have a major impact. In June 2013, the Egyptian government discussed using special forces to destroy a dam that Ethiopia was building on the Blue Nile because it feared that this would affect the availability of water in Egypt.

Resource pressures will affect the poorer states and thus will be an element in their stability and military planning. The situation will also be the case for their wealthier counterparts. The development and coordination of military and civilian strategies and policies to protect and further national interests is a prime requirement of security, one already highlighted by the serious issues of confronting energy provision and security. These issues span from the domestic to the international, from the provision and security of sufficient generating and storage capacity at home to the security of energy flows from abroad. War and society as a theme certainly relates to the consequences of resource issues.

Unfortunately, it is difficult to ensure an overall strategy, not least because the exigencies of consumers and, indeed, many companies in terms of the provision of supplies are frequently short term. There are important exceptions with the long-term development of oil and gas fields, but there are also short-term commercial and risk-management strategies that are less happy in their consequences. In the case of piracy, a growing problem in the early twenty-first century, insurance may lessen the financial penalty to the individual company of the seizure of oil or natural gas tankers by pirates, but that method does not provide the necessary national capacity. There is a parallel with defense as a whole in that short-term issues in the late 2000s and early 2010s, notably the operational needs of the Iraq and Afghanistan commitments, threatened the long-term requirements for naval capability.

Risk management in the field of energy flows is itself problematic because an interruption in energy supplies represents a challenge to national interests and security that is far graver than a check for a particular episode of force projection. Moreover, the very context for energy security is unstable because rising needs for energy, and a failure to match them with production, increase the vulnerability both of the individual state and of the entire international economic order. A lack of energy surpluses also means that the disruption of production in particular markets, or the cutting of specific flows, cannot be so readily handled by seeking alternative capacity. Energy may be fungible, which limits the challenge posed by developments in individual producers, such as Iran or Venezuela, but that situation depends on other sources being available.

In the event of a crisis, an international collaborative effort will be required to provide the necessary military security to complement interventionist purchasing and transport arrangements. Such an effort will require the guarantee of military force and, given the volume of energy that moves on and under the sea, because pipelines are a key security issue, that guarantee can only be provided by navies and their airpower. Naval cutbacks would leave the major powers unable to take the effective role that is necessary if their national interests and the international free-trading order are to be protected.

Technological capabilities will also probably change, notably with the specifications of weaponry and delivery systems and the nature of soldiery. The former may include chemical warfare and electromagnetic pulses and the latter genetic manipulation and possibly cloning. Social norms will clearly be highly significant for changes to the nature of soldiery.

The extent to which current planning centers on future threats means that we must assess views of the future, but the latter is unpredictable and indeterminate and, as a result, views of future circumstances have often proven mistaken. At present, much of the assessment of future high-tech confrontation or war depends on two concepts, that of synergy or profitable combination, which relates essentially to the means of conflict, and that of information warfare, which relates to the means and the redefinition of goals. Both synergy and information warfare are seen as important to the rivalry of major powers.

The rivalry between the major powers was a suppressed theme after the end of the Cold War, but became more overt in the 2010s. Indeed, the revival of this rivalry became more significant in the 2000s even while the War on Terror engaged attention. A deterioration of relations affecting China, India, Russia, and the United States suggested new military issues and threats, both involving relations between these powers and affecting their capacity to deal with others, as the United States discovered with Syria in 2012: Russian opposition limited America's options. There were earlier public shows of friction, such as, in 2007–2008, Russian opposition to American plans to extend the ballistic missile shield to cover Eastern Europe and to encourage Georgia and Ukraine to join NATO. Russia's successful attack on Georgia in 2008 was an aspect of this confrontation, as Georgia looked to the United States for support. The cooling of relations between the United States and China is of particular significance because the alignment between the two in the 1970s had brought crucial improvements to their strategic position. The concept of synergy suggests that in any future conflict, success will hinge on the ability to achieve an effective combination of land, air, sea, cyber, and space forces and that this ability requires the development of new organizational structures, appropriate systems of command, control, communications, and information appraisal and analysis, and the careful training of commanders and units accordingly. The heavy American investment in military infrastructure in space in the 2000s and 2010s, including the Advanced Extremely High Frequency Program, indicated the commitment to such a synergy. In response to the development of antisatellite technology, there was the need for continued advances, for instance, against antisatellite radio-jamming techniques. The idea of synergy suggests that instead of treating developments in weaponry in isolation, their impact is to be multiplied by careful cooperation within and outside of new organizational structures.

A sense of new possibilities as already present was captured by the interest in information or cyber-warfare. With cyber-attacks, we are already in the stage of actuality, not speculation. For example, there have been Chinese attacks on American and Japanese military and economic attacks, as well as a Russian cyber-assault on Estonia. Both Russian and China have been particularly active in this field, and this activity is clearly designed to provide a means to offset the conventional advantages enjoyed by the United States.

As of yet, however, this technology has not reached the state of any fully fledged conflict. Therefore, what it will amount to in practice is unclear. Electronic warfare across a broad range certainly suggests the possibility of destroying the organizational processes of a target society and, therefore, has an almost science-fiction quality to it. These possibilities are related to the idea that the so-called RMA did not really occur in the 1990s and early 2000s, but is actually occurring now. Against this view, it can be suggested, both for the alleged RMA and for changes now, that revolutionary change is generally always just over the horizon, with present predictions and promises brought to fruition in future success. In part, moreover, the idea of revolutionary change is centrally bound up with the way in which advocates of particular policies and weapons proclaim the value of their recommendations. Allowing for this, there is something very different about the relationship between humans and lethality suggested by weapons in which the destructiveness of this lethality is not so much a matter of physical destruction.

Cyberwarfare is an instance of the staging of novelty. Into the 2010s, most of the technologies of warfare, both for weapons and for weapon systems, still focused on devices and machines invented and deployed in the first half of the twentieth century. This was true of aircraft, poison gas, tanks, aircraft carriers, rockets, and nuclear armaments, all of which, however newly developing, were legacy systems. By the 2010s, however, there was growing interest in later technologies, not least technologies that would make earlier weapons and platforms redundant or seriously compromised. In addition to cyber-warfare, there was interest in smart means of transporting munitions to the target, as well as the tactical, operational, and strategic capabilities of electromagnetic pulses and the development of designer materials with inherent capabilities to sense and modify their behavior or functionality.

Moreover, looking to the future instead of focusing on past weapons systems, it is possible that different types of combatants will be created in the forms of robots, cyborgs, and clones. It is more likely that advances in knowledge of the brain and genetic engineering may alter what can be expected from human warriors. The latter, like other humans in the future, will probably be enhanced organic entities with cybernetic implants. Increased knowledge of the brain may also provide opportunities for action against combatants. The world of robotics is already present in the form of automatic weapons that can be controlled from a distance, including not only drones but also weaponry on aircraft that is not under the control of the pilot.

There will be links between new and future weapons, but there are still significant differences among, for example, electromagnetic pulses, robotic vehicles such as drones, and altering the fighting characteristics of soldiers. To link all the changes in some revolution in military affairs is misleading, not least because there may be contradictions between the supposed constituents, for example, serious competing resource demands. There are also the issues posed by the financial crisis that gathered pace in the West in the late 2000s.

The crises of American and European public finances are especially relevant, with economic and fiscal problems greatly exacerbated by structural and contingent political

Boston Dynamics' Atlas robot takes on an irregular surface in a "terrain negotiation exercise," August 2013.

problems. For example, what NATO will, or even can, look like after the Euro crisis is a question as pertinent as any discussion about the consequences for NATO of the "Arab Spring." Similarly, it is unclear whether Anglo-French plans for military cooperation will be affected, indeed weakened, by not only fiscal crises but also the extent to which the political resolution of the Euro crisis binds France closer to Germany. That, moreover, will be a Germany whose decision to move away from its own nuclear power will make it even more dependent on Soviet natural gas (as well as French nuclear power).

One likely consequence will be the continued longevity of legacy systems as opposed to an emphasis on completely new developments. In cost terms, for example, far more would probably be gained from developing drone technology than from building F35s or Eurofighters. Moreover, unmanned aircraft will not require the large flights decks and hangers that manned aircraft do at sea. However, the possibility of moving to new systems will be compromised by the difficulties that financially strapped governments will face in discarding less effective but nevertheless on-stream developments.

As far as military tasking is concerned, a key consequence of the economic and fiscal crises will be their overlap and interaction with the consequences of the hitherto unprecedented population rise. Meeting the resulting demands for resources and jobs will be much harder in this context of a reshaping of geopolitics, and this may well accentuate domestic problems in a number of states. The resulting instability will create a problem for the militaries of many states and may also exacerbate the issues raised by failed states: in sum, a new geopolitics and new strategic issues.

There are also the much more specific issues posed by tasking. The choice of technology and doctrine will vary greatly depending on whether symmetrical warfare is assumed or counterinsurgency. In judging capability, this raises the more general issue of fitness for purpose because that criterion of effectiveness necessarily varies across states and other combatants, as well as with reference to their range of activity. The increase in population will certainly pose issues for military and political effectiveness, while also ensuring that much conflict is focused on urban areas. The latter will contribute greatly to a congested battle space, and such a battle space will lessen technological advantages and complicate military options.

There is no reason to believe that the process and pace of future change will be limited or inconsequential. However, the imponderables include not only human capability but also the availability of the necessary resources, especially energy and materials. The resources issue emerges very clearly in the failure to develop capability in space to the anticipated extent. So many of the bold ideas advanced in the 1980s have not been brought to fruition. It is likely that the unpredictability of change will continue to be a key element in warfare and military capability.

READING LIST

Jeremy Black, *War and the New Disorder in the 21st Century*, London, Continuum, 2004.

TWELVE

CONCLUSIONS

This book has demonstrated the global significance of war over the past century and the extent to which the history of the world cannot be understood unless due weight is placed on the formative role of war and wars. At the same time, this book has also shown that there is no single experience of war. Indeed, the exact opposite is true. For both the military and civilians, there is an enormous variety in what happened, why it happened, and how it was experienced. Death and suffering may seem to be common features, but the experience and perception vary greatly by societies and cultures.

To turn to the more specific question of how, faced by the varied nature of war, states and militaries sought best to prepare themselves is to appreciate the extent to which fitness for purpose at the level of the individual military was different, notably depending on the social and political contexts, the nature of the opponent, and the tasking involved. Whereas the central narrative (and related analysis) involved in discussing war, that focused on "high-tempo," symmetrical warfare, remains significant today, not least because of the rise of China and its rivalry with the United States, it is apparent that it is also necessary to devote more attention to "little wars," counterinsurgency, and civil conflict. If, for example, Creighton Abrams is most prominent as American commander in Vietnam from 1968 to 1972, he had also led troops in quelling disturbances in Mississippi in 1962–1963. This need, which arises from the range of states and societies involved, to devote attention to such commitments suggests a multiple approach to military modernity and an emphasis on its diversity.

As a result of the variety of present-day circumstances, most aspects of past doctrine, organization, and practice appear to prefigure aspects of the present, and there is no single pattern of modernization and no one assessment of significance. Key elements—tasking and fitness—arose from the extent to which conflict within states was as important as war between them. This point is underplayed in

Western discussion of war over the past century but is of great significance, notably for postindependence Africa, as well as for other states, both those that were colonies and others.

The role of force in much (but not all) colonial rule and decolonization, and in the modern perception of both, underlines the extent to which the historical narratives of individual states involve discussion of their history over the past century in terms of valorous struggle against oppression. Whether or not the scholarly emphasis should be on such struggle, it is highly significant in public accounts. This significance, in turn, appears to underline the more general importance of violence in both national and international history.

Force also plays a key role as a framer of modern society across much of the world. For example, the two world wars were partly responsible for female emancipation. World War I transformed the position in Britain for women having the vote: before the war, the political order was opposed, whereas women gained the right to vote in 1918. In World War II, there was also a mobilization of women by the Allies, whereas the Axis preferred to rely on the slave labor of prisoners of war and coerced civilians while treating women in a traditional fashion. The women who received the Honor Cross of the German Mother beginning in 1939 for having numerous children were under the would-be panoptic vision of a regime for which the home front was truly a front line of racial conflict.

In contrast, the workplace offered women in the Allied countries a degree of freedom they did not always find in the household and certainly more money. A 1944 report, "Women at Work," from the British government's Wartime Social Survey, produced evidence from questionnaires that war work was popular for women, first for the pay and second for friendship. The previous year, the Mass Observation Survey noted that in London pubs there was a free and easy atmosphere in which men and women paired off. The films British *Waterloo Road* (1944) and *Brief Encounter* (1945) suggested that the war was offering new possibilities for relationships between the sexes, even at the cost of marriages.

War as the cause of social liberalization may not be the first theme that comes to mind, but it captures the extent to which the change and disruption brought by conflict shook existing social structures and beliefs. For the women and men who were the victims of war, both directly and as relatives, friends, and community members, this was no consolation. Yet, the consequences of conflict were not simply suffering and grief, and its history is not therefore simply a terrible aspect of the century, one treated as its dark side. Indeed, such a marginalization is totally inappropriate because war and its causes, course, and consequences helped determine not only individual and collective experience, but also major transformations in political fortunes and structures. Indeed, without the wars of the century, it is clear that its political history would have been very different; the same is probable, although to a lesser extent, for the social, economic, and cultural history of the century.

Moreover, war was, and is, crucially important as a source of the visual images of strife that have been used to record and encourage attitudes about identity and

The My Lai Massacre, December 1, 1969, photographed by Ron Haeberle and published by *Life* magazine shortly thereafter.

value. This is true both of positive images and of darker counterparts. Thus, the reality of conflict in the Vietnam War was brought home to the American public with photographs such as that of Eddie Adams of the execution of a Viet Cong prisoner by a South Vietnamese policeman and Nick Ut's picture of a nine-year-old girl running from a napalm attack. Media coverage was an important aspect of the relationship between warfare and societies.

Conflict at the front was linked to the state of war economies at home. In particular, the ability to mobilize and deploy resources is a key element, although it should not lead to an underplaying of developments in fighting effectiveness. The direction of influence was not one way because changes in social and cultural norms also affected the context and nature of warfare. The absence of military experience at the senior or, in many cases, any level was not restricted to the current leadership of major Western states, but was more generally a feature of their political, administrative, and social elites. These no longer reflected the ethos (and often composition) of the landowner–warrior nexus that had been so important in the West down to the early twentieth century and that in some senses represented a tradition looking back to the "Barbarian" Invasions that brought on the fall of the (western) Roman Empire. The tales of epic heroism of, for example, the times of Genghis Khan and Richard the Lionheart in the twelfth century were repeated in the world of print of the nineteenth and early twentieth centuries, but have largely disappeared since. In Britain, the valorous novels of George Alfred Henty and Captain W. E. Johns (the latter the creator of Biggles) were replaced in public libraries beginning in the 1960s by exemplary tales of a new political correctness: charitable, humane, and, crucially, no longer a masculine preserve. Smaller families have made every child precious, and the cult of youth in modern Western consumer culture is not a cult of organized violence. There is no equivalent to the child soldiers of Iran or Somalia. Instead, there is an emphasis on hedonism and individual rights, neither of which is conducive to militarism or bellicosity. The glorification of sacrifice in war that preceded and followed World War I finds few modern echoes.

An emphasis on such cultural factors, on the significance of cultures and attitudes for military developments, is not intended as any denial that other factors play a major role, but instead rests on a conviction that the extent and intensity of bellicist values are important not only in creating a general context for international relations, but also in sustaining the view that war is an instrument of policy and in determining how disputes between and within states were treated. It is important to understand the values that in some, but not all, contexts make compromise unacceptable, force appear necessary and even desirable, and war seem crucial to identity and self-respect. This remains the challenge today. The techniques of diplomatic management can help solve some crises, but others reflect a willingness, sometimes even a desire, to kill and be killed that cannot be ignored. In many states, civilian leaders were more reluctant than hitherto to employ force against their citizens. Troops and paramilitaries continued to be deployed to tackle regional separatism, as in Ulster, Corsica, and Kashmir in the 1990s, but European governments preferred to rely on the police to maintain internal order. The Communist governments of the Soviet Union and Eastern Europe used far less force resisting their overthrow beginning in 1989 than they had earlier exerted in seeking to maintain it in East Germany (1953), Hungary (1956), Czechoslovakia (1968), and Poland (1981). The use of troops in labor disputes is less common than in the early twentieth century. This more hesitant resort to force domestically affects foreign policy.

At the same time, the situation varied greatly at the global level. Despite the efforts of international institutions, there was no uniformity of values. Partly as a result, conflict and its consequences are key features not only in the making of the modern world, but also in its character today. There is no reason to assume that this situation will change.

CREDITS

Chapter 1
Courtesy of the Library of Congress, 1; © jcarillet/iStock, 8; Courtesy of the Library of Congress, 10.

Chapter 2
© Imperial War Museums (Q 14140), 12; Courtesy of the Library of Congress, 18; Courtesy of the Library of Congress, 20; Courtesy of the Library of Congress, 22; Courtesy of the Library of Congress, 26; Courtesy of the Library of Congress, 30; Courtesy of the Library of Congress, 32; Courtesy of the Library of Congress, 34; Courtesy of the Library of Congress, 38.

Chapter 3
Courtesy of the Library of Congress, 42; Popperfoto/Getty Images, 46; Courtesy of the Library of Congress, 49; © Imperial War Museums (Q 67814), 51; Courtesy of the Library of Congress, 54; Courtesy of the Library of Congress, Prints and Photographs Division, LC-USZ62-132597, 60.

Chapter 4
Courtesy of the Library of Congress, 67; Courtesy of the Library of Congress, 72; Courtesy of the Library of Congress, Prints and Photographs Division, LC-USZ62-75083, 74; Courtesy of the Library of Congress, 77; Courtesy of Everett Collection, Inc., 82; Courtesy of the Library of Congress, 84; Courtesy of the Library of Congress, Prints and Photographs Division, LC-DIG-ppmsca-18614, 86; Courtesy of the Library of Congress, 89; © Fine Art Images / Heritage Images / Imagestate, 90; Courtesy of the Library of Congress, 92.

Chapter 5
© Hulton-Deutsch Collection/CORBIS, 94; Popperfoto/Getty Images, 96; Courtesy of the Library of Congress, 100; Courtesy of the Library of Congress, 102; Courtesy of the Library of Congress, Prints and Photographs Division, LC-USZ62-136142, 109; Courtesy of the Library of Congress, 115.

Chapter 6
Courtesy of the Library of Congress, 118; Courtesy of the Library of Congress, 120; Courtesy of the Library of Congress, Prints and Photographs Division, LC-USZ62-128852, 128; Courtesy of the Library of Congress, 131; Courtesy of the Library of Congress, 135; Courtesy of the Library of Congress, 139.

Chapter 7
© Bettmann/CORBIS, 142; Photo by Kaveh Kazemi/Getty Images, 147; Courtesy of the Library of Congress, 149; © Anonymous/AP/AP/Corbis, 152; AP Photo/File, 155.
Chapter 8
© Peter Turnley/Corbis, 157; © Louie Psihoyos/CORBIS, 159; © Manca Juvan/In Pictures/Corbis, 163; © epa/Corbis, 167; © Corinne Dufka/Reuters/Corbis, 169.
Chapter 9
© Stephen Morrison/epa/Corbis, 173; © Per-Anders Pettersson/Corbis, 176; © U.S. Marine Corps/epa/Corbis, 180; © Zurab Kurtsikidze/epa/Corbis, 185.
Chapter 10
© JAYANTA SHAW/Reuters/Corbis, 189; © Erbin News/NurPhoto/NurPhoto/Corbis, 191; © STR/Reuters/Corbis, 196; © Wong Maye-E/AP/Corbis, 198.
Chapter 11
© Oktay Ortakcioglu/iStock, 203; © Andrew Innerarity/Reuters/Corbis, 207.
Chapter 12
The LIFE Images Collection/Getty Images, 211.

INDEX

Page numbers followed by the italicized letters *i* and *p* indicate material found in illustrations or photographs.